HEALTH POLICY

Revolutionizing Wellness: Navigating the Future of Health Policy for Radical Change

ABSTRACT

"No nation is born a loser or a winner, but Nations are born a chooser." The current state of sub-Saharan Africa's (SSA) healthcare system is ominous, and a drastic change from its moribund status is needed to make access to quality and affordable healthcare a human right of all citizens. Access to quality and affordable healthcare should be the right of every citizen of any society. Providing universal healthcare for all citizens of any society has both meaning and validity in addressing society's socioeconomic concerns. Sub-Saharan Africa (SSA) stands at a critical juncture in its health policy journey.

Adebowale Awosika-Olumo MD., MS., MPH., PhD., FACE

Table of Contents

Foreword

In an era of unprecedented global health challenges, the urgency for transformative and forward-thinking health policies has never been greater. Across Sub-Saharan Africa, healthcare systems are at a crossroads, facing complex issues that demand innovative solutions, bold leadership, and a radical reimagining of how healthcare is delivered and sustained. Within this landscape, "Revolutionizing Wellness: Navigating the Future of Health Policy for Radical Change" emerges as an essential and timely contribution.

This book, authored by my dear brother, Dr Adebowale Awosika-Olumo—known affectionately as "Cousin Debo"—is more than just an academic analysis; it is a deeply personal and passionately crafted blueprint for change. Dr Awosika-Olumo has always been a visionary. His curiosity and dedication to making a difference were evident when I met him. I vividly recall our conversations about healthcare—his aspirations, frustrations, and unwavering commitment to improving health systems for those who need them most. His drive was not just about theoretical policy shifts but about real, actionable change that could transform lives. This book is a testament to that commitment.

Despite considerable progress, healthcare systems in Sub-Saharan Africa continue to grapple with significant obstacles—persistent health disparities, economic constraints, limited infrastructure, and systemic inefficiencies. These challenges are not just policy dilemmas but ethical imperatives that demand urgent and courageous action. Incremental adjustments will not suffice. A radical overhaul of how healthcare is structured, financed, and delivered is essential to building a future where quality healthcare is not a privilege but a fundamental right.

This book provides a compelling and thought-provoking roadmap to achieving that vision. It delves into crucial policy instruments, including global budgeting, universal access to care, and micro-budget allocation—all foundational elements in creating a sustainable, efficient, and equitable healthcare system. Dr Awosika-Olumo masterfully articulates the importance of global budgeting to ensure continuous and sufficient funding, reducing financial unpredictability while fostering private-sector engagement.One of the book's most insightful contributions is its distinction between public health preventive care and clinical care services. Governments can strategically allocate resources to strengthen disease prevention, maternal and child health programs, infrastructure development, nutrition initiatives, and ethical clinical research. The emphasis on preventive healthcare enhances population health and reduces long-term medical costs, creating a more resilient system.

Equally compelling is the book's exploration of universal health coverage (UHC) as an indispensable tool for achieving healthcare equity. Dr Awosika-Olumo presents a well-reasoned argument for government oversight in licensing providers, maintaining quality assurance, and creating a competitive yet fair market for healthcare delivery. He highlights how UHC can eliminate financial barriers, streamline administrative costs, and ensure healthcare services reach those most in need.

Importantly, this book does not ignore the complex ethical questions accompanying healthcare reform in resource-constrained settings. How do we fairly ration healthcare when resources are limited? How can moral reasoning guide policy decisions to ensure justice and equity? How can public engagement shape a system that reflects the values and needs of the people it serves? These are critical dilemmas that demand thoughtful, inclusive, and ethically grounded solutions—questions that this book challenges policymakers and healthcare professionals to confront head-on.

Beyond policy and economics, this book is also a call to action. It challenges governments, healthcare leaders, and all stakeholders to embrace a new paradigm that is not just reactive but visionary, not just incremental but revolutionary. It urges us to harness the power of technology, innovation, and strategic planning to create a healthcare system that is both sustainable and just.

As we stand at this pivotal moment in healthcare history, the insights and strategies outlined in this book serve as a guiding light. To truly revolutionize wellness and build a future where healthcare is a universal right, the innovative approaches presented here must be embraced, refined, and, most importantly, implemented.

To all who read this book—whether you are a policymaker, a healthcare professional, an advocate, or simply someone who cares about the future of global health—I encourage you to engage deeply with its ideas. Let it challenge you. Let it inspire you. Moreover, most importantly, let it propel you toward action.

The future of healthcare in Sub-Saharan Africa—and indeed, the world—depends on all of us.

Michael Adekunle Charles

Dr. Michael Adekunle Charles is an experienced diplomat, medical doctor, and public health expert, serving as the CEO of the RBM Partnership to End Malaria — the most prominent global platform for coordinated action toward a world free from malaria. Charles has many years of experience leading the organization's African malaria coordination, providing technical, managerial, and operational support.

Acknowledgments

This book would not have been possible without so many people's love, support, and encouragement.

First and foremost, to my incredible wife—Morounsayo Awosika-Olumo, your unwavering belief in me, patience, and constant support have been my anchors throughout this journey. To my children (Ademusoyo, Adedayo, and Oluwademiladeayo), and my darling health policy wonk niece—Derin Aladesanmi all inspire me daily with curiosity and boundless energy, thank you for reminding me why I do what I do. Your love is my greatest motivation.

To my colleagues and peers in the social media groups I belong to—your insights, discussions, and shared wisdom have been invaluable in shaping my thoughts and deepening my understanding. The sense of community and collaboration you provide is truly priceless.

To my family members, friends, mentors, and all those who have offered guidance, encouragement, or even a simple word of motivation along the way—thank you. Your belief in this project helped bring it to life.

Lastly, to my readers, this book would be just words on a page without you. Thank you for taking this journey with me.

With gratitude,
Debo Awosika-Olumo

Contributors

Dr. Morounsayo Awosika-Olumo PhD., MD., MPH

Clinical research epidemiology

Baylor College of Medicine

Houston, Texas

About the Author

Dr. Adebowale Awosika-Olumo is a visionary leader, entrepreneur, and public health consultant dedicated to advancing emerging-market healthcare and environmental solutions. As the President and CEO of GHMIGROUP INC., Dr. Awosika-Olumo has spearheaded innovative initiatives that bridge health equity gaps and promote sustainable development.

In addition to corporate leadership, Dr. Awosika-Olumo is a contributing faculty member at Walden University and a professor of global health at the University of Maryland Global Campus. His academic work focuses on global health challenges, public health epidemiology, health outcomes and equity, sustainability, and the integration of artificial intelligence in healthcare.

A Fellow of the American College of Epidemiology, Dr. Awosika-Olumo has made significant contributions to the field of public health, influencing policies, improving healthcare accessibility, and fostering collaborations across industries. His expertise spans epidemiology, health equity, and the application of emerging technologies to address pressing health challenges worldwide.

Beyond professional and academic endeavors, Dr. Awosika-Olumo actively engages with professional networks and social media communities, contributing to thought leadership and discussions that drive meaningful change. His passion for transformative solutions and commitment to health equity are at the heart of this book, offering readers valuable insights into building a more inclusive and sustainable future.

Dr. Awosika-Olumo lives with his wife and with the support of his children, whose unwavering support fuels their mission to create a lasting impact in the world.

Chapter 1: The Need for Change

Navigating the Future of Health Policy for Radical Change in Sub-Saharan Africa

This illustration depicts the future of health policy in sub-Saharan Africa, focused on radical change. The image features a diverse group of African healthcare professionals and policymakers gathered around a futuristic digital map of Africa, showcasing health innovations such as telemedicine and mobile clinics. The background blends a modern city skyline with traditional African landscapes, symbolizing the integration of technology and culture.

Vignette: The Crossroads of Transformation

Dr. Amina Kwesi stood before a diverse group of stakeholders in the bustling capital of Zandoria, a fictional sub-Saharan African nation. As the newly appointed Minister of Health, she faced the daunting task of overhauling a healthcare system plagued by chronic underfunding, widespread disparities, and a crippling brain drain of medical professionals.

Zandoria's health challenges were manifold: high maternal and infant mortality rates, a persistent HIV/AIDS epidemic, rising non-communicable diseases, and frequent outbreaks of infectious diseases. However, Dr. Kwesi saw an opportunity for radical change.

She envisioned a future where cutting-edge technology merged with traditional healing practices, artificial intelligence empowered community health workers, and preventive care took center stage. Implementing such sweeping reforms required navigating complex political landscapes, addressing deeply rooted cultural beliefs, and securing sustainable funding in a resource-constrained environment.

As Dr. Kwesi prepared to unveil her ambitious 10-year plan, she knew the road ahead would be fraught with challenges. Success would demand innovation and consensus among diverse stakeholders—from village elders to international donors, from traditional healers to tech entrepreneurs.

Questions:

1. How can Dr. Kwesi effectively integrate modern technological solutions with traditional healing practices to create a healthcare system that is both culturally acceptable and scientifically sound? What potential conflicts might arise, and how can they be mitigated?
2. Given Zandoria's limited resources, what strategies can Dr. Kwesi employ to prioritize and address the nation's multiple health challenges? How can she ensure that focusing on specific areas does not neglect other critical health needs?
3. Considering the ongoing brain drain of healthcare professionals, what innovative approaches can Dr. Kwesi implement to build and retain a skilled healthcare workforce? How might these approaches challenge conventional models of medical education and practice?
4. How can Dr. Kwesi design and implement a health financing system that ensures universal health coverage while remaining sustainable in Zandoria's economic context? What role might public-private partnerships, international aid, and community-based insurance schemes play in this system?

"No nation is born a loser or a winner, but Nations are born a chooser."

The current state of sub-Saharan Africa's (SSA) healthcare system is dire, necessitating a drastic shift from its moribund status to ensure quality and affordable healthcare becomes a fundamental right for all citizens. Universal healthcare access is both a moral imperative and a practical necessity in addressing society's socio-economic concerns.

Sub-Saharan Africa (SSA) stands at a critical juncture in its health policy journey. Despite notable progress in improving overall health outcomes, the region continues to grapple with challenges that impede its path toward a healthier future. The need for radical change is not just warranted but essential, as persistent health disparities, economic constraints, and systemic inefficiencies demand a revolutionary approach to wellness and healthcare policy. This chapter delves into the pressing issues, innovative solutions, and actionable strategies needed to propel sub-Saharan Africa toward a transformative era in health policy.

Disproportional Disease Burden

This chapter examines the disproportionate disease burden in sub-Saharan Africa, exploring its challenges and perspectives.

Introduction

This overview of the health disparities faced by sub-Saharan Africa highlights the region's disproportionate share of the global disease burden. This introduction will set the stage for a deeper exploration of the factors contributing to this imbalance and the impact of healthcare delivery systems.

Understanding the Disease Burden in Sub-Saharan Africa

This section quantifies the region's disease burden using key statistics and recent findings. It highlights the leading causes of morbidity and mortality, including infectious diseases, malnutrition, and emerging non-communicable diseases. The goal is to provide a clear understanding of the region's health challenges and the scale of its disease burden.

Factors Contributing to the Disproportionate Disease Burden

This section will delve into the socio-economic factors

contributing to sub-Saharan Africa's health disparities, such as poverty, limited access to clean water, and inadequate sanitation. It also examines the challenges posed by weak healthcare infrastructure and environmental factors affecting health. Understanding these contributing factors is crucial for addressing the disproportionate disease burden in the region.

Impact of Healthcare Delivery on Disease Burden

This section analyzes the state of healthcare systems in sub-Saharan Africa, including the role of international aid and local governance in healthcare delivery. Success stories and notable improvements in healthcare access and outcomes will be highlighted. This section aims to understand how healthcare delivery impacts the disease burden in the region and what can be learned from successful initiatives.

Strategies for Addressing the Disproportionate Disease Burden

This section outlines policy recommendations for strengthening healthcare systems, the importance of education, community health programs, and preventive measures. Additionally, it discusses the role of technology and innovation in transforming healthcare delivery in sub-Saharan Africa. Strategies for addressing the disproportionate disease burden will be examined, aiming to provide actionable solutions for policymakers and stakeholders.

Adult health in developing countries receives little attention in public health discussions. In low- and middle-income countries (LMICs), adult health (ages 20–59) is essential for the well-being of both younger and older populations and for sustainable development. Cost-effective prevention, early detection, and treatment strategies are paramount for improving adult health

(Awosika-Olumo, 2003; Okoroiwu et al., 2020; Shah et al., 2019), especially given the high rate of premature deaths in LMICs.

For example, while overall cancer incidence is lower in LMICs than in high-income countries (HICs), cancer-related mortality is significantly higher, particularly among individuals aged 65 or younger (Torre, 2016; Ghoncheh, 2016). This premature mortality leads to lost productivity and exacerbates economic hardship (WHO, 2016).

Sub-Saharan Africa region is notable for having some of the highest rates of preventable neonatal and maternal mortality, as well as deaths from infectious diseases, antimicrobial-resistant infections, and malnutrition on a global scale. Despite recent economic growth leading to positive changes like rapid urbanization, increased alcohol and tobacco consumption, and a rising prevalence of non-communicable diseases (which now account for over 37% of all deaths), new challenges are emerging (Health in Africa 2024; WHO, 2022). As life expectancy increases in African populations, the number of individuals living with multiple chronic health conditions, also known as multi-morbidity, is also on the rise (Health in Africa 2024). Although this concept is still being explored, recent studies have shown significant connections in Africa between multi-morbidity and factors such as urbanization, female gender, age over 50, and higher education levels.

The impact of rising multi-morbidity on Africa's health systems is uncertain, highlighting the need for public health initiatives to adapt to this evolving landscape. Historically, health programs have primarily focused on treating individual diseases, but the current situation necessitates a shift toward diagnosing and managing patients with overlapping health conditions. This transformation is essential for effectively addressing the intricate health needs of African populations and ensuring the sustainability and flexibility of healthcare systems in the region.

Healthcare financing remains a major challenge in sub-Saharan Africa. Stenberg et al. (2017) found that among 67 low- and middle-income countries—accounting for 95% of the global population in this category—there is an annual funding shortfall of over $370 billion to achieve the Sustainable Development Goal (SDG)—ensuring healthy lives and promote well-being for all at all ages health targets. Approximately half of these low-medium-income countries are in SSA, where the gap in health financing is particularly severe (Jeetoo & Jaunky, 2023).

Despite comprising 16% of the global population and carrying 23% of the world's disease burden, Africa received only 1% of total global health expenditure in 2015. Regarding per capita spending, the world allocates ten times more resources to healthcare than Africa (Jeetoo & Jaunky, 2023).

Current State of Health in Sub-Saharan Africa

This illustration depicts the current state of health in Sub-Saharan Africa. This image contrasts a busy urban hospital with overcrowded waiting areas against a rural clinic with limited resources, highlighting disparities in healthcare access. The background blends traditional huts with modern buildings, symbolizing the coexistence of old and new elements.

Vignette: Current State of Health in Sub-Saharan Africa

Sub-Saharan Africa faces numerous health challenges but shows signs of progress and potential for improvement. Infectious, non-communicable, and socio-economic factors shape the region's health landscape. Despite these challenges, ongoing efforts are being made to enhance healthcare systems and improve health outcomes.

Questions

1. What primary health challenges does sub-Saharan Africa currently face?

2. How has life expectancy in sub-Saharan Africa changed in recent years?

3. What role do socio-economic factors play in the health outcomes of sub-Saharan Africa?

4. What strategies are being implemented to improve health systems in sub-Saharan Africa?

5. How do health disparities within sub-Saharan Africa affect different populations?

Background

Stark contrasts mark sub-Saharan Africa's health landscape. Life expectancy figures and health outcomes trail significantly behind global averages, influenced by complex, interwoven factors. Poverty, limited access to healthcare, and nutritional deficiencies create a compounded crisis, exacerbating disease burden and mortality rates—particularly among the most vulnerable populations such as women and children (Jiang et al., 2024).

Despite its vast natural and human resources, the region continues to struggle with a high prevalence of infectious diseases, further aggravated by inadequate healthcare infrastructure and services. Additionally, disparities between and within countries highlight the uneven distribution of healthcare resources, making the fight against health inequities an uphill battle (Oladipo et al., 2022).

Introduction

In this present day, the sub-Saharan Africa region continues to confront many health challenges, albeit with progress evident in certain areas. This introductory segment establishes the backdrop for a thorough examination of the health landscape in sub-Saharan Africa, primarily focusing on prevalent health concerns such as infectious diseases such as HIV and malaria and emerging contagious threats, alongside the escalating burden posed by non-communicable diseases.

By gaining an insight into the present health status, we can unravel the intricate web of factors contributing to the region's health challenges and deliberatively explore potential pathways toward enhanced health outcomes.

The health panorama of sub-Saharan Africa in 2023 depicts a blend of advancements and persistent hurdles. Noteworthy achievements have been observed, specifically in the realm of combating HIV, with Eastern and Southern Africa registering a remarkable 57% decline in new infections (Fuseini et al., 2021; Müllerschön et al., 2019; Okoye et al., 2021). Despite these triumphs, the region remains embroiled in challenges revolving around infectious diseases, malnutrition, and the burgeoning threat posed by non-communicable diseases (NCDs) (Fuseini et al., 2021; Scott & Webb, 2014). Delving into the pivotal health benchmarks and metrics that delineate the current health status of sub-Saharan Africa will shed light on the health dynamics prevalent in the region and lay a solid foundation for comprehending the encompassing health challenges it faces.

Major Health Issues Confronting the Region

The health landscape of sub-Saharan Africa is fundamentally characterized by its ongoing struggle against infectious diseases, exacerbated by the emergence of novel pathogens and the surge in non-communicable diseases (NCDs) (Amu et al., 2024; Arhin & Asante-Darko, 2023; Hollingworth et al., 2023).

Infectious diseases have long stood as the primary adversary of the region, with HIV/AIDS, malaria, and diarrheal diseases leading the forefront in terms of morbidity and mortality rates

(Oladipo et al., 2022). Recent years have witnessed the emergence of ailments such as Ebola, cholera, meningitis, and the global menace of COVID-19, adding layers of complexity to the region's health crisis(Moyo et al., 2023).

Concurrently, the looming threat of NCDs is on the upswing, with a growing portion of deaths attributed to ailments unrelated to infections ("Health in Africa," 2024). Malnutrition, intricately interlinked with poverty, remains a pervasive issue, exerting a significant influence on the health outcomes of millions (Azevedo, 2017; "Health in Africa," 2024; Moyo et al., 2023).

This segment seeks to unravel the intricate fabric of the significant health issues in sub-Saharan Africa, underscoring the critical imperative for multidimensional approaches to healthcare and disease prevention.

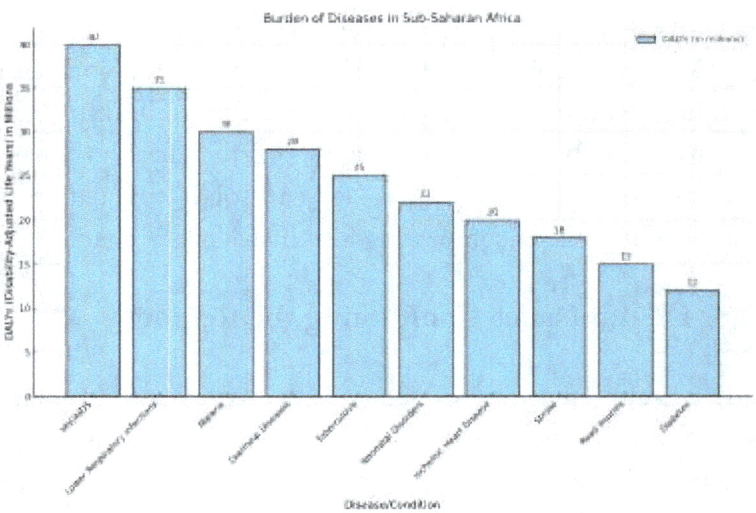

Challenges Facing the Health Care System

The healthcare landscape in Africa faces several challenges, notably issues with financial accessibility. Out-of-pocket spending comprises 36% of healthcare expenses, leading to a $66 billion annual financial gap. From 2000 to 2015, African governments allocated an average of 7.2% of their budgets to healthcare, though funding distribution varies among countries. Nigeria, Congo, Egypt, and South Africa have differing healthcare funding approaches. Nigeria heavily relies on out-of-pocket payments (77%), with minimal government funding (14%). Congo and Egypt also depend significantly on out-of-pocket expenses (48% and 60%, respectively). Nigeria and Congo receive limited external funding (8%) for healthcare. In contrast, South Africa allocates 54% of healthcare spending from government sources, reducing out-of-pocket payments to just 8%. The issue of high out-of-pocket healthcare spending is particularly prominent in Nigeria, Congo, and Egypt, while South Africa has a more balanced funding model with lower reliance on out-of-pocket expenses (Erlangga et al., 2023; Frimpong et al., 2022; Utan, 2021).

Three core challenges encapsulate the healthcare dilemma in sub-Saharan Africa: inadequate human resources, insufficient budget allocations, and poor leadership and management (Achoki, 2016; Blaise & Yongsi, 2023; Cassell, 2019; Larson, 2018; Oleribe et al., 2019; Zekeng, 2016). The shortage of skilled healthcare professionals exacerbates the inability to meet the healthcare needs of a rapidly growing population, while meager health budgets limit the scope and quality of services. Leadership gaps further erode the efficacy of healthcare delivery, impeding the implementation of comprehensive health policies and reforms (Oleribe et al., 2019). Addressing these fundamental issues is pivotal to reshaping the health landscape in sub-Saharan Africa, fostering environments where innovations can thrive and lead to substantial health improvements.

The healthcare systems in sub-Saharan Africa face numerous challenges that hinder the delivery of modern care and ultimately undermine the population's well-being. Unequal access to quality healthcare, as highlighted by Blaise (2023), is a prominent issue plaguing the region. This inequality stems from various factors, such as disparities in wealth, geography, and education, leaving certain communities and individuals without proper medical attention. Consequently, health disparities are exacerbated, perpetuating cycles of poor health. Furthermore, sub-Saharan Africa's healthcare systems grapple with poor governance, pervasive corruption, and extreme poverty, as noted by Cassell (2019). These systemic issues contribute to a need for more transparency and accountability, ultimately hindering the efficient allocation of resources needed for healthcare provision. More investment in the healthcare sector, often due to limited budgetary allocations, is needed to ensure the systems are equipped to meet the growing demand for quality care.

Leadership and human resource shortages further compound these challenges. Oleribe (2019) emphasizes the importance of effective leadership in implementing sustainable healthcare policies and driving essential reforms. However, inadequate leadership and management skills hinder improvements in healthcare services, preventing the establishment of a robust and resilient system (Oleribe et al., 2019).

The "double burden" of traditional tropical diseases and non-communicable diseases presents additional obstacles to healthcare systems in sub-Saharan Africa (Larson, 2018). While the region faces a heavy burden from infectious diseases such as malaria, HIV/AIDS, and tuberculosis, non-communicable diseases such as diabetes, cardiovascular diseases, and cancer are also on the rise. This dual challenge requires comprehensive and integrated healthcare approaches to address both communicable and non-communicable diseases (Larson, 2018). To combat these intricate challenges, scholars and professionals have proposed community-based delivery of health services and the establishment of local research institutes (Zekeng, 2016). Community-based approaches aim to bring healthcare services closer to the people, ensuring accessibility and culturally appropriate care (Zekeng, 2016). Additionally, the development of local research institutes fosters capacity-building and knowledge generation within the region. These institutions enable evidence-based decision-making and contribute to tailored and effective healthcare interventions by researching regional health priorities (Zekeng, 2016).

Despite the countless obstacles, progress has been made in tackling critical health issues in sub-Saharan Africa. Achoki (2016) highlights the advancements made in child survival rates as well as the management of HIV/AIDS and tuberculosis. These successes are a testament to the resilience and determination of healthcare professionals, policymakers, and communities in the region (Achoki, 2016). By leveraging these achievements and building upon them, sub-Saharan Africa can strive towards improved healthcare outcomes for its population, ensuring a healthier future for all. Strengthening healthcare resilience is imperative in the face of epidemics and other healthcare crises, focusing on capacity-building, enhancing healthcare worker training, and improving access to essential medical supplies and technology.

In summary, this section scrutinizes the systemic challenges embedded within the healthcare framework of sub-Saharan Africa, accentuating the pressing need for reforms and international collaboration to surmount these obstacles and forge a more robust, resilient healthcare system.

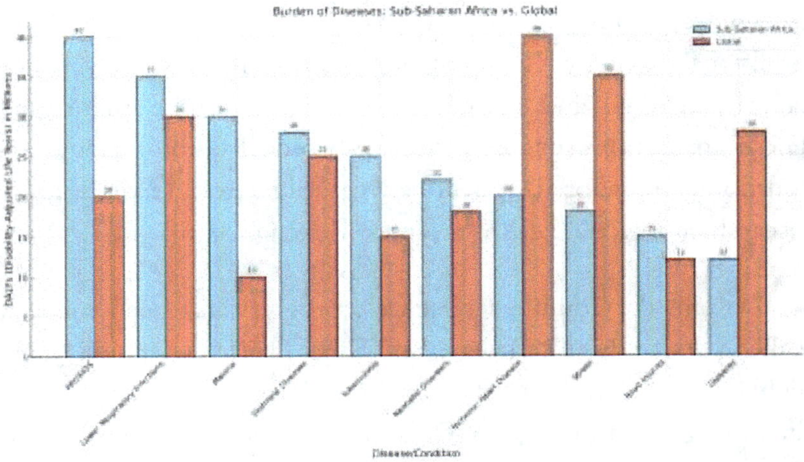
Burden of Diseases: Sub-Saharan Africa vs. Global

Innovative Solutions for a Healthier Future

This depicts diverse people collaborating around a large, light oak table. On the table are a DNA double helix model, a futuristic-looking medical device (e.g., a sleek scanner or monitor), several tablets displaying health data graphs, and a few scattered notebooks—natural light streams in from a large window behind them, creating a warm, optimistic atmosphere.

Introduction

The path to a healthier future in sub-Saharan Africa depends on adopting innovative health solutions tailored to the region's unique challenges. Digital health technologies stand out as a beacon of hope, potentially revolutionizing healthcare delivery by improving access, reducing costs, and enhancing the quality of care. From mobile health applications facilitating remote patient monitoring to digital platforms streamlining health records management, the digital transformation of healthcare could bridge the gap between under-resourced communities and quality healthcare services.

Beyond technology, increasing healthcare funding and fostering effective leadership are also essential. Public-private partnerships could unlock new funding avenues, ensuring healthcare systems are adequately equipped and staffed. Meanwhile, cultivating a cadre of capable health leaders could drive the changes needed to dismantle barriers to efficient healthcare delivery, ensuring policies are crafted and executed with precision and foresight.

African healthcare systems face numerous challenges, including inadequate human resources, budgetary constraints, and poor leadership (Oleribe, 2019). These issues have been exacerbated by the COVID-19 pandemic, highlighting the need for a paradigm shift in healthcare organizations (Blaise, 2023). Innovative strategies such as integrating traditional African medicine (Blaise, 2023) and using disruptive technologies like telemedicine and medical drones (Oppong, 2020) have been proposed to address these challenges. Adopting a comprehensive health system-strengthening action framework has also been suggested (Ibeneme et al., 2020). However, these efforts must be supported by improved governance, reduced corruption, and increased health financing (Cassell, 2019; Tewolde, 2019).

African healthcare systems face many challenges that hinder their ability to provide adequate care to their populations. These challenges include a need for more human resources, constraints in budget allocation, and ineffective leadership (Oleribe, 2019). The COVID-19 pandemic has further exacerbated these issues, underscoring the urgent need for a paradigm shift in healthcare organizations (Blaise, 2023). To address these pressing challenges, several innovative strategies have been proposed. One such strategy is integrating traditional African medicine, an approach advocated by Blaise (2023). Drawing upon the rich healing traditions and knowledge of African indigenous medicine, this approach combines traditional remedies with modern medical practices to enhance healthcare outcomes. Disruptive technologies like telemedicine and medical drones have also been suggested to overcome logistical hurdles in healthcare delivery (Oppong, 2020). These technologies have the potential to bridge geographical barriers, improve access to healthcare services, and reduce costs, particularly in remote and underserved areas.

Moreover, experts have recommended adopting a comprehensive health system-strengthening action framework (Ibeneme, 2020). This framework aims to address the root causes of the challenges faced by African healthcare systems by strengthening various healthcare system components, such as infrastructure, workforce capacity, supply chains, and information systems. By implementing this framework, healthcare systems can become more resilient and better equipped to handle emergencies like the pandemic. However, for these efforts to succeed, they must be supported by improved governance, reduced corruption, and increased health financing (Cassell, 2019; Tewolde, 2019). Effective and accountable governance ensures that healthcare resources are allocated efficiently and transparently while addressing corruption, which safeguards the integrity of healthcare systems. Adequate health financing is crucial for sustained investment in infrastructure, human resources, and technological advancements, enabling the implementation and improvement of innovative healthcare strategies.

In conclusion, African healthcare systems face numerous challenges worsened by the COVID-19 pandemic. To address these challenges and improve healthcare outcomes, the integration of traditional medicine, the utilization of disruptive technologies, and the adoption of a comprehensive health system-strengthening action framework have been recommended. However, these initiatives must be supported by improved governance, reduced corruption, and increased health financing. By implementing these measures, African healthcare systems can strive toward achieving better healthcare for their populations.

Innovative Approaches for a Healthier Tomorrow

This illustration showcases the progress in mRNA technology. It features a modern laboratory with diverse scientists and researchers working collaboratively on mRNA vaccines and treatments. The scene includes advanced laboratory equipment, digital screens displaying molecular structures, and vials labeled with mRNA samples, highlighting the innovative and collaborative atmosphere.

Introduction

The healthcare sector is constantly evolving and is driven by innovation. Moving forward, we must understand how these advancements are reshaping healthcare to be more effective, inclusive, and sustainable. From revolutionary mRNA technology to the embrace of telehealth services, the landscape is undergoing rapid changes. This session aims to illuminate these groundbreaking solutions and examine their potential to mold a healthier future for everyone.

Progress in mRNA Technology

The COVID-19 pandemic underscored the remarkable capabilities of mRNA technology, initially through the development of vaccines. However, mRNA's versatility extends far beyond this, offering a bright outlook for treating various diseases, including influenza and cancer. Progressively moving forward, researchers are committed to leveraging this technology to create more precise therapies, potentially transforming our approach to many medical conditions.

The emergence of messenger RNA (mRNA) technology has sparked a revolution in the field of biotechnology, reshaping the landscape of medicine and therapeutics. By harnessing the process of protein synthesis within the body, mRNA technology enables the design of mRNA sequences that instruct cells to produce specific proteins. This breakthrough has profound implications for medicine, especially in the rapid development of vaccines. By providing the body with the blueprint to produce antigens and stimulate an immune response, mRNA technology eliminates the need for traditional attenuated or inactivated pathogens (Garcia et al., 2022; Lin et al., 2023; Malhotra, 2022).

The journey of mRNA technology from a theoretical concept to a pivotal tool in modern medicine can be traced through several significant milestones. Over half a century ago, scientists first uncovered the role of mRNA in translating DNA into proteins. However, it was only in the 1990s that researchers began exploring mRNA's therapeutic potential. Early challenges such as stability and effective delivery mechanisms initially impeded progress. Nevertheless, the development of lipid nanoparticles (LNPs) in the early 2000s provided a viable method for delivering mRNA molecules, propelling the field forward. Key figures, including Katalin Karikó and Drew Weissman, made notable contributions by investigating modified nucleosides, enhancing mRNA's stability, and reducing its immunogenicity. These advancements paved the way for the development of mRNA vaccines and therapeutics (Badieyan & Evans, 2019; Du et al., 2023; Rhym et al., 2023).

The pivotal role of mRNA technology was thrust into the global spotlight with the rapid development and deployment of COVID-19 vaccines. Biotechnology companies like Moderna and Pfizer-BioNTech capitalized on mRNA technology to swiftly design and manufacture vaccines in response to the pandemic. These vaccines introduce a piece of mRNA into the body that encodes the coronavirus spike protein, thus prompting the immune system to recognize and combat the virus. The unprecedented speed of vaccine development and their efficacy in preventing COVID-19 infections and reducing their severity have unequivocally demonstrated the immense potential of mRNA technology in addressing public health crises (Ackerman et al., 2021; Aquino-Jarquin, 2022; Jamous & Alhomoud, 2023).

Beyond vaccines, mRNA technology applies to various medical treatments and prophylactics. For instance, mRNA is used in cancer therapies to direct cells to produce tumor antigens, stimulating an immune response against cancer cells. Researchers are also exploring mRNA-based therapies for genetic disorders, seeking to provide instructions for producing deficient proteins or enzymes due to genetic mutations. The versatility of mRNA technology offers the tantalizing prospect of personalized medicine, wherein treatments can be tailored to an individual's genetic makeup, thus opening up new horizons in therapeutic interventions(Lin et al., 2023; Rzymski, 2023; Zhou, 2024). The future of mRNA technology holds immense promise in various domains beyond its current applications. One potential avenue includes the development of personalized cancer vaccines customized to target an individual's unique tumor profile, offering a more targeted and practical approach to cancer treatment. Additionally, mRNA technology could revolutionize regenerative medicine by providing instructions for cellular repair and tissue or organ replacement. Another exciting prospect is the development of mRNA-based treatments for autoimmune diseases, guiding the body to modulate its immune response. As research progresses, the flexibility and adaptability of mRNA technology may unlock breakthroughs in areas yet unimagined, firmly establishing its position as a cornerstone in the next generation of medical treatments(Catanzaro et al., 2019; Imran et al., 2022; Rus et al., 2022).

In conclusion, mRNA technology has ushered in a new era in biotechnology and medicine, transforming how vaccines and therapeutics are developed. From its historical milestones to its current applications in COVID-19 vaccines and other medical treatments, the potential of mRNA technology is vast. As we navigate toward the future, the prospects of personalized medicine, regenerative medicine, and innovative approaches to disease management all lie within the realm of mRNA technology. With its proven efficacy, adaptability, and transformative impact, it is evident that mRNA technology is shaping the future of medicine with unwavering confidence.

The Emergence of Telehealth

This image depicts a diverse group of patients using videoconferencing to consult with a doctor from the comfort of their homes.

Telehealth has rapidly become a fundamental aspect of modern healthcare, providing patients with unprecedented access to medical services from the comfort of their homes. The surge in telemedicine adoption has been driven by the COVID-19 pandemic and a growing recognition of its convenience and efficiency. Looking ahead, telehealth is poised to become a staple, further integrating into regular healthcare delivery, thus enhancing accessibility and alleviating pressure on traditional healthcare systems.

This broad spectrum of remote healthcare services includes both clinical and non-clinical applications. Clinical services encompass video consultations, while non-clinical services include administrative meetings, training, and continuing medical education (Ali, 2024; Olorunsogo et al., 2024). The emergence of telehealth marks a pivotal shift in healthcare delivery, offering convenience, accessibility, and efficiency. It allows patients to receive care from the comfort of their homes, reducing the need for physical travel and enabling healthcare professionals to extend their reach beyond traditional clinical settings.

Exploring the evolution of telehealth, we will examine its historical milestones, technological advancements, and profound global impact on patients and healthcare systems (Al-Bataineh et al., 2023; Ng et al., 2022; Sharma et al., 2022). The journey of telehealth from a novel idea to a mainstream healthcare service has been long and fascinating. It began with early experiments in the 1960s when healthcare providers started exploring the possibility of delivering healthcare services over a distance. One of the earliest instances of telehealth was using a two-way television to conduct medical consultations, a project initiated by the Nebraska Psychiatric Institute in collaboration with Norfolk State (Janjua et al., 2021; Sood et al., 2016).

Over the years, telehealth has experienced significant milestones that have shaped its evolution. The advent of the internet and advancements in telecommunications technology in the 1990s and early 2000s played a pivotal role in expanding the capabilities of telehealth services. This period saw the introduction of more sophisticated telehealth systems, capable of transmitting high-quality video and audio for remote consultations, along with the ability to capture and share medical data electronically (Meza & Rodríguez, 2018; Vacas-Aguilar, 2020; Ziaie et al., 2000).

The development of mobile health (mHealth) applications and wearable technology further propelled the telehealth industry forward, making it possible for patients to monitor their health and communicate with healthcare providers in real-time. These technological milestones have not only made telehealth more accessible but have also enhanced the quality of remote healthcare (Cerda et al., 2024; Pennell et al., 2017; Pham et al., 2023).

Technological breakthroughs in digital communication, mobile computing, and wearable devices have primarily fueled telehealth's rapid expansion. Smartphones and the internet have played a transformative role, turning telehealth from a concept into a practical solution for millions of patients worldwide (Alleema et al., 2023; Pham et al., 2023; Singh et al., 2023). Innovative mobile applications have enabled patients to easily schedule virtual consultations, access medical records, and receive reminders for medication and appointments. Wearable devices, such as fitness trackers and smartwatches, have become vital tools for continuous health monitoring, providing real-time data on heart rate, activity levels, and other health metrics directly to healthcare providers (Argunova et al., 2024; Martinez et al., 2024; Moonga, 2023).

Additionally, the development of secure, scalable software platforms has been crucial. These platforms not only support video consultations but also ensure the safe transmission of medical data, adhering to privacy regulations such as HIPAA in the United States. Such advancements have expanded the scope of telehealth services, making it possible to remotely manage various conditions, from mental health issues to chronic disease management (Patange et al., 2023).

Utilization of Artificial Intelligence and Data Integration

Introduction

Integrating Artificial Intelligence (AI) in healthcare is pivotal for advancing medical diagnostics. These cutting-edge technologies, particularly AI algorithms, stand out for their unparalleled precision and efficiency in unraveling the complexities of medical data (Seth et al., 2023). This chapter delves into how AI algorithms are transforming diagnostic processes, significantly enhancing the accuracy of medical diagnostics. The objective is to shed light on the symbiotic relationship between AI and healthcare, illustrating how AI-driven solutions set new standards in diagnostic excellence, patient care, and medical research while providing reassurance about the quality of medical diagnostics.

Understanding AI Algorithms

AI algorithms epitomize the powerful convergence of computer science and healthcare, integrating machine learning

(ML), deep learning (DL), and comprehensive medical expertise (Asif Naveed, 2023). At their core, these algorithms rely on sophisticated mathematical models and rules meticulously designed to process and analyze complex datasets. One of their most significant attributes is their exceptional adaptability—an innovative capability reshaping the medical landscape. These algorithms learn from the vast amounts of data they encounter, enhancing their accuracy and efficiency in identifying patterns and anomalies (Janga et al., 2022).

Artificial intelligence (AI) facilitates an in-depth examination of extensive databases—including medical records, imaging studies, and clinical research—allowing for the extraction of critical information that informs diagnosis, prognosis, and treatment planning. Whether deployed to address specific medical conditions or to facilitate broader healthcare initiatives, AI algorithms provide indispensable insights across diverse medical scenarios (Iqbal et al., 2023). Their transformative potential not only augments clinical decision-making but also paves the way for innovations in patient care and healthcare delivery. As such, the role of AI in medicine is no longer a matter of possibility but a reality actively shaping the future of healthcare.

AI in Medical Data Analysis

The deployment of AI algorithms in medical data analysis leverages their sophisticated capabilities to navigate the complexities inherent in health-related data effectively. This encompasses examining electronic health records (EHRs), genomic sequences, imaging data, and notes from healthcare providers (Khan et al., 2023). AI's ability to analyze large datasets rapidly and accurately is of paramount importance, particularly for diseases that exhibit subtle symptoms or necessitate integrating information from multiple sources to arrive at a precise diagnosis.

For instance, AI has demonstrated remarkable advancements in radiology by interpreting X-rays and MRI scans to identify abnormalities such as tumors or fractures. The precision with which AI achieves these tasks matches and often surpasses that of human experts (Gomes et al., 2023; Lin et al., 2024). Furthermore, in oncology and cardiology, AI's ability to analyze genetic markers and heart scans facilitates the early detection of potentially life-threatening conditions. Such early interventions are critical for improving patient outcomes and optimizing treatment strategies. The integration of AI into medical data analysis represents a transformative shift in healthcare, driving advancements in diagnostic accuracy and patient care.

Enhancing Diagnostic Accuracy with AI

The substantial impact of AI on improving diagnostic accuracy is evident across multiple medical disciplines. Its ability to analyze complex medical data with exceptional precision has led to remarkable advancements in diagnosing conditions ranging from cancer to cardiovascular diseases and beyond.

For instance, in oncology, AI algorithms play a crucial role in the early detection of malignancies, enabling timely interventions before the disease progresses to advanced stages (Geevarghese et al., 2024). In neurology, these algorithms are instrumental in examining brain scans for indicators of stroke, Alzheimer's disease, and other neurodegenerative disorders, often identifying subtle changes that manifest prior to clinical symptoms (Quandt et al., 2023). Furthermore, AI's influence extends to routine diagnostics, such as blood tests and health screenings, underscoring its transformative potential in preventive healthcare. By predicting health risks based on biochemical markers and genetic information, AI can revolutionize how we approach health maintenance and disease prevention (Alowais et al., 2023; Bohr &

Memarzadeh, 2020).

Additionally, integrating AI into diagnostic workflows not only enhances accuracy but also significantly reduces the time required for diagnosis. This dual benefit ultimately leads to improved patient outcomes and greater overall efficiency within healthcare systems (Al Kuwaiti et al., 2023). The evidence is clear: AI is poised to be a game-changer in medical diagnostics.

Challenges and Limitations

In recent years, the emergence of AI-driven mobile applications has dramatically reshaped various healthcare domains, particularly in personalized cancer care (Iqbal et al., 2023; Seth et al., 2023). These applications are designed to offer customized treatment plans, facilitate timely diagnoses, and improve ongoing cancer management processes. However, despite AI's profound potential to revolutionize healthcare diagnostics, several challenges and limitations warrant careful consideration. One of the foremost concerns revolves around data privacy and security. AI algorithms typically require access to extensive amounts of personal medical data (Powell, 2020), raising critical issues regarding protecting this sensitive information from unauthorized access and breaches. Safeguarding patient data is not merely an operational hurdle; it is paramount to maintaining trust in health systems utilizing AI technologies. Furthermore, the accuracy of AI algorithms is intricately linked to the quality and diversity of the training data. Inadequate or biased training datasets can result in skewed outcomes, adversely affecting diagnostic accuracy for specific patient populations. Addressing these biases is essential to ensure equitable healthcare delivery and optimize AI's effectiveness across diverse groups. Additionally, integrating AI into clinical settings requires significant investment in both technology and the training of healthcare professionals. This necessity poses a substantial barrier to the widespread adoption of AI solutions in practice (Powell, 2020). Addressing these economic barriers is crucial to realizing the full benefits of AI in healthcare. Lastly, the ethical implications of relying on AI for critical healthcare decisions cannot be overlooked. This reliance highlights the urgent need for continuous oversight, transparency, and accountability in AI-driven diagnostics. As we advance into the era of AI in healthcare, these challenges must be systematically addressed to harness AI's transformative potential while ensuring the integrity and safety of healthcare delivery.

The Future of AI in Healthcare

Looking ahead, the impact of AI in healthcare is set to expand, driven by ongoing technological advancements and a growing understanding of its potential benefits. Cutting-edge research is focused on developing more sophisticated AI algorithms capable of predicting diseases even before symptoms manifest, shifting the focus from treatment to prevention. Efforts are also underway to improve the interoperability between AI systems and existing healthcare infrastructure, ensuring seamless integration. The future may see AI playing a central role in personalized medicine, customizing treatments and interventions based on an individual's genetic makeup, lifestyle, and risk factors, thereby elevating the efficacy of healthcare delivery to unprecedented levels (Al Kuwaiti et al., 2023; Alowais et al., 2023; Bohr & Memarzadeh, 2020; Johnson et al., 2021). The journey of AI in healthcare is just beginning, with its full potential yet to be realized. This progression toward an AI-infused future promises improved diagnostic accuracy and comprehensive enhancements in patient care and medical research.

The integration of AI in predicting cancer is poised to grow as technology evolves. Researchers are exploring how AI algorithms, in combination with wearable devices and mobile applications, can monitor health parameters and detect early signs of disease. Additionally, combining AI with blockchain could enhance data security and privacy, promoting better collaboration among healthcare providers and researchers (Kolluri et al., 2024; Shah et al., 2022). AI can potentially transform cancer detection and diagnosis by analyzing complex datasets and identifying patterns indicative of early cancer stages. It assists healthcare professionals in interpreting medical images, genomic data, and other critical factors, leading to more accurate and timely diagnoses. However, it is crucial to address the challenges and limitations to ensure AI's ethical and responsible use in healthcare. Ongoing research, collaboration, and innovation in AI technology are essential for making significant progress in the early detection and treatment of cancer (Abhilasha et al., 2024; Derraz et al., 2024; Geevarghese et al., 2024).

Personalized cancer care, also known as precision oncology, focuses on tailoring medical treatment to the individual characteristics of each patient. AI-driven mobile applications are vital in achieving this personalized approach by leveraging vast data to predict outcomes, suggest treatments, and monitor patient progress (Srivastava R., 2023). However, for these AI-driven apps to be effective in personalized cancer care, they must overcome various challenges, such as data integration from diverse sources, patient privacy concerns, and the need for user-friendly interfaces. This section will delve into the benefits and significance of using AI in personalized cancer care while highlighting the critical need to understand the existing gaps to improve these technologies (Chakraborty et al., 2023; Derraz et al., 2024; Powell, 2020; Shah et al., 2022). AI-driven mobile applications for cancer care have gained prominence due to their potential to enhance diagnostic accuracy, optimize treatment protocols, and improve patient outcomes. These applications utilize machine learning algorithms, natural language processing, and computer vision to analyze patient data, including medical histories, genetic information, and imaging results. Notable AI-driven apps in cancer care include IBM Watson for Oncology, which provides evidence-based treatment recommendations, and Cancer Guide, which offers personalized care plans (Abhilasha et al., 2024; Derraz et al., 2024; Shah et al., 2022; Srivastava R., 2023). Despite their advancements, these applications face several limitations that impact their efficacy in real-world settings.

Ensuring Healthcare Data Security

As healthcare systems accumulate vast amounts of sensitive patient data, the importance of cybersecurity becomes increasingly evident. Data security innovations are designed to prevent breaches and maintain patient confidentiality. Key measures being implemented include advanced encryption techniques, secure data transmission protocols, and comprehensive cybersecurity training for healthcare professionals. These strategies are crucial for maintaining the trust and privacy of individuals, which are integral to establishing a secure and reliable healthcare system. By prioritizing cybersecurity, healthcare organizations safeguard sensitive information and reinforce the foundational tenets of patient care and trust that are essential in healthcare. The commitment to robust cybersecurity practices ensures that patient data remains intact, fostering a secure environment where patients can confidently receive care.

Promoting Sustainable Healthcare Solutions

The healthcare industry is progressively prioritizing sustainable solutions, acknowledging the significant role that environmental factors play in public health. This transition toward sustainability encompasses several key strategies, including waste reduction, energy conservation, and the adoption of green building designs. Furthermore, numerous organizations are actively exploring innovative technologies that facilitate the use of recyclable materials and mitigate pollution. These sustainable practices enhance the planet's health and offer substantial long-term cost savings and efficiency improvements for healthcare facilities. This commitment to sustainability positions the healthcare sector as a leader in environmental stewardship, ultimately benefiting public health and the economy.

Wearable Technology and Remote Health Monitoring

Wearable technology and remote health monitoring devices have fundamentally changed how individuals use their health data. These advancements empower patients by providing real-time insights into critical health metrics, facilitating proactive healthcare and wellness management. As technology continues to evolve, increasingly sophisticated wearables are being developed to monitor various health parameters, including heart rate, glucose levels, and sleep patterns. The future of wearable technology lies in its ability to predict health issues before they escalate into more serious conditions, representing a significant advancement in preventative healthcare. This evolution enhances individual health management and revolutionizes the broader approach to public health.

Case Studies: Success Stories in Health Policy Reforms

Across sub-Saharan Africa, notable success stories in health policy reform provide valuable insights and lessons for other regions. A prime example is Rwanda, where a comprehensive health system transformation has been achieved through community-based health insurance schemes and substantial investments in healthcare infrastructure. These initiatives have led to marked improvements in health outcomes for the population. Additionally, Ethiopia's Health Extension Program exemplifies how effective leadership and robust community engagement can drive significant advancements in health. By prioritizing preventive and primary curative services at the community level, the program has successfully enhanced the overall health status of its citizens. These cases illustrate the potential of targeted policies and strategic investments to stimulate positive change within health systems. The results achieved in Rwanda and Ethiopia serve as a compelling testament to the impact that well-designed health initiatives can have on the welfare of communities (Mac-Seing et al., 2020; Mhazo & Maponga, 2022; Odoch et al., 2022).

Strategies for Implementing Radical Change

A comprehensive and multifaceted strategy is vital for effectively navigating the future landscape of health policy, particularly in pursuit of transformative change. Advocating for political support and steadfast commitment is imperative, especially in increasing budget allocations for health initiatives. Concurrently, leaders in healthcare management must prioritize capacity building and integrating best practices in healthcare delivery systems. Moreover, harnessing international partnerships and embracing digital health innovations can be powerful catalysts for successfully implementing transformative policies and programs. The path toward a reimagined wellness ecosystem in sub-Saharan Africa requires a unified and strategic approach, emphasizing the critical importance of collaboration, innovation, and commitment across all sectors and levels. Through these concerted efforts, we can drive the systemic changes necessary to improve health outcomes and achieve lasting regional advancements.

Bibliography

A Review of AI in Breast Cancer Detection. (2024). *International Journal of Innovative Research in Computer Science and Technology.* ttps://api.semanticscholar.org/CorpusID:269399913Abhilasha, A. Narang, & Priyanka Vashisht. (2024). A Review of AI in Breast Cancer Detection. *International Journal of Innovative Research in Computer Science and Technology (IJIRCST), 12*(2), 126–129. https://doi.org/doi:10.55524/ijircst.2024.12.2.22
Achoki, T. (2016). *Revisiting Health System Performance Assessment in Africa.* https://api.semanticscholar.org/CorpusID:79109646

Ackerman, M., Henry, D., Finon, A., Binois, R., & Estève, É. (2021). Persistent maculopapular rash after the first dose of Pfizer-BioNTech COVID-19 vaccine. *Journal of the European Academy of Dermatology and Venereology, 35*, e423–e425.

Al-Bataineh, R. T., Al-Hammouri, M. M., & Al-Jaraideh, W. K. (2023). Perspective of healthcare providers on assessing the quality and accessibility of health services for chronic diseases in Jordan during Covid-19: A mixed method study. *BMC Health Services Research, 23.* https://api.semanticscholar.org/CorpusID:261067884

Ali, M. M. (2024). Telehealth, The Light at The End of The Tunnel-A Ray of Hope for Rural and Remote Healthcare. *International Journal of Clinical Studies and Medical Case Reports.* https://api.semanticscholar.org/CorpusID:262208253

Alleema, N. N., Chaturvedi, A., Nanda, A. K., Josephson,

P. J., Buttar, A. M., & Komarasamy, D. (2023). Computation Offloading for Image Compression in Mobile Edge Computing Using a Deep Belief Network Based on the Markov Approximation Algorithm. *Mobile Networks and Applications*, 1–15.

Aquino-Jarquin, G. (2022). The patent dispute over the breakthrough mRNA technology. *Frontiers in Bioengineering and Biotechnology, 10*. https://api.semanticscholar.org/CorpusID:253260706

Argunova, Y. A., Lyapina, I. N., Zvereva, T. N., & Barbarash, O. L. (2024). Modern information technology in cardiac rehabilitation. Applications for mobile devices (review). *Fundamental and Clinical Medicine*. https://api.semanticscholar.org/CorpusID:266942660

Azevedo, M. J. (2017). The State of Health System(s) in Africa: Challenges and Opportunities. In *Historical Perspectives on the State of Health and Health Systems in Africa, Volume II: The Modern Era* (pp. 1–73). Springer International Publishing. https://doi.org/10.1007/978-3-319-32564-4_1

Badieyan, Z. S., & Evans, T. (2019). Concise Review: Application of Chemically Modified mRNA in Cell Fate Conversion and Tissue Engineering. *Stem Cells Translational Medicine, 8*, 833–843.

Blaise, H., & Yongsi, N. (2023). For a shift of paradigm in healthcare systems in sub-Saharan Africa: Moving from current unequal access to modern care to sustainable health systems encompassing African traditional medicine. *World Journal of Advanced Research and Reviews*. https://api.semanticscholar.org/CorpusID:259851132

Bywater, T. J., Berry, V., Blower, S. L., Bursnall, M., Cox, E., Mason-Jones, A. J., McGilloway, S., McKendrick, K., Mitchell, S. B., Pickett, K. E., Richardson, G., Solaiman, K., Teare, M., Walker, S., & Whittaker, K. A. (2022). A randomized controlled trial of a proportionate universal parenting program delivery model (E-SEE Steps) to enhance child social-emotional wellbeing. *PLoS ONE, 17*. https://api.semanticscholar.org/CorpusID:247953035

Cadet, K., Baker, D. R., & Brown, A. (2023). A qualitative assessment of provider satisfaction and experiences with a COVID-19 community mobile health clinic outreach model in underserved Baltimore neighborhoods. *SAGE Open Medicine*, *11*. https://api.semanticscholar.org/CorpusID:256779948

Cassell, L. T., & Cassell, A. K. (2019). Health Care Assessment of Health Care Delivery and Outcome- A West African Review. *Saudi Journal of Medicine*, *04*(11), 710–714.

Catanzaro, J., logix, L. C. M. G. M. M. U. N., & Dickens, A. (2019). Regenerative Medicine Revolution By Personalized Design. *Biosciences*. https://api.semanticscholar.org/CorpusID:208583155

Cerda, I. H., Thérond, A., Moreau, S., Studer, K., Donjow, A. R., Crowther, J. E., Mazzolenis, M. E., Lang, M., Tolba, R., Gilligan, C., Ashina, S., Kaye, A. D., Yong, R. J., Schatman, M. E., & Robinson, C. L. (2024). Telehealth and Virtual Reality Technologies in Chronic Pain Management: A Narrative Review. *Current Pain and Headache Reports*, 1–12.

Chakraborty, C., Pal, S., Bhattacharya, M., Dash, S., & Lee,

S. S. (2023). Overview of Chatbots with special emphasis on artificial intelligence-enabled ChatGPT in medical science. In *Frontiers in Artificial Intelligence* (Vol. 6). Frontiers Media SA. https://doi.org/10.3389/frai.2023.1237704

Crusan, A. C., Lilja, K., Walters, T., & Baumler, M. D. (2021). *Barriers to Using Telehealth During a Pandemic Versus In-Person Appointments to Conduct Nutrition Assessments in a Community Health Clinic Setting.* https://api.semanticscholar.org/CorpusID:236270419

Derraz, B., Breda, G., Kaempf, C., Baenke, F., Cotte, F., Reiche, K., Köhl, U., Kather, J. N., Eskenazy, D., & Gilbert, S. (2024). New regulatory thinking is needed for AI-based personalized drug and cell therapies in precision oncology. *Npj Precision Oncology, 8*(1). https://doi.org/10.1038/s41698-024-00517-w

Du, X., Yada, E., Terai, Y., Takahashi, T., Nakanishi, H., Tanaka, H., Akita, H., & Itaka, K. (2023). Comprehensive Evaluation of Lipid Nanoparticles and Polyplex Nanomicelles for Muscle-Targeted mRNA Delivery. *Pharmaceutics, 15.* https://api.semanticscholar.org/CorpusID:261644848

Erlangga, D., Powell-Jackson, T., Balabanova, D., & Hanson, K. (2023). Determinants of government spending on primary healthcare: A global data analysis. *BMJ Global Health, 8.* https://api.semanticscholar.org/CorpusID:265507606

Frimpong, A. O., Amporfu, E., & Arthur, E. (2022). Effects of Public and External Health Spending on Out-of-Pocket Payments for Healthcare in Sub-Saharan Africa. *Health Policy and Planning.* https://api.semanticscholar.org/CorpusID:251622975

Garcia, B., Padgett, K. E., & Russo, J. L. A. (2022). Development of the COVID-19 (SARS-CoV-2) mRNA Vaccines: Translational Medicine at its Best. *Journal of Medical - Clinical Research & Reviews.* https://api.semanticscholar.org/CorpusID:251674684

Geevarghese, R., Bodard, S., Razakamanantsoa, L., Marcelin, C., Petre, E. N., Dohan, A., Kastler, A., Frandon, J., Barral, M., Soyer, P., & Cornelis, F. H. (2024). Interventional Oncology: 2024

Göksu, G. G. (2023). A retrospective overview of the Journal of Public Budgeting, Accounting and Financial Management using bibliometric analysis. *Journal of Public Budgeting, Accounting & Financial Management.* https://api.semanticscholar.org/CorpusID:257609022

Health in Africa. (2024). *Nature Communications*, *15*(1), 967. https://doi.org/10.1038/s41467-024-45268-1

Ibeneme, S., Ongom, M., Ukor, N., & Okeibunor, J. (2020). Realigning Health Systems Strategies and Approaches; What Should African Countries Do to Strengthen Health Systems for the Sustainable Development Goals? *Frontiers in Public Health*, *8*.

Imran, S. A. M., Hamizul, M. H. A. M., Bariah, A. A. N. K., Zaman, W. S. W. K., & Nordin, F. (2022). Regenerative Medicine Therapy in Malaysia: An Update. *Frontiers in Bioengineering and Biotechnology*, *10*. https://api.semanticscholar.org/CorpusID:248399542

IoT Integration in Telemedicine: Investigating the Role of Internet of Things Devices in Facilitating Remote Patient Monitoring and Data Transmission. (2023). *International*

Internal Medicine Journal.
https://api.semanticscholar.org/CorpusID:266302757

Jamous, Y. F., & Alhomoud, D. A. (2023). The Safety and Effectiveness of mRNA Vaccines Against SARS-CoV-2. *Cureus, 15*.
https://api.semanticscholar.org/CorpusID:262206021

Janjua, S., Carter, D., Threapleton, C. J. D., Prigmore, S., & Disler, R. T. (2021). Telehealth interventions: Remote monitoring and consultations for people with chronic obstructive pulmonary disease (COPD). *The Cochrane Database of Systematic Reviews*, *7*, CD013196.

Jeetoo, J., & Jaunky, V. C. (2023). Divergence of healthcare expenditure in sub-Saharan Africa. *Journal for Studies in Economics and Econometrics*, *47*(1), 75–105.
https://doi.org/10.1080/03796205.2023.2185664

Khan, A., Wu, J., Choi, E., Graber-Naidich, A., Henry, S., Wakelee, H. A., Kurian, A. W., Liang, S.-Y., Leung, A., Langlotz, C., Backhus, L. M., & Han, S. S. (2023). Abstract P068: A hybrid modelling approach for abstracting CT imaging indications by integrating natural language processing from radiology reports with structured data from electronic health records. *Cancer Prevention Research*, *16*(1_Supplement), P068–P068.
https://doi.org/10.1158/1940-6215.PrecPrev22-P068

Kolluri, S. , Patil, S. C. , Kasula, B. Y. , Jiwani, N. , &, & Kiruthiga, T. (2024). Development of Consistent Followup and Analysis of Level of Cancer Detection Using Wearables With AI Technology. *IEEE International Conference on Computing, Power and Communication Technologies (IC2PCT)*, 310–415.

Larson, P. S. (2018). Access to Health Care in Sub-Saharan Africa: Challenges in a Changing Health Landscape in a Context of Development. *Health in Ecological Perspectives in the Anthropocene.* https://api.semanticscholar.org/CorpusID:133937897

Lin, F., Lin, E. Z., Anekoji, M., Ichim, T. E., Hu, J., Marincola, F. M., Jones, L. D., Kesari, S., & Ashili, S. (2023). Advancing personalized medicine in brain cancer: Exploring the role of mRNA vaccines. *Journal of Translational Medicine, 21.* https://api.semanticscholar.org/CorpusID:265259289

Mac-Seing, M., Zinszer, K., Omenka, C. O., Beaudrap, P. D., Mehrabi, F., & Zarowsky, C. (2020). Pro-equity legislation, health policy and utilisation of sexual and reproductive health services by vulnerable populations in sub-Saharan Africa: A systematic review. *Global Health Promotion*, *27*, 97–106.

Malhotra, A. (2022). Curing the pandemic of misinformation on COVID-19 mRNA vaccines through real evidence-based medicine—Part 1. *Journal of Insulin Resistance, 5.* https://api.semanticscholar.org/CorpusID:252895592

Martinez, B., Velazquez, A., & Vital, D. (2024). Self-Powered Wearable Devices Integrated with Virtual Reality Simulation Clinics: A Novel Approach to Healthcare Modernization. *2024 United States National Committee of URSI National Radio Science Meeting (USNC-URSI NRSM)*, 140–140.

Mehboob, R. (2023). Approaches and challenges in Public Health. *Pakistan Journal of Health Sciences.*

https://api.semanticscholar.org/CorpusID:265090441

Meza, J. L. R., & Rodríguez, C. J. V. (2018). HISTORIA DE LA INGENIERÍA INDUSTRIAL. *Enfoques, Teorías y Perspectivas de La Ingeniería Industrial y Sus Programas Académicos.* https://api.semanticscholar.org/CorpusID:239905466

Mhazo, A. T., & Maponga, C. C. (2022). Beyond political will: Unpacking the drivers of (non) health reforms in sub-Saharan Africa. *BMJ Global Health, 7*(12). https://doi.org/10.1136/bmjgh-2022-010228

Mishra, V., Ugemuge, S., & Tiwade, Y. (2023). Artificial intelligence changing the future of healthcare diagnostics. *Journal of Cellular Biotechnology.* https://api.semanticscholar.org/CorpusID:261020441

Mooney, K. E., Bywater, T. J., Hinde, S., Richardson, G., Wright, J., Dickerson, J., & Blower, S. L. (2023). A quasi-experimental effectiveness evaluation of the 'Incredible Years Toddler' parenting programme on children's development aged 5: A study protocol. *PLOS ONE, 18.* https://api.semanticscholar.org/CorpusID:263061719

Moonga, J. (2023). Digital Biomarkers and Wearable Neurotechnologies: A Cost of Privacy and Security for Alzheimer's Patients. *Alzheimer's & Dementia, 19.* https://api.semanticscholar.org/CorpusID:259167262

Moyo, E., Mhango, M., Moyo, P., Dzinamarira, T., Chitungo, I., & Murewanhema, G. (2023). Emerging infectious disease outbreaks in Sub-Saharan Africa: Learning from the past and present to be better prepared for future outbreaks. *Frontiers in Public Health, 11.*

https://www.frontiersin.org/journals/public-health/articles/10.3389/fpubh.2023.1049986

Musiega, A., Nyawira, L., Tsofa, B., Njuguna, R. G., Munywoki, J., Hanson, K., Mulwa, A., Molyneux, S., Maina, I., Normand, C., Jemutai, J., & Barasa, E. W. (2023). Budget monitoring, accountability practices and their influence on the efficiency of county health systems in Kenya. *PLOS Global Public Health*, *3*. https://api.semanticscholar.org/CorpusID:265254830

Ng, B. P., Park, C., Silverman, C. L., Eckhoff, D. O., Guest, J. C., & Díaz, D. A. (2022). Accessibility and utilisation of telehealth services among older adults during COVID-19 pandemic in the United States. *Health & Social Care in the Community*. https://api.semanticscholar.org/CorpusID:245801623

Odoch, W. D., Senkubuge, F., Masese, A. B., & Hongoro, C. (2022). How are global health policies transferred to sub-Saharan Africa countries? A systematic critical review of literature. *Globalization and Health*, *18*. https://api.semanticscholar.org/CorpusID:247027875

Okoroiwu, H. U., Uchendu, K. I., & Essien, R. A. (2020). Causes of morbidity and mortality among patients admitted in a tertiary hospital in southern Nigeria: A 6 year evaluation. *PLOS ONE*, *15*(8), 1–15. https://doi.org/10.1371/journal.pone.0237313

Oleribe, O. O., Momoh, J., Uzochukwu, B. S., Mbofana, F., Adebiyi, A. O., Barbera, T. A., Williams, R., & Taylor-Robinson, S. D. (2019). Identifying Key Challenges Facing Healthcare Systems In Africa And Potential Solutions. *International Journal of General Medicine*, *12*, 395–403.

Olorunsogo, T. O., Balogun, O. D., Ayo-Farai, O., Ogundairo, O., Maduka, C. P., Okongwu, C. C., & Onwumere, C. (2024). Reviewing the evolution of U. S. telemedicine post-pandemic by analyzing its growth, acceptability, and challenges in remote healthcare delivery during Global Health Crises. *World Journal of Biology Pharmacy and Health Sciences.* https://api.semanticscholar.org/CorpusID:267166597

Oppong, J. (2020). Disruptive Technologies and the African Health-Care Crisis: A Path to Sustainability. In *Disruptive Technologies, Innovation and Development in Africa* (pp. 117–145). Springer International Publishing.

Patange, A., Mahesan, K. V., Manjula, C., Donald, C., Babu, S. A., Peroumal, V., & Arumugam, M. (2023). Advancements in optical steganography for secure medical data transmission in telehealth systems. *Optical and Quantum Electronics*, *55*, 1–13.

Pennell, N. A., Dicker, A. P., Tran, C., Jim, H. S. L., Schwartz, D., & Stepanski, E. (2017). mHealth: Mobile Technologies to Virtually Bring the Patient Into an Oncology Practice. *American Society of Clinical Oncology Educational Book. American Society of Clinical Oncology. Annual Meeting*, *37*, 144–154.

Pham, H.-S., Le, H. S., & Hoang, T. A. (2023). Propose technology and management model of mobile cloud computing for the Vietnam national digital transformation program. *Ministry of Science and Technology, Vietnam.* https://api.semanticscholar.org/CorpusID:261190943

Powell, A. (2020). Risks and benefits of an AI revolution in medicine-Harvard Gazette. *The Harvard Gazette.*

Rhym, L. H., Manan, R. S., Koller, A., Stephanie, G., & Anderson, D. G. (2023). Peptide-encoding mRNA barcodes for the high-throughput in vivo screening of libraries of lipid nanoparticles for mRNA delivery. *Nature Biomedical Engineering*, *7*, 901–910.

Rus, V., Nguyen, V. P., Shriver, M. C., Degrezia, M., Alhassan, E., Passetti, M., Thomas, A., & Rus, H. G. (2022). Effect of methotrexate on response to Covid-19 mRNA vaccines in patients with Autoimmune Inflammatory Rheumatic Diseases: A longitudinal study. *The Journal of Immunology*. https://api.semanticscholar.org/CorpusID:255707784

Rzymski, P. (2023). The pivotal role of uridine modifications in the development of mRNA technology. *Journal of Medical Science*. https://api.semanticscholar.org/CorpusID:266121594

Shah, S. C., Kayamba, V., Peek, R. M., & Heimburger, D. (2019). Cancer Control in Low- and Middle-Income Countries: Is It Time to Consider Screening? *Journal of Global Oncology*, *5*, 1–8. https://doi.org/10.1200/JGO.18.00200

Shah, U. , Biswas, M. R. , Alzubaidi, M. S. , Ali, H. , Alam, T. , Househ, M. , &, & Shah, Z. (2022). Recent Developments in Artificial Intelligence-Based Techniques for Prostate Cancer Detection_ A Scoping Review. *Studies in Health Technology and Informatics*, *289*, 268–271.

Sharma, P., Shaikh, A. A., Sao, A., & Rohilla, N. (2022). Using Technology Acceptance Model, Analyzing the Role of Telehealth Services in the Healthcare Industry During COVID-19. *Asia Pacific Journal of Health Management*.

https://api.semanticscholar.org/CorpusID:251268844

Singh, A. V., Bansod, G., Mahajan, M., Dietrich, P. M., Singh, S. P., Rav, K., Thissen, A., Bharde, A. M., Rothenstein, D., Kulkarni, S., & Bill, J. (2023). Digital Transformation in Toxicology: Improving Communication and Efficiency in Risk Assessment. *ACS Omega*, *8*, 21377–21390.

Sood, V. R., Baig, A. H., & Gururajan, R. (2016). *What factors determine healthcare professionals' (HCPs) acceptance of mobile devices for telehealth: A qualitative study conducted in Queensland, Australia.* https://api.semanticscholar.org/CorpusID:78216151

Srivastava, R. (2022). Applications of artificial intelligence multiomics in precision oncology. *Journal of Cancer Research and Clinical Oncology*, *149*, 503–510.

Srivastava R. (2023). Applications of artificial intelligence multiomics in precision oncology. *Journal of Cancer Research and Clinical Oncology*, *149*(1), 503–510. https://doi.org/https://doi.org/10.1007/s00432-022-04161-4

Tewolde, M., & Weldeyohannes, M. (2019). Health Care Systems in Africa: Achievements, Challenges and Policy Implications for Achieving Sustainable Development Goal 3. *The International Journal of Humanities & Social Studies*, *7*(2).

Utan, O. E. (2021). Patterns of African Healthcare Funding: Investment Implications for Public-Private Partnerships. *TEXILA INTERNATIONAL JOURNAL OF PUBLIC HEALTH.*

https://api.semanticscholar.org/CorpusID:240743121

Vacas-Aguilar, F. (2020). 5G como oportunidad para la ruptura del duopolio en el mercado móvil. *Profesional De La Informacion, 28.* https://api.semanticscholar.org/CorpusID:212880825

Zekeng, E. G. (2016). *Healthcare Systems in Sub-Saharan Africa: Focusing on community-based delivery (CBD) of health services and the development of local research institutes.* https://api.semanticscholar.org/CorpusID:20567468

Zhou, H. (2024). mRNA Vaccines in Cancer Treatment. *MedScien.* https://api.semanticscholar.org/CorpusID:266831629

Ziaie, B., Jagannathan, S., Yokoyama, K., Murray, P. J., Venetsanopoulos, A. N., Al-Rwashidi, H., & Mitchell, J. B. (2000). *Guest Editorial Special Issue on Mobile Telemedicine and Telehealth Systems T.* https://api.semanticscholar.org/CorpusID:73772659

Chapter 2: Global and Macro-Budgeting for Healthcare

Illustration of global and macro-budgeting for healthcare, depicting a collaborative atmosphere among diverse policymakers, economists, and healthcare professionals as they analyze financial data and global health metrics.

Vignette: Navigating the Complexities of Global and Macro-Budgeting in Healthcare

Background:

The island nation of Azura, with a population of 5 million, is undergoing significant healthcare reform. The government aims to transition from a fragmented, fee-for-service model to a more integrated, globally budgeted system. This shift is driven by the need to control escalating healthcare costs, improve access to care, and enhance health outcomes for its citizens.

The Challenge:

Azura's healthcare **expenditures have grown from 8% to 12% of its GDP over the past decade, outpacing economic growth. The current system is plagued by inefficiencies, including an overreliance** on specialized care, long waiting times for non-emergency procedures and significant disparities in health access and outcomes across different socio-economic groups.

The Task:

As a member of Azura's Healthcare Reform Task Force, you are tasked with developing a global and macro-budgeting framework. This framework must address the following objectives:

1. Cost Containment: Implement mechanisms to control healthcare spending without compromising quality.

2. Equitable Access: Ensure that all citizens access necessary healthcare services, regardless of socio-economic status.

3. Quality Improvement: Promote high-quality care focusing on patient outcomes and satisfaction.

4. Sustainability: Develop a long-term financing model considering Azura's economic growth and fiscal capacity.

5. Stakeholder Engagement: Foster collaboration and buy-in among healthcare providers, patients, and the broader community.

Questions for Discussion:

1. What are the critical steps in establishing a global budget for Azura's healthcare system, and how can it be structured to incentivize cost-effective, high-quality care?

2. How can macro-budgeting tools and techniques be applied to forecast healthcare expenditures, and what factors should be considered in these projections?

3. In designing the global budget, how can Azura prioritize preventive care and public health initiatives to reduce the burden of chronic diseases and improve population health?

4. What strategies can be employed to ensure the equitable distribution of healthcare resources, address the needs of vulnerable populations, and reduce health disparities?

5. How can the success of the global and macro-budgeting approach be measured, and what adjustments might be necessary based on ongoing evaluation and feedback?

Introduction

"A leader ceases to lead as soon as they fail to inspire their followers to dream big and face future challenges with courage." The current healthcare funding sources in sub-Saharan African countries could be more inspiring and reveal a need for foresight by the leaders and planners.

Given the above observations, with emphasis on individual and human dignity, I am suggesting actions that safeguard and improve the health and vitality of people in general and the labor force in particular.

Global budgeting involves allocating a fixed budget to a

specific entity, like a department or hospital, for a set period to control costs and promote efficiency. In contrast, macro budgeting focuses on a broader economic scale, considering factors like GDP growth and inflation rates to guide governmental budget policies and allocations (Murray, 2022). Global budgeting is applied at the organizational level, emphasizing internal cost management, while macro budgeting operates at the national or regional level to influence the entire economy (International Monetary Fund (IMF), n.d.). The primary goal of global budgeting is to manage costs within a predefined limit, while macro budgeting aims to steer a country or region's economic health and fiscal position (Murray, 2022). These distinct financial management strategies serve different purposes, allowing entities and governments to manage finances at different scales to achieve their objectives effectively.

Healthcare Budgeting is a critical framework for managing financial resources within the healthcare sector. It ensures that funds are allocated efficiently to improve patient care while maintaining financial sustainability. Global and macro-budgeting have gained prominence among various budgeting approaches for their strategic implications on healthcare financing (Chen et al., 2021). Global budgeting in healthcare involves allocating a predetermined lump sum to a healthcare provider or a group of providers for a set period, typically a year. This budget is meant to cover all healthcare services based on historical spending patterns, demographics, and the health needs of the population served (Yang et al., 2021). For instance, hospitals in certain regions operate under global budgets, enabling them to focus on delivering comprehensive care without the pressure to increase volume (Behera & Dash, 2019; Chen et al., 2021). This system encourages healthcare providers to optimize resource allocation, prioritize preventive care, and invest in community health initiatives. Global healthcare budgeting revolutionizes the allocation of resources and delivery of comprehensive care (Murray, 2022; Pany et al., 2022; Yang et al., 2021). This is a predetermined lump sum, meticulously calculated, entrusted to healthcare providers for a fixed period, usually a year. This budget, carefully crafted using historical spending patterns, demographics, and the unique health needs of the population served, ensures that every dollar is maximized for optimal impact.

Imagine hospitals operating under this global budgeting system, free from the pressure of increasing patient volume. Liberated from the relentless pursuit of numbers, healthcare providers can now focus solely on what truly matters—delivering high-quality care. No longer burdened by the pressure to generate revenue, they can channel their energy towards optimization, excellence, and innovation. This bold approach to budgeting encourages healthcare providers to become resource allocation experts, efficiently distributing funds where they are most needed (Pany et al., 2022). They can strategically invest in preventive care initiatives—a powerful weapon against the rise of chronic diseases. The system undergoes a tectonic shift towards long-term wellness by addressing health issues at their root rather than simply treating symptoms.

Nevertheless, there is more. Global budgeting fosters a sense of responsibility within healthcare providers, empowering them to think beyond the confines of their walls. With surplus funds available, they can embark on community health initiatives, reaching out to underserved populations and ensuring access to quality care is not just a privilege for some but a right for all.

Confidently, I embrace this transformative concept of global budgeting in healthcare and recognize its potential to reshape the landscape of the healthcare industry. In this landscape, outcomes matter more than volume, where resources are optimized, and where the health and well-being of our communities are prioritized above all else. So, let us forge ahead, boldly embracing global budgeting as the catalyst for change. With unwavering determination, this will create a healthcare system not confined by financial constraints but propelled by the limitless potential of human compassion, innovation, and a shared mission to enhance the lives of those we serve.

Understanding Global Budgeting

Global budgeting in healthcare refers to the allocation of a fixed financial resource to a specific healthcare institution or system for a defined period. This lump sum is intended to cover all necessary services, incentivizing providers to focus on efficiency and the quality of care. Examples include Taiwan's national health insurance program, which, facing financial deficits, implemented global budgeting to manage expenditures effectively (Yang et al., 2021).

Global budgeting is a strategic financial management approach used in healthcare systems to control costs and allocate resources efficiently. Macro-budgeting, on the other hand, focuses on the broader economic perspective of healthcare expenditure across a nation or large region. It considers the optimal distribution of resources concerning the gross domestic product (GDP) and overall public health goals. Research shows that, on a macro level, many economies—excluding the United States—tend to underspend on healthcare, highlighting the need for a balanced approach to budget allocation (Pany et al., 2022).

One critical element of global budgeting is establishing a designated healthcare account. This account serves as a centralized repository for all healthcare-related funds, allowing for better tracking and management of expenses. By consolidating financial resources in a designated healthcare account, healthcare organizations can streamline budgeting processes, monitor spending patterns, and ensure resources are allocated effectively to meet the population's needs. Furthermore, a designated healthcare account enhances transparency and accountability in resource allocation, as it provides a clear overview of how funds are utilized across various healthcare services and programs. This level of financial visibility enables decision-makers to identify areas of overspending or inefficiency, making it easier to make informed budgetary adjustments and optimize resource utilization.

Global and macro-budgeting in healthcare are essential for effective management and policy-making. This strategic methodology involves large-scale allocation of financial resources to address healthcare needs at national or international levels. Decision-makers engaged in global and macro-budgeting must consider several factors, such as population health trends, disease burdens, emerging health threats, and existing healthcare infrastructure. By systematically analyzing these components, policymakers can make informed decisions about the efficient distribution of financial resources, ensuring the healthcare needs of the population are met (Behera & Dash, 2019; Glassman et al., 2023; Murray, 2022; Pany, n.d.; Yang et al., 2021). The significance of this strategic approach cannot be overstated, as it lays the foundation for robust healthcare systems capable of effectively responding to diverse health challenges.

Advantages of Global and Macro-Budgeting

Global and macro-budgeting are robust methodologies offering several significant healthcare management advantages. These approaches not only facilitate control over healthcare costs but also enhance the efficiency of resource allocation and the overall quality of service delivery. They serve as strategic instruments for healthcare administrators and policymakers, enabling them to achieve financial sustainability within healthcare systems.

A notable benefit of global and macro-budgeting is their capacity to promote equity and access to healthcare services for all individuals, irrespective of socio-economic status or geographic location. Policymakers can make strides toward universal healthcare coverage and reduce health disparities by prioritizing resource allocation based on population health needs rather than individual patient characteristics. This approach ensures that resources are directed where they are most needed, ultimately advancing equitable healthcare for all (Behera & Dash, 2019; Murray, 2022; Yang et al., 2021).

Challenges and Considerations in Implementing Global and Macro-Budgeting Approaches

Implementing global and macro-budgeting approaches in healthcare presents several challenges and considerations that must be addressed for successful outcomes. One significant obstacle is the resistance from healthcare providers accustomed to fee-for-service models. Additionally, determining appropriate budget levels can be complex and fraught with difficulties, particularly when it comes to ensuring that the quality of care is consistently maintained. A notable example of these budgeting challenges can be found in Benin's universal health coverage project, which underscores the imperative of strategic purchasing and efficient expenditure processes (Paul et al., 2020).

Moreover, global and macro-budgeting are crucial for optimizing healthcare spending and resource allocation. By identifying areas characterized by inefficiency or waste, decision-makers can conduct thorough analyses of healthcare expenditures and outcomes, thereby pinpointing opportunities for improvement. This enables the reallocation of resources to areas that can significantly impact population health (Alebachew et al., 2023; Debie et al., 2022).

Global budgeting in healthcare represents a pivotal advancement toward achieving sustainable and equitable healthcare systems. With careful design and implementation, it provides a viable pathway to controlling healthcare costs while ensuring the delivery of high-quality care to all individuals. As nations strive to balance the increasing demands for healthcare services with the necessity of maintaining fiscal responsibility, global and macro-budgeting will undoubtedly play a more prominent role in shaping the future of healthcare financing and delivery. Future trends indicate a sustained emphasis on innovative budgeting strategies to address the dual challenges of rising healthcare costs and evolving care demands. Consequently, global and macro-budgeting are set to play a profound role in the financial management of healthcare systems worldwide, with a focus on sustainability and equity.

In conclusion, global and macro-budgeting are essential for broadly shaping healthcare systems and policies. By prioritizing equity, access, and efficiency, decision-makers can enhance population health outcomes and promote sustainable healthcare systems. Furthermore, global budgeting, alongside a designated healthcare account, emerges as an invaluable financial management tool for healthcare organizations seeking to control costs and optimize resources. By consolidating funding from diverse sources and centralizing financial management practices, healthcare systems can improve operational efficiency, enhance financial transparency, and ultimately provide superior quality care to patients (Yang et al., 2021).

Bibliography

Alebachew, A., Abdella, E., Abera, S., Dessie, E., Mesele, T., Mitiku, W., Muñoz, R., Opuni, M., Teplitskaya, L., Walker, D. G., & Gilmartin, C. (2023). Costs and resource needs for primary health care in Ethiopia: evidence to inform planning and budgeting for universal health coverage. *Frontiers in Public Health, 11.* https://doi.org/https://doi.org/10.3389/fpubh.2023.1242314

Behera, D. K., & Dash, U. (2019). Impact of macro-fiscal determinants on health financing: empirical evidence from low-and middle-income countries. *Global Health Research and Policy, 4*(1). https://doi.org/10.1186/s41256-019-0112-4

Chen, S., Kuhn, M., Prettner, K., Bloom, D. E., & Wang, C. (2021). Macro-level efficiency of health expenditure: Estimates for 15 major economies. *Social Science and Medicine, 287.* https://doi.org/10.1016/j.socscimed.2021.114270

Debie, A., Khatri, R. B., & Assefa, Y. (2022). Contributions and challenges of healthcare financing towards universal health coverage in Ethiopia: a narrative evidence synthesis. *BMC Health Services Research, 22*(1). https://doi.org/10.1186/s12913-022-08151-7

Glassman, A., Keller, J. M., & Smitham, E. (2023). *The Future of Global Health Spending Amidst Multiple Crises.*

Murray, R. (2022). Hospital Global Budgets_ A Promising State Tool for Controlling Health Care Spending _ Commonwealth Fund. *Commonwealth Fund.* https://doi.org/https://doi.org/10.26099/98xk-am95

Bichachi, R. (2024). *Healthcare & Hospital Budgeting Guide for 2024.* https://www.netsuite.com/portal/resource/articles/financial-management/healthcare-budgeting.shtml

Campbell, M., Escobar, O., & Fenton, C. et al. (2018). The impact of participatory budgeting on health and wellbeing. *BMC Public Health, 18*(822). https://doi.org/https://doi.org/10.1186/s12889-018-5735-8

Daniels, N. (2016). Resource Allocation and Priority Setting. In W. H. Barrett D, Ortmann L, & et al., Dawson A (Eds.), *Public Health Ethics: Cases Spanning the Globe.* Springer.

Güngör Göksu, G. (2023). A retrospective overview of the Journal of Public Budgeting, Accounting and Financial Management using bibliometric analysis. In *Journal of Public Budgeting, Accounting and Financial Management* (Vol. 35, Issue 2, pp. 264–295). Emerald Publishing. https://doi.org/10.1108/JPBAFM-04-2022-0061

Homauni, A., Markazi-Moghaddam, N., Mosadeghkhah, A., Noori, M., Abbasiyan, K., Zargar, S., & Jame, B. (2023). Budgeting in Healthcare Systems and Organizations: A Systematic Review. In *Iran J Public Health* (Vol. 52, Issue 9). https://creativecommons.org/licenses/by-nc/4.0/

International Monetary Fund (IMF). (n.d.). *Guidelines for Public Expenditure Management--Section 3--Budget Preparation.* Retrieved April 24, 2024, from https://www.imf.org/external/pubs/ft/expend/guide3.htm.

Janga, V., Wako, D. , A. , Genale, A. , S. , Sundaram, B. , Pandey, A. , & Karthika, P. (2022). Artificial Intelligence in Cloud Technology and Wireless Network Technology using Health Care System. *6th International Conference on Trends in Electronics and Informatics (ICOEI), 1-7.*

Murray, R. (2022). *Hospital Global Budgets: A Promising State Tool for Controlling Health Care Spending | Commonwealth Fund Hospital Global Budgets: A Promising State Tool for Controlling Health Care Spending.*

https://www.commonwealthfund.org/publications/issue-briefs/2022/mar/hospital-global-budgets-state-tool-controlling-spending

Musiega, A., Nyawira, L., Tsofa, B., Njuguna, R. G., Munywoki, J., Hanson, K., Mulwa, A. , Molyneux, S. , Maina, I. , Normand, C. , Jemutai, J. , & & Barasa, E. (2023). Budget monitoring, accountability practices and their influence on the efficiency of county health systems in Kenya. *PLOS Global Public Health*, *3*(11). https://doi.org/https://doi.org/10.1371/journal.pgph.0001908

Pany, M., Biniek, J. &, & Neuman, J. (2022). *Price Regulation, Global Budgets, and Spending Targets_ A Road Map to Reduce Health Care Spending and Improve Affordability.* (https://www.kff.org/health-costs/report/priceregulation- global-budgets-and-spending-targets-a-road-map-to-reduce-health-care-spending-and-improveaff ordability/view/footnotes/#footnote-555524-44)

Seixas, B. V., Regier, D. A., & Bryan, S. et al. (2021). Describing practices of priority setting and resource allocation in publicly funded health care systems of high-income countries. *BMC Health Serv Res*, *21*(90). https://doi.org/https://doi.org/10.1186/s12913-021-06078-z

Sultana, S., Hossain, M. E., Khan, M. A., Saha, S. M., Amin, M. R., & & Haque Prodhan, M. M. (2024). Effects of healthcare spending on public health status: An empirical investigation from Bangladesh. *Heliyon*, *10*(1). https://doi.org/https://doi.org/10.1016/j.heliyon.2024.e24268

UNICEF. (2019). *Guidelines for Developing a Health Budget Brief.* https://www.unicef.org/esa/media/3821/file/Guidelines-Developing-a-Health-Budget-Brief-March-2019.pdf

Yuan, X., Shi, C., & Wang, Z. (2022). The Optimization of Hospital Financial Management Based on Cloud Technology and Wireless Network Technology in the Context of Artificial Intelligence. *Wireless Communications and Mobile Computing, 2022.* https://doi.org/10.1155/2022/9998311

Paul, E., Sambiéni, N. E., Wangbe, JP., & et al. (2020). Budgeting challenges on the path towards universal healthcare coverage the case of Benin. *Health Econ Rev, 10*(28). https://doi.org/https://doi.org/10.1186/s13561-020-00286-9

Yang, S. W., Chu, K. C., & Kreng, V. B. (2021). The impact of global budgeting on the efficiency of healthcare under a single-payer system in Taiwan. *International Journal of Environmental Research and Public Health, 18*(20). https://doi.org/10.3390/ijerph182010983

Chapter 3: Micro-Budget Allocation and Public Health

This illustration depicts micro-budget allocation and public health, highlighting the collaborative efforts of healthcare professionals, community leaders, and financial planners in a modern office setting. This scene emphasizes the importance of detailed financial planning in improving public health outcomes.

Vignette: Strategic Micro-Budgeting for Enhanced Public Health in Sub-Saharan Africa

In the heart of sub-Saharan Africa, the fictional country of Azalia is grappling with pressing public health issues, including high malaria rates, limited access to clean water, and a shortage of healthcare professionals.

To tackle these challenges, the Azalian Ministry of Health has embarked on an innovative micro-budget allocation strategy. This approach involves distributing targeted funds to local health districts, enabling them to address specific health needs and implement community-driven solutions.

Key Components:

Decentralized Funding: By allocating micro-budgets directly to local health districts, Azalia aims to ensure that resources are utilized efficiently and in response to immediate health concerns.

Community Engagement: Local health committees, comprising community leaders and healthcare workers, identify priority areas and manage the allocated funds.

Health Worker Training: A portion of the micro-budget is dedicated to training healthcare workers in disease management, preventive care, and community health education.

Partnerships and Collaborations: Azalia is fostering partnerships with NGOs and international health organizations to leverage additional resources, expertise, and support for its micro-budget initiatives.

Outcome-Based Evaluation: The Ministry of Health has established clear indicators to measure the impact of micro-budget allocations on public health outcomes, ensuring accountability and informing future budgeting decisions.

Questions for Discussion:

1. What are the potential benefits and challenges of implementing a decentralized micro-budget allocation strategy in Azalia, and how can these challenges be addressed?
2. How can Azalia ensure that micro-budget allocations align with national health priorities while addressing local health needs and disparities?

3. How can community engagement and participation in the budgeting process enhance the effectiveness and sustainability of public health interventions in Azalia?
4. How can technology improve the transparency, efficiency, and management of micro-budget allocations in Azalia's public health sector?
5. How can the outcomes and lessons learned from Azalia's micro-budget allocation strategy inform and improve public health budgeting practices in other sub-Saharan African countries?

This vignette offers a framework for discussing the strategic use of micro-budget allocation in enhancing public health outcomes in sub-Saharan Africa, focusing on community engagement, decentralization, and partnerships.

Introduction

Micro-budgeting is a pivotal strategy in financial planning that significantly influences public health initiatives. Public health programs can achieve optimal outcomes and extend their reach by emphasizing efficient resource management, even with limited funds (Daniels, 2016; UNICEF, 2019). This chapter will elucidate the concept of micro-budget allocation, highlighting its critical importance in public health and its potential to foster more sustainable and effective health interventions.

In public health, micro-budgeting involves allocating small, targeted financial resources within the broader context of health budgets. In contrast to macro-budgeting, which typically encompasses large-scale funding for entire health programs or departments, micro-budgeting narrows its focus to specific projects, interventions, or areas of need within the public health domain (Bichachi, 2024; Daniels, 2016; Seixas et al., 2021). This targeted approach allows for precise funding distributions, ensuring that available resources are directed toward addressing specific service gaps (Campbell et al., 2018; Daniels, 2016; Homauni et al., 2023).

The significance of micro-budgeting lies in its ability to utilize finite resources effectively, stimulate innovation, enhance accountability, and aid adaptability during fiscal constraints. It is a strategic method that empowers health policymakers and administrators to maximize the impact of each dollar spent in pursuit of public health objectives (Bichachi, 2024; Campbell et al., 2018; Homauni et al., 2023; Musiega et al., 2023; Seixas et al., 2021; UNICEF, 2019). The concept of micro-budget allocation is particularly relevant in public health, as it pertains to the careful distribution of limited financial resources designed to address health needs at a granular level. This practice entails meticulously allocating funds toward specific programs or interventions to improve health outcomes for targeted populations within constrained financial parameters.

Successful micro-budget allocation strategies in public health demand an intricate understanding of community health needs, the cost-effectiveness of various interventions, and the prospective impact of allocated funds on health outcomes. By assessing where to direct limited resources based on critical factors such as disease burden, population demographics, and existing infrastructure, policymakers can significantly amplify the effectiveness of their budget allocations in tackling urgent health challenges (Daniels, 2016; Homauni et al., 2023; Sultana et al., 2024; UNICEF, 2019).

A strategic approach is essential to achieve effective micro-budget allocation in public health. This involves prioritizing interventions with the highest likelihood of yielding positive health outcomes, optimizing resource utilization through cost-effective methodologies, and continuously monitoring the effectiveness of allocated funds in reaching established health objectives. By embracing a data-driven and evidence-based framework, decision-makers can ensure that scarce resources are employed efficiently to address the most pressing public health issues (Bichachi, 2024; Campbell et al., 2018; Daniels, 2016; Homauni et al., 2023; Seixas et al., 2021; UNICEF, 2019).

How Micro-Budgets are Allocated in Public Health

Micro-budgeting is an essential strategy in the financial planning landscape, playing a vital role in the effectiveness of public health initiatives. By prioritizing efficient resource management, public health programs can optimize outcomes and broaden their reach, even when constrained by limited financial resources (Daniels, 2016; UNICEF, 2019). This chapter elucidates the concept of micro-budget allocation, demonstrating its importance in public health and its potential to foster sustainable and impactful health interventions.

In public health, micro-budgeting involves allocating small, targeted financial resources within the broader context of health budgets. Unlike macro-budgeting, which typically addresses large-scale funding for entire health programs or departments, micro-budgeting narrows its focus to specific projects, interventions, or areas of need (Bichachi, 2024; Daniels, 2016; Seixas et al., 2021). This targeted approach enables precise funding distribution, ensuring that resources are directed toward addressing specific service gaps (Campbell et al., 2018; Daniels, 2016; Homauni et al., 2023).

The significance of micro-budgeting lies in its ability to effectively utilize finite resources, stimulate innovation, enhance accountability, and facilitate adaptability during periods of fiscal constraint. It serves as a strategic tool that empowers health policymakers and administrators to ensure that every dollar spent contributes effectively to public health objectives (Bichachi, 2024; Campbell et al., 2018; Homauni et al., 2023; Musiega et al., 2023; Seixas et al., 2021; UNICEF, 2019).

Micro-budget allocation is particularly pertinent within the public health sphere, as it involves carefully distributing limited financial resources to address health needs at a granular level. This practice requires meticulous allocation of funds toward specific programs or interventions that directly improve health outcomes for targeted populations, all while adhering to constrained financial parameters. Successful micro-budget allocation strategies demand an intricate understanding of community health needs, the cost-effectiveness of various interventions, and the projected impact of allocated funds on health outcomes. By strategically assessing where to direct limited resources—taking into consideration critical factors such as disease burden, population demographics, and existing infrastructure—policymakers can significantly enhance the effectiveness of their budget allocations in addressing urgent health challenges (Daniels, 2016; Homauni et al., 2023; Sultana et al., 2024; UNICEF, 2019).

Achieving effective micro-budget allocation in public health necessitates a rigorous strategic approach. This involves prioritizing interventions that are most likely to yield positive health outcomes, optimizing resource utilization through cost-effective methodologies, and continuously monitoring the effectiveness of allocated funds in achieving established health objectives. By embracing a data-driven and evidence-based framework, decision-makers can confidently ensure that scarce resources are employed efficiently to tackle the most pressing public health issues (Bichachi, 2024; Campbell et al., 2018; Daniels, 2016; Homauni et al., 2023; Seixas et al., 2021; UNICEF, 2019).

Impact of Micro-Budgets on Public Health Outcomes

Micro-budgets significantly influence public health outcomes by facilitating targeted funding and implementing focused programs. The effectiveness of this financial strategy is supported by numerous case studies and success stories across various domains of public health (Campbell et al., 2018; Musiega et al., 2023; Seixas et al., 2021; Sultana et al., 2024).

For instance, strategically allocating micro-budgets to vaccination campaigns in underserved areas has been instrumental in preventing outbreaks of vaccine-preventable diseases. This approach not only saves lives but also reduces healthcare costs. However, the impact of micro-budgets is not without its challenges. Chronic underfunding of public health initiatives can lead to significant limitations, obstructing the attainment of desired health outcomes (Sudari et al., 2022). Additionally, misallocation of resources and inadequate planning can undermine the effectiveness of these financial allocations (Forbinake et al., 2023; Paul et al., 2020).

Despite these obstacles, participatory budgeting has emerged as an effective strategy, allowing community members to influence how public funds are allocated for health services. This involvement can potentially enhance the efficiency and overall impact of micro-budget allocations on health outcomes. By empowering communities to engage in the budgetary process, we can ensure that financial resources are utilized in ways that genuinely benefit public health, thereby leading to improved health outcomes at the grassroots level.

Micro-Costing as a Tool for Public Health Economics

Micro-costing is a fundamental aspect of public health economics, providing a comprehensive method for estimating the costs associated with healthcare interventions and programs. This approach entails detailed tracking and analysis of each resource and its corresponding expenses, allowing for precise calculation of total expenditures. In the context of public health, where resources are frequently constrained, micro-costing is invaluable for ensuring efficient resource allocation (Alebachew et al., 2023; Debie et al., 2022; Homauni et al., 2023; Yang et al., 2021).

Establishing a standardized framework for micro-costing is essential to ensure consistency and comparability across various programs and studies. A prominent example of effective micro-costing can be seen in the Incredible Years Toddler Parenting Program (Bywater et al., 2022). Through meticulous data collection and cost analysis, this program exemplifies how micro-costing can yield crucial insights into the financial implications of public health interventions (Bywater et al., 2022). Such insights are vital for policymakers and health administrators, enabling them to make informed decisions regarding resource allocation and ultimately supporting the development of more effective and sustainable public health initiatives.

Moreover, the successful implementation of micro-budget allocations in public health depends heavily on collaboration and coordination among diverse stakeholders, including government agencies, non-profit organizations, healthcare providers, and community members (Mehboob, 2023). By fostering partnerships and leveraging collective expertise, resources, and networks, these stakeholders can collectively enhance the impact of budget allocations, ultimately improving population health and well-being.

Micro-Budget Allocation and Public Health: An In-depth Analysis

Public Health Budget allocation is crucial for ensuring that healthcare services are effective and accessible to the population. Micro-budget allocation is a focused approach within this broader spectrum, emphasizing the distribution of financial resources to specific, often smaller-scale health initiatives or departments. It involves earmarking funds for narrowly defined health projects or programs (Daniels, 2016).

Unlike macro or global budgeting, which deals with more extensive financial plans across entire health systems or countries, micro-budget allocation targets specific areas of need, allowing for more precise and potentially impactful spending (Homauni et al., 2023). This section will explore how micro-budget allocation is defined and how it differs from other budgeting methods.

Various mechanisms are employed to manage and allocate micro-budgets in public health settings. These range from competitive grant processes to targeted funding for health issues. Understanding these mechanisms is critical to grasping the operational aspects of micro-budget allocation. This section will examine these mechanisms, including the criteria used for fund allocation and distribution methods.

In public health, micro-budget allocation offers several advantages, including greater flexibility in addressing specific health challenges, piloting innovative projects, and enhancing spending accountability. By focusing on well-defined areas, micro-budgets contribute to more targeted and effective public health interventions. Examples of successful micro-budgeting in healthcare will be highlighted to illustrate these benefits (Barroy et al., 2018; CMS.gov, n.d.; Kaplan & Porter, 2011; Murray, 2022).

Challenges and Limitations

Despite its advantages, micro-budget allocation also comes with significant challenges and limitations. These may include difficulties in assessing the impact of funded projects, potential biases in fund allocation, and challenges in scaling successful interventions. This section will discuss the obstacles healthcare administrators and policymakers face when implementing micro-budget strategies.

In conclusion, micro-budget allocation plays a critical role in managing public health finances. While it promises targeted and efficient healthcare spending, achieving these outcomes requires careful planning, evaluation, and oversight. The future of micro-budget allocation in public health will likely depend on how well these challenges are addressed and the extent of innovation in budgeting practices.

Furthermore, micro-budget allocation in public health is a vital process that requires a strategic, evidence-based approach to optimizing the utilization of limited financial resources to address health needs effectively. By prioritizing interventions, optimizing resource allocation, and fostering collaboration among stakeholders, decision-makers can maximize the impact of budget allocations in promoting public health and achieving positive health outcomes.

Strategies for Effective Micro-Budget Allocation

Introduction

Micro-budget allocation presents an opportunity to enhance public health outcomes through targeted financial strategies. Specific techniques can be implemented to harness its full potential, including refining evaluation methods for funded projects, enhancing transparency in the budget allocation process, and promoting collaborations across various health departments (Glover & Naylor, 2023; Murray, 2022). This chapter outlines several strategies to maximize the effectiveness of micro-budget allocation within public health settings.

Challenges and Limitations

While the advantages of micro-budget allocation are substantial, they are not without significant challenges and limitations. Key issues may include difficulties in assessing the impact of funded projects, potential biases in allocating funds, and obstacles encountered in scaling successful interventions (Kaplan & Porter, 2011; PHCPI, n.d.). Addressing these challenges is crucial for realizing the full benefits of micro-budgeting.

In summary, micro-budget allocation is essential for effective public health finance management. Although it promises targeted and efficient healthcare expenditures, achieving these desired outcomes necessitates meticulous planning, rigorous evaluation, and ongoing oversight (Homauni et al., 2023). The future of micro-budget allocation in public health will largely depend on the capacity to address these challenges and innovate budgeting practices. Adopting a strategic, evidence-based approach is imperative to ensure that scarce financial resources are utilized optimally to meet health needs. By prioritizing interventions, optimizing resource distribution, and fostering collaboration among stakeholders, decision-makers can significantly enhance the impact of budget allocations in promoting public health and improving health outcomes (Homauni et al., 2023).

The healthcare sector consistently confronts the challenge of delivering high-quality care while operating under stringent budgetary constraints (Barroy et al., 2018; Glover & Naylor, 2023b; Murray, 2022). This challenge is amplified for organizations relying on micro-budgets. However, with strategic and effective micro-budget allocation, even the most minor healthcare providers can sustain high standards of patient care while ensuring financial viability (Glover & Naylor, 2023a; Murray, 2022; PHCPI, n.d.). This article delves into pragmatic strategies that healthcare administrators can employ to optimize micro-budget allocation, ultimately achieving superior outcomes for patients and their organizations.

Understanding Micro-Budgets in Healthcare

Micro-budgets in healthcare represent the minimal financial resources allocated to the operations and services of small-scale healthcare providers (Barroy et al., 2018; CMS.gov, n.d.; Glover & Naylor, 2023b; Kaplan et al., 2011). These budgets are distinguished by their precise and tailored nature, often designed to address specific needs or objectives within a limited scope. Although micro-budgets present certain limitations, they empower healthcare organizations to concentrate on vital areas, prioritize patient-centered approaches, and implement innovative solutions to enhance efficiency. The effective management of micro-budgets is paramount, as it has direct implications for both the quality of patient care and the sustainability of operations (CMS.gov, n.d.; Glover & Naylor, 2023a; Kaplan et al., 2011; Murray, 2022; Organization for Economic Co-operation and Development [OECD], 2023). By judiciously allocating and managing these limited resources, healthcare providers can optimize their impact and deliver high-quality care, affirming the critical role micro-budgets play in the overall healthcare landscape.

Critical Strategies for Effective Budget Allocation

Prioritization of Needs: Prioritizing needs is essential in effectively managing micro-budgets within healthcare settings. Organizations must undertake comprehensive assessments to accurately identify and rank various healthcare needs based on their urgency and potential impact on patient care. These assessments allow administrators to discern which areas necessitate immediate financial support, thus ensuring that available resources are allocated efficiently. Healthcare administrators must focus on high-priority services and equipment that demonstrably affect patient outcomes in a landscape of financial constraints. By directing funds toward these critical areas, administrators can enhance the quality of care provided, ultimately leading to better patient health outcomes. This strategic approach optimizes using limited resources and promotes a culture of accountability and responsiveness within the organization. Moreover, leveraging data-driven methodologies to guide these prioritization efforts can significantly improve decision-making processes. By using frameworks that assess patient needs, service demand, and clinical effectiveness, healthcare administrators can ensure funding decisions align with organizational goals and improve patient care. Therefore, systematically identifying and prioritizing healthcare needs is a cornerstone in micro-budget management. Emphasizing this strategy enables healthcare administrators to navigate financial limitations while safeguarding the quality of patient care, fostering a sustainable and impactful healthcare environment (Barroy et al., 2018; CMS.gov, n.d.; Kaplan et al., 2011; Walsh, 2016).

Adopting a Patient-Centered Approach: Adopting a patient-centered approach in healthcare administration is imperative for enhancing the quality of care and optimizing resource allocation. Effective management in this realm must prioritize the patient's well-being, positioning the patient as the central focus of healthcare delivery. By doing so, healthcare administrators not only facilitate improvements in care pathways but also ensure that access to services is equitable and the overall patient experience is markedly enriched (Bichachi, 2024; CMS.gov, n.d.; Forbinake et al., 2023; Kaplan & Porter, 2011; UNICEF, 2019; Walsh, 2016).

In today's complex healthcare landscape, particularly within systems constrained by financial limitations, organizations must adopt a strategic framework for resource allocation that emphasizes high-priority needs. A rigorous assessment must be undertaken to identify and rank healthcare requirements based on urgency and their potential impact on patient outcomes. This systematic evaluation allows administrators to discern critical areas that warrant immediate financial support, thereby ensuring that resources are directed toward initiatives that yield the most significant benefits for patient care.

Furthermore, a data-driven methodology should be implemented to enhance the prioritization process. By utilizing frameworks that analyze patient needs, service demand, and clinical effectiveness, healthcare administrators can align funding decisions with organizational objectives, ultimately improving patient outcomes. This approach optimizes resource utilization and fosters a culture of accountability and responsiveness within healthcare organizations.

In practice, directing funds toward high-priority services and essential equipment demonstrably affects the quality of care provided. Healthcare administrators can significantly improve patient health outcomes by focusing on these critical areas, ensuring that care is both practical and sustainable. Therefore, the systematic identification and prioritization of healthcare needs is a foundational element in successfully managing micro-budgets within healthcare settings. Emphasizing this strategic approach enables healthcare administrators to navigate financial limitations while safeguarding patient care quality.

By committing to a patient-centered model that prioritizes

patients' needs and experiences, healthcare organizations can create a sustainable and impactful environment that not only meets today's challenges but also sets the stage for future improvements in healthcare delivery (Barroy et al., 2018; CMS.gov, n.d.; Kaplan et al., 2011; Walsh, 2016).

Utilizing Technology and Data Analytics: In the contemporary landscape of healthcare administration, integrating technological advancements and data analytics is a pivotal mechanism for optimizing budget allocation. As healthcare costs continue to escalate, it becomes increasingly imperative for administrators to leverage these tools to enhance both financial efficiency and patient care outcomes.

Budgeting software plays a fundamental role in this process. Such software enables administrators to systematically track expenditures, forecast future financial needs, and allocate resources effectively across various departments. This systematic approach, supported by real-time data, allows for the identification of spending patterns and trends, facilitating more strategic decision-making. Consequently, healthcare administrators can ensure that funds are directed toward areas with the highest impact on patient care.

Moreover, the application of data analytics extends beyond mere budgeting functions. Predictive analytics allows healthcare organizations to analyze historical data and trends to forecast future needs. By utilizing algorithms and statistical models, administrators can anticipate changes in patient demand, optimize staffing levels, and identify potential areas for cost savings. This proactive approach enables healthcare organizations to respond efficiently to current challenges and prepare for future demands in an ever-evolving healthcare environment.

The impact of these technologies on resource management is

profound. By employing a data-driven approach, administrators can make informed decisions that prioritize financial sustainability and high-quality patient care. The correlation between effective budget allocation and improved patient outcomes is well-documented, underscoring technology and data analytics' vital role in enhancing the efficiency and effectiveness of healthcare services.

Utilizing advanced technology and robust data analytics is no longer optional but essential for successful budget management in healthcare. Adopting budgeting software and predictive analytical tools empowers administrators to optimize resource allocation, significantly enhancing patient outcomes and organizational efficiency. As supported by the literature (CMS.gov, n.d.; Glover & Naylor, 2023b; Kaplan et al., 2011; PHCPI, n.d.; Walsh, 2016), the integration of these tools represents a critical advancement in the field of healthcare administration, ensuring that resources are utilized effectively to meet the dynamic needs of patients and the healthcare system at large.

Engaging Stakeholders in the Budgetary Process: Engaging stakeholders in the budgetary process is critical to effective financial management in organizations, particularly within healthcare settings. Involving a diverse range of stakeholders—including employees, patients, and community members—in budget discussions cultivates a culture of transparency and inclusivity, as evidenced by recent studies (Daniels, 2016; Homauni et al., 2023; Seixas et al., 2021). The significance of stakeholder involvement cannot be overstated. By actively participating in the budgetary process, stakeholders gain a deep understanding of the institution's financial challenges and opportunities. This engagement fosters a sense of ownership among participants as they realize their contributions can directly influence financial decisions and resource allocation. Such ownership is crucial, as individuals who feel invested in the budgetary process are more likely to support and commit to the institution's financial and operational goals.

Moreover, collective engagement promotes sustainable budgeting practices. When stakeholders collaborate, they bring diverse perspectives and insights that can lead to more innovative solutions for resource allocation. By allowing various voices to be heard, organizations can uncover areas for cost efficiencies or potential revenue enhancements that may not have been apparent to management alone. This collaborative approach improves the quality of budget decisions and ensures that they are aligned with the needs and priorities of those they serve. Furthermore, fostering an inclusive budgeting process enhances accountability. Stakeholders engaged in the conversation can hold each other and management accountable for the decisions made during budget development. This level of scrutiny minimizes wastage and encourages responsible stewardship of institutional resources. Engaging stakeholders in the budgeting process enhances transparency and inclusiveness and cultivates a supportive environment characterized by shared responsibility. The result is a more committed workforce and a community that feels valued and heard, ultimately leading to more effective and sustainable financial practices. Emphasizing this collaborative approach in future budget discussions will undoubtedly yield significant benefits for organizations, positioning them for continued success amidst an ever-evolving landscape.

Case Studies: Success Stories in Micro-Budgeting

Community Health Clinic Optimization: A small community health clinic in a rural area confronted significant budget constraints. By strategically prioritizing primary care services and harnessing the capabilities of telehealth technologies, the clinic successfully extended its reach and enhanced patient care without incurring substantial expenditure increases. The application of effective micro-budget allocation improved operational efficiency and elevated patient satisfaction scores (Cadet et al., 2023; Crusan et al., 2020).

Urban Hospital Resource Management: An urban hospital adopted a strategic micro-budgeting framework, concentrating on high-demand areas such as emergency and outpatient services. By utilizing data analytics to monitor patient flow and resource utilization, the hospital was able to optimize staffing and supplies, thereby minimizing waste and eliminating unnecessary expenses. This focused approach to resource allocation enabled the hospital to redirect savings towards upgrading medical equipment, ultimately leading to a marked improvement in the quality of care delivered (Alahmar & Benlamri, 2020).

Tools and Software for Efficient Budget Management

Integrating budgeting tools and software has fundamentally transformed financial management within healthcare organizations. Today, various robust platforms are specifically designed for healthcare budgeting and financial planning. These advanced tools streamline the budget allocation process, ensuring accuracy and efficiency through features such as historical data analysis, predictive analytics, and customizable budget templates. By automating and optimizing many of the manual processes traditionally associated with budget planning, these tools empower healthcare administrators to prioritize strategic decision-making. The shift from manual to automated processes enhances operational efficiency and enables organizations to allocate resources more effectively. This, in turn, promotes better financial health for the organization and significantly improves patient outcomes.

Adopting these innovative budgeting solutions is no longer optional—it is essential for healthcare organizations aiming to thrive in an increasingly complex financial landscape. Embracing such technologies positions healthcare entities to navigate challenges more adeptly while achieving their core mission of delivering quality patient care.

Bibliography

Alahmar, A., & Benlamri, R. (2020). Optimizing Hospital Resources using Big Data Analytics with Standardized e-Clinical Pathways. *2020 IEEE Intl Conf on Dependable, Autonomic and Secure Computing, Intl Conf on Pervasive Intelligence and Computing, Intl Conf on Cloud and Big Data Computing, Intl Conf on Cyber Science and Technology Congress (DASC/PiCom/CBDCom/CyberSciTech)*, 650–657. https://doi.org/10.1109/DASC-PICom-CBDCom-CyberSciTech49142.2020.00112

Alebachew, A., Abdella, E., Abera, S., Dessie, E., Mesele, T., Mitiku, W., Muñoz, R., Opuni, M., Teplitskaya, L., Walker, D. G., & Gilmartin, C. (2023). Costs and resource needs for primary health care in Ethiopia: evidence to inform planning and budgeting for universal health coverage. *Frontiers in Public Health, 11*. https://doi.org/https://doi.org/10.3389/fpubh.2023.1242314

Barroy, H., Dale, E., Sparkes, S., & Kutzin, J. (2018). *BUDGET MATTERS FOR HEALTH: KEY FORMULATION AND CLASSIFICATION ISSUES HEALTH FINANCING POLICY BRIEF No 4 BUDGETING IN HEALTH*. http://apps.who.int/bookorders.

Bartsch, S. M. , Ferguson, M. C. , McKinnell, J. A. , O'Shea, K. J. , Wedlock, P. T. , Siegmund, S. S. , & Lee, B. Y. (2020). The Potential Health Care Costs And Resource Use Associated with Covid 19 in the United States. *Health Affairs (Project Hope)*, *39*(6), 927935. https://doi.org/10.1377/hlthaff.2020.00426

Bichachi, R. (2024). *Healthcare & Hospital Budgeting Guide for 2024.* https://www.netsuite.com/portal/resource/articles/financial-management/healthcare-budgeting.shtml

Brownson, R. C., Fielding, J. E., & Green, L. W. (2018). Building Capacity for Evidence-Based Public Health: Reconciling the Pulls of Practice and the Push of Research. *Annual Review of Public Health*, *39*, 27–53. https://doi.org/10.1146/annurev-publhealth-040617-014746

Bywater, T., Berry, V., Blower, S., Bursnall, M., Cox, E., Mason-Jones, A., McGilloway, S., McKendrick, K., Mitchell, S., Pickett, K., Richardson, G., Solaiman, K., Teare, M. D., Walker, S., & Whittaker, K. (2022). A randomized controlled trial of a proportionate universal parenting program delivery model (E-SEE Steps) to enhance child social-emotional wellbeing. *PLoS ONE*, *17*(4 April). https://doi.org/10.1371/journal.pone.0265200

Cadet, K., Baker, D. R., & Brown, A. (2023). A qualitative assessment of provider satisfaction and experiences with a COVID-19 community mobile health clinic outreach model in underserved Baltimore neighborhoods. *SAGE Open Medicine*, *11*. https://doi.org/10.1177/20503121231152090

Campbell, M., Escobar, O., & Fenton, C. et al. (2018). The impact of participatory budgeting on health and wellbeing. *BMC Public Health*, *18*(822). https://doi.org/https://doi.org/10.1186/s12889-018-5735-8

Clark, E. C., Neumann, S., Hopkins, S., Kostopoulos, A., Hagerman, L., & Dobbins, M. (2024). Changes to Public Health Surveillance Methods Due to the COVID-19

Pandemic: Scoping Review. In *JMIR Public Health and Surveillance* (Vol. 10, Issue 1). JMIR Publications Inc. https://doi.org/10.2196/49185

CMS.gov. (n.d.). *Total Cost of Care and Hospital Global Budgets Defining key terms.* https://www.cms.gov/priorities/innovation/key-concepts/total-cost-care-and-hospital-global-budgets

Collins, T., Akselrod, S., Bloomfield, A., Gamkrelidze, A., Jakab, Z., & Placella, E. (2020). Rethinking the COVID-19 pandemic: Back to public health. *Annals of Global Health, 86*(1), 1–7. https://doi.org/10.5334/aogh.3084

Congressional Research Service. (2019). *Federal Grants to State and Local Governments: A Historical Perspective on Contemporary Issues.* https://crsreports.congress.gov

Crusan, A. C., Lilja, K. C., Walters, T., & Baulmer, M. (2020). Barriers to Using Telehealth During a Pandemic Versus In-Person Appointments to Conduct Nutrition Assessments in a Community Health Clinic Setting. *2020 IEEE Intl Conf on Dependable, Autonomic and Secure Computing, Intl Conf on Pervasive Intelligence and Computing, Intl Conf on Cloud and Big Data Computing, Intl Conf on Cyber Science and Technology Congress (DASC/PiCom/CBDCom/CyberSciTech),* 650–657.

Dabestani, N. M., Leidner, A. J., Seiber, E. E., Kim, H., Graitcer, S. B., Foppa, I. M., & Bridges, C. B. (2019). A review of the cost-effectiveness of adult influenza vaccination and other preventive services. In *Preventive Medicine* (Vol. 126). Academic Press Inc. https://doi.org/10.1016/j.ypmed.2019.05.022

Daniels, N. (2016). Resource Allocation and Priority Setting.

In W. H. Barrett D, Ortmann L, & et al., Dawson A (Eds.), *Public Health Ethics: Cases Spanning the Globe*. Springer.

Debie, A., Khatri, R. B., & Assefa, Y. (2022). Contributions and challenges of healthcare financing towards universal health coverage in Ethiopia: a narrative evidence synthesis. *BMC Health Services Research*, *22*(1). https://doi.org/10.1186/s12913-022-08151-7

Forbinake, N. A., Enongene, J. M., Nchinjoh, S. C., Orock-Benem, V. T., Engelberg, S., & Chinitz, D. (2023). Reallocation of Cameroon's Public Health Budget from the Central Administration to Regional Level: Is it Worthwhile? *The Open Public Health Journal*, *16*(1). https://doi.org/10.2174/18749445-v16-e230419-2022-196

Glover, R. E., & Naylor, N. R. (2023). The WHO costing and budgeting tool for national action plans on antimicrobial resistance—a practical addition to the Whole toolkit. *JAC-Antimicrobial Resistance*, *5*(3). https://doi.org/10.1093/jacamr/dlad064

Güngör Göksu, G. (2023). A retrospective overview of the Journal of Public Budgeting, Accounting and Financial Management using bibliometric analysis. In *Journal of Public Budgeting, Accounting and Financial Management* (Vol. 35, Issue 2, pp. 264–295). Emerald Publishing. https://doi.org/10.1108/JPBAFM-04-2022-0061

Homauni, A., Markazi-Moghaddam, N., Mosadeghkhah, A., Noori, M., Abbasiyan, K., Zargar, S., & Jame, B. (2023). Budgeting in Healthcare Systems and Organizations: A Systematic Review. In *Iran J Public Health* (Vol. 52, Issue 9). https://creativecommons.org/licenses/by-nc/4.0/

Institute for Health Metrics and Evaluation. (2024). *Global Burden of Disease 2021 Findings from the GBD 2021 Study.*

Janga, V. , Wako, D. A. , Genale, A. S. , Sundaram, B. B. , Pandey, A. , & & Karthika, P. (2022). Artificial Intelligence in Cloud Technology and Wireless Network Technology using Health Care System. *6th International Conference on Trends in Electronics and Informatics (ICOEI),* 1–7. https://doi.org/10.1109/ICOEI53556.2022.9776658.

Johns Marquisha, & Rosenthal Jill. (2024). *How the Affordable Care Act Improved Access to Preventive Health Services - Center for American Progress.*

Kaplan, R. S., & Porter, M. E. (2011). The Big Idea_ How to Solve the Cost Crisis in Health Care. *Harvard Business Review.* https://hbr.org/2011/09/how-to-solve-the-cost-crisis-in-health-care

Maciosek, M. V., LaFrance, A. B., Dehmer, S. P., McGree, D. A., Flottemesch, T. J., Xu, Z., & Solberg, L. I. (2017). Updated priorities among effective clinical preventive services. *Annals of Family Medicine, 15*(1), 14–22. https://doi.org/10.1370/afm.2017

Maciosek, M. V., LaFrance, A. B., St. Claire, A. W., Keller, P. A., Xu, Z., & Schillo, B. A. (2020). The 20-year impact of tobacco price and tobacco control expenditure increases in Minnesota, 1998-2017. In *PLoS ONE* (Vol. 15, Issue 3). Public Library of Science. https://doi.org/10.1371/journal.pone.0230364

MacIosek, M. V., Lafrance, A. B., St Claire, A., Xu, Z., Brown, M., & Schillo, B. A. (2020). Twenty-year health and economic impact of reducing cigarette use: Minnesota 1998-

2017. *Tobacco Control*, *29*(5), 564–569. https://doi.org/10.1136/tobaccocontrol-2018-054825

Mehboob, R. (2023). Approaches and challenges in Public Health. *Akistan Journal of Health Sciences*, *4*(10). https://doi.org/https://doi.org/10.54393/pjhs.v4i10.899

Murray, R. (2022). *Hospital Global Budgets: A Promising State Tool for Controlling Health Care Spending | Commonwealth Fund Hospital Global Budgets: A Promising State Tool for Controlling Health Care Spending.* https://www.commonwealthfund.org/publications/issue-briefs/2022/mar/hospital-global-budgets-state-tool-controlling-spending

Musiega, A., Nyawira, L., Tsofa, B., Njuguna, R. G., Munywoki, J., Hanson, K., Mulwa, A., Molyneux, S., Maina, I., Normand, C., Jemutai, J. , & & Barasa, E. (2023). Budget monitoring, accountability practices and their influence on the efficiency of county health systems in Kenya. *PLOS Global Public Health*, *3*(11). https://doi.org/https://doi.org/10.1371/journal.pgph.0001908

Ng, N. Y., & Ruger, J. P. (2014). Ethics and Social Value Judgments in Public Health. In *Encyclopedia of Health Economics* (pp. 287–291). Elsevier. https://doi.org/10.1016/B978-0-12-375678-7.00415-6

Nicholson, W. K., Silverstein, M., Wong, J. B., Barry, M. J., Chelmow, D., Coker, T. R., Davis, E. M., Jaén, C. R., Krousel-Wood, M., Lee, S., Li, L., Mangione, C. M., Rao, G., Ruiz, J. M., Stevermer, J. J., Tsevat, J., Underwood, S. M., & Wiehe, S. (2024). Screening for Breast Cancer: US Preventive Services Task Force Recommendation Statement. In *JAMA*

(Vol. 331, Issue 22, pp. 1918–1930). American Medical Association. https://doi.org/10.1001/jama.2024.5534

Nwobu, O. A. (2021). *Corporate Social Responsibility and the Public Health Imperative: Accounting and Reporting on Public Health.* https://doi.org/http://dx.doi.org/10.5772/intechopen.94356

Paul, E., Sambiéni, N. E., Wangbe, JP., & et al. (2020). Budgeting challenges on the path towards universal healthcare coverage_the case of Benin. *Health Econ Rev, 10*(28). https://doi.org/https://doi.org/10.1186/s13561-020-00286-9

PHCPI. (n.d.). *Funding & Allocation of Resources _ PHCPI.*

Seixas, B. V., Regier, D. A., & Bryan, S. et al. (2021). Describing practices of priority setting and resource allocation in publicly funded health care systems of high-income countries. *BMC Health Serv Res, 21*(90). https://doi.org/https://doi.org/10.1186/s12913-021-06078-z

Sharma, K. P., Grosse, S. D., Maciosek, M. V., Joseph, D., Roy, K., Richardson, L. C., Jaffe, H., & Sharma, K. P. (2020). Preventing Breast, Cervical, and Colorectal Cancer Deaths: Assessing the Impact of Increased Screening. *Preventing Chronic Disease, 17*. https://doi.org/10.5888/pcd17.200039

Sudari, F., Priskilla, I., Febiola, M., & Sinuraya, R. K. (2022). Strategies to improve the vaccine distribution and community awareness of taking COVID-19 vaccine in rural areas in Indonesia. *Pharmacia, 69*(2), 543–553. https://doi.org/10.3897/pharmacia.69.e81525

Sultana, S., Hossain, M. E., Khan, M. A., Saha, S. M., Amin, M. R., & & Haque Prodhan, M. M. (2024). Effects of healthcare spending on public health status: An empirical investigation from Bangladesh. *Heliyon*, *10*(1). https://doi.org/https://doi.org/10.1016/j.heliyon.2024.e24268

UNICEF. (2019). *Guidelines for Developing a Health Budget Brief.* https://www.unicef.org/esa/media/3821/file/Guidelines-Developing-a-Health-Budget-Brief-March-2019.pdf

Vollset, S. E., Ababneh, H. S., Abate, Y. H., Abbafati, C., Abbasgholizadeh, R., Abbasian, M., Abbastabar, H., Abd Al Magied, A. H. A., Abd ElHafeez, S., Abdelkader, A., Abdelmasseh, M., Abd-Elsalam, S., Abdi, P., Abdollahi, M., Abdoun, M., Abdullahi, A., Abebe, M., Abiodun, O., Aboagye, R. G., … Murray, C. J. L. (2024). Burden of disease scenarios for 204 countries and territories, 2022–2050: a forecasting analysis for the Global Burden of Disease Study 2021. *The Lancet*, *403*(10440), 2204–2256. https://doi.org/10.1016/S0140-6736(24)00685-8

Walsh, K. (2016). Managing a budget in healthcare professional education. *Annals of Medical and Health Sciences Research*, *6*(2), 71. https://doi.org/10.4103/2141-9248.181841

Ward, Z. J., & Goldie, S. J. (2024). Global Burden of Disease Study 2021 estimates_ implications for health policy and research. *Lancet*, *403*(10440), 1958–1959. https://doi.org/https://doi.org/10.1016/S0140-6736(24)00812-2

World Health Organization. (2020). *WHO methods and data sources for global burden of disease estimates 2000-2019.*

http://www.who.int/gho/mortality_burden_disease/en/index.html

Yang, S. W., Chu, K. C., & Kreng, V. B. (2021). The impact of global budgeting on the efficiency of healthcare under a single-payer system in Taiwan. *International Journal of Environmental Research and Public Health, 18*(20). https://doi.org/10.3390/ijerph182010983

Yuan, X., Shi, C., & Wang, Z. (2022). The Optimization of Hospital Financial Management Based on Cloud Technology and Wireless Network Technology in the Context of Artificial Intelligence. *Wireless Communications and Mobile Computing, 2022.* https://doi.org/10.1155/2022/9998311

Chapter 4: The Importance of Public Health and Preventive Care

This illustration depicts the importance of public health and preventive care in Sub-Saharan Africa. It illustrates healthcare workers providing education and medical services in a rural village setting, emphasizing the positive impact of preventive care on community well-being.

Vignette: The Importance of Public Health and Preventive Care in Sub-Saharan Africa

In the fictional country of Savannia, located in sub-Saharan Africa, health officials are grappling with a complex array of public health challenges. High rates of infectious diseases, maternal and child mortality, and an increasing burden of non-communicable diseases are straining the country's limited healthcare resources. Recognizing the critical need for change, Savannia's Ministry of Health has launched an ambitious initiative to strengthen public health infrastructure and promote preventive care.

The "Healthy Horizons" initiative aims to shift the healthcare paradigm from a reactive, treatment-based approach to a proactive, prevention-oriented system. Key components of the program include:

1. Expanding vaccination coverage for children and adults
2. Implementing community-based health education programs
3. Improving access to clean water and sanitation facilities
4. Enhancing maternal and child health services
5. Promoting early screening and management of non-communicable diseases

Health officials closely monitor the program's impact on various health indicators and community engagement levels as the program rolls out. They hope that by prioritizing public health and preventive care, Savannia can significantly improve health outcomes and reduce the long-term burden on its healthcare system.

Questions:

1. What are the potential long-term benefits of shifting towards a prevention-oriented healthcare system in Savannia, and how might these benefits extend beyond health to impact the country's overall development?
2. How can Savannia effectively address cultural beliefs or practices that may hinder the adoption of preventive health measures, and what strategies can be employed to ensure community buy-in?
3. Given the limited resources in many sub-Saharan African countries, how can Savannia prioritize and allocate funds between immediate healthcare needs and long-term preventive care initiatives?

4. How can technology enhance public health and preventive care efforts in Savannia, particularly in remote or underserved areas?
5. How can Savannia measure the success of its "Healthy Horizons" initiative, and what indicators should be used to evaluate both short-term progress and long-term impact on population health?

This vignette highlights the critical importance of public health and preventive care in sub-Saharan Africa, encouraging thoughtful discussion on strategies to improve health outcomes and create sustainable healthcare systems in resource-limited settings.

Introduction

Public health represents the collective efforts to improve community health and well-being. Public health and preventive care are pivotal in promoting and maintaining the well-being of individuals and communities. These concepts encompass various strategies to prevent diseases, promote healthy behaviors, and improve overall population health. The significance of public health and preventive care cannot be overstated, as they help reduce healthcare costs, increase life expectancy, and enhance the quality of life for both individuals and communities.

This chapter aims to comprehensively analyze the existing research on the importance of public health and preventive care. By reviewing various studies, articles, and reports, it highlights the significance of these practices in addressing public health challenges and improving population health. Furthermore, it explores the existing research on the importance of public health and preventive care, focusing on aspects such as disease prevention, health promotion, and the role of healthcare systems in supporting these efforts.

Disease prevention is one of the primary objectives of public health and preventive care. Numerous studies have shown the effectiveness of preventive measures in reducing the burden of diseases. For example, vaccination programs have substantially decreased the incidence of vaccine-preventable diseases. Lifestyle modifications and behavior changes are also necessary for disease prevention, with regular physical activity being shown to reduce the risk of chronic diseases (Abdullah et al., 2023; Pavlović et al., 2022; Nyiramana, 2024).

Public health campaigns and interventions promoting physical activity and healthy lifestyle choices are crucial in preventing these conditions. Public health and preventive care also promote health and well-being through various strategies.

Health promotion activities empower individuals and communities to improve their health and make informed decisions. Education and awareness campaigns are essential for disseminating information and promoting healthy behaviors. For example, health education programs have been effective in increasing smoking cessation rates. Mental health promotion is another important aspect of public health efforts, with school programs showing positive outcomes regarding improved mental health and reduced psychological distress among students. While public health and preventive care primarily focus on population-based interventions, healthcare systems support these endeavors (Fluxa et al., 2022; Sharma R. et al., 2018; Larson et al., 2006).

Integrating public health initiatives with healthcare systems is essential for disease prevention and health promotion. Primary care providers play a crucial role in delivering preventive services, such as screenings and vaccinations. Collaboration between public health agencies and healthcare systems is necessary to ensure comprehensive preventive care.

Healthcare systems should prioritize preventive care by implementing policies that support its delivery. Reimbursement policies that incentivize preventive services have been shown to increase utilization rates significantly. Public health and preventive care are vital in preventing diseases, promoting health, and improving overall population well-being.

This review emphasizes the importance of various preventive measures, the role of healthcare systems in supporting preventive care, and the need for collaboration between public health agencies and healthcare providers. Prioritizing public health and preventive care can lead to reduced healthcare costs, improved population health outcomes, and enhanced quality of life for individuals and communities.

Public health and preventive care are integral components of healthcare systems, aiming to prevent diseases, promote health, and improve overall population well-being. Moreover, various preventive measures should be emphasized, such as vaccination, lifestyle modifications, and health education programs. Additionally, the role of healthcare systems in supporting preventive care delivery and the need for collaboration between public health agencies and healthcare providers have been emphasized. By prioritizing public health and preventive care, societies can reduce healthcare costs, enhance population health outcomes, and improve the quality of life for individuals and communities.

The Importance of Public Health

Vignette: The Importance of Public Health

The flickering fluorescent lights of the community clinic hummed a monotonous tune. Maria, eight months pregnant and juggling a toddler on her hip, shifted nervously. The waiting room air, thick with the scent of antiseptic and anxiety, felt heavy in her lungs. She would come for her flu shot, following a recommendation from the brightly colored posters plastered across the bus she took—posters she had usually ignored. However, this year, with little Leo clinging to her like a koala, the message about protecting vulnerable populations resonated.

Across from her, an elderly man coughed into a tissue, his face etched with worry. A teenager with a pierced nose scrolled through their phone, seemingly oblivious to the posters detailing the symptoms of measles. A young mother breastfed her baby—a quiet island of serenity in the bustling room. Maria wondered about their stories, their reasons for being here. Were they, like her, motivated by a sudden awareness of their interconnectedness—a fragile understanding of shared health risks?

Suddenly, a piercing cry shattered the waiting room's uneasy peace. A child, no older than three, wailed inconsolably, his mother whispering soothing words. Maria watched, her heart aching. She thought of Leo—his infectious giggle, his tiny hands reaching for hers. She thought of the future, a future she desperately wanted to be healthy and safe for him.

The clinic door opened, and a nurse called her name. As Maria walked towards the examination room, questions swirled in her mind:

Questions

1. How can public health initiatives effectively reach and educate diverse communities, particularly those distrusting medical institutions or facing language barriers?
2. What are the long-term economic benefits of investing in preventative healthcare, such as vaccinations and health education programs, compared to treating illnesses after they arise?
3. How can public health officials balance individual freedoms with the need to implement measures that protect the collective well-being, particularly during outbreaks of infectious diseases?
4. Beyond vaccinations, what role does access to clean water, nutritious food, and safe housing play in ensuring public health, and how can these needs be addressed equitably?
5. In an increasingly interconnected world, how can global cooperation and resource sharing strengthen public health systems and prevent the spread of international health threats?

Public health encompasses a wide range of activities aimed at preventing diseases, prolonging life, and promoting health at the population level. It involves assessing and monitoring health issues, formulating policies, and implementing interventions to improve health outcomes. Numerous studies have emphasized the importance of public health in reducing morbidity and mortality rates (Singh et al., 2020; Safarpour et al., 2019; O'Connell et al., 2005).

A study by Brownson et al. (2018) examined the impact of public health interventions on population health. The authors found that public health efforts, such as immunizations, tobacco control, and injury prevention, have significantly contributed to declining mortality rates and overall health improvements. This study emphasizes the crucial role of public health interventions in preventing diseases and promoting healthier lifestyles (Brownson et al., 2018).

Furthermore, the World Health Organization (WHO) recognizes the importance of public health in achieving global health goals. The WHO's report on the global disease burden highlights the significance of public health interventions in reducing the prevalence of communicable and non-communicable diseases (World Health Organization, 2020). It emphasizes the need for comprehensive public health strategies to address various health challenges faced by populations worldwide (World Health Organization, 2020).Public health and preventive care are crucial components of a comprehensive healthcare system that aims to promote the well-being of individuals and communities. Investing in strengthening public health infrastructure is critical in all countries, regardless of income level, as public health systems are the first line of defense during pandemics (Collins et al., 2020).

Public health focuses on promoting healthcare equity, quality, and accessibility, as well as controlling diseases caused by various organisms (Nwobu, 2021). It is a collective social effort that involves population surveillance, regulation of determinants of health, and the provision of essential health services, with an emphasis on prevention.

Preventive care focuses on proactive measures to prevent diseases and promote health, primarily through screenings, vaccinations, and health education. It aims to identify risk factors and early signs of diseases to facilitate timely interventions. Numerous studies have demonstrated the effectiveness of preventive care in improving health outcomes and reducing healthcare costs.

A study by Maciosek et al. (2017) examined the cost-effectiveness of preventive care interventions in the United States. The authors found that preventive services, such as cancer screenings and vaccinations, were highly cost-effective in preventing diseases and reducing healthcare expenditures (Maciosek et al., 2017). This study highlights the economic benefits of preventive care and emphasizes its importance in healthcare policy planning.

Moreover, health promotion is crucial in preventive care, as it empowers individuals to make healthier choices and adopt positive behaviors (Maciosek et al., 2017). The Ottawa Charter for Health Promotion emphasizes the significance of health promotion in addressing the underlying determinants of health, including social, economic, and environmental factors. By promoting healthy lifestyles and creating supportive environments, health promotion efforts contribute to disease prevention and overall well-being (Maciosek et al., 2020; Maciosek et al., 2020; Nicholson et al., 2024; Sharma et al., 2020).

The exercise of government authority for the health of its population raises ethical issues, such as public welfare, individual autonomy, freedom, privacy, confidentiality, equitable distribution of benefits and burdens, transparency, and public accountability (Ng & Ruger, 2014).

The COVID-19 pandemic underscored the importance of

public health and preventive care in protecting populations from infectious diseases. Public health measures, such as widespread testing, contact tracing, and quarantine protocols, were instrumental in controlling the spread of the virus. Preventive measures effectively reduced transmission rates, including mask-wearing, hand hygiene, and social distancing (Collins et al., 2020).

The COVID-19 pandemic highlighted the importance of prioritizing core public health capacities, improving international cooperation and coordination, addressing health inequities, and enhancing health literacy(Collins et al., 2020). These measures will ensure that health systems and communities are better prepared for the disruptions that future disease outbreaks will inevitably bring.

A study by Bartsch et al. (2020) examined the impact of various public health interventions on COVID-19 outcomes in the United States. The authors found that a combination of testing, contact tracing, and mask-wearing could significantly reduce the number of cases and deaths(Bartsch et al., 2020). This study emphasizes the critical role of public health interventions in mitigating the impact of infectious diseases.

Public health is not solely the government's responsibility; it is the responsibility of individuals and society to prioritize public health. Governments have taken on these public health responsibilities differently, reflecting different political cultures, disease environments, and pressures from civil society(Maciosek et al., 2020; MacIosek et al., 2020; Vollset et al., 2024).

Public health measures have concentrated on four main areas: controlling hazards in the physical environment, ensuring the quality of food and water, preventing the transmission of infectious diseases, and providing vaccinations and other individual preventive services. (Collins et al., 2020; Ng & Ruger,

2014).

Public health and preventive care are essential components of a well-functioning healthcare system that promotes individuals' and communities' overall health and well-being.

Funding Priorities in Preventive Care

Funding for preventive care is a crucial pillar of public health, ensuring that resources are allocated judiciously to combat and prevent various health issues affecting communities. One significant initiative in this area is the Preventive Health and Health Services Block Grant, which grants communities the autonomy to address their most pressing health needs through targeted policies, systemic changes, and environmental initiatives (Congressional Research Service, 2019). This funding mechanism acknowledges the diverse health challenges different communities face, allowing for tailored responses that improve health outcomes.

Furthermore, the Affordable Care Act (ACA) represents a transformative investment in preventive healthcare, designating $15 billion over ten years to this critical area (Johns et al., 2024). This substantial financial commitment supports community and clinical prevention initiatives, research, and public health infrastructure improvements. Such investments are fundamental in establishing a framework for sustainable and effective preventive health interventions.

The impact of these funding initiatives is profound, prioritizing essential services such as vaccinations, tobacco cessation programs, and maternal and infant health services (Dabestani et al., 2019; Maciosek et al., 2020; Nicholson et al., 2024; Sharma et al. 2020). By focusing on these areas, public health policymakers can adopt a strategic approach that maximizes the use of available resources, ensuring that interventions are directed toward where they will have the greatest impact. This is particularly critical for under-resourced and vulnerable communities, which often bear the highest burden of health disparities.

In conclusion, funding for preventive care is more than just a financial allocation—it is a strategic investment in community health and a commitment to addressing urgent health challenges. These programs play an integral role in enhancing public health and ensuring equitable healthcare by empowering local initiatives and aligning substantial funding with targeted health outcomes. Evidence strongly supports the assertion that well-directed funding significantly improves overall public health.

Examples of Successful Public Health Interventions

Public health interventions encompass strategies to improve community health outcomes, from targeted disease prevention campaigns to comprehensive initiatives to enhance overall well-being.

Vaccination programs stand out as one of the most effective interventions. These programs have played a critical role in eradicating or substantially reducing numerous vaccine-preventable diseases, such as smallpox and polio, ultimately saving countless lives (Dabestani et al., 2019; Maciosek et al., 2017). Similarly, tobacco control measures—including smoking bans, taxation, and widespread public education campaigns—have proven to be highly effective in reducing smoking prevalence and associated health complications (Maciosek et al., 2020).

Initiatives focused on maternal and infant health have also played a key role in lowering mortality rates and improving health outcomes for both mothers and their children. Additionally, the

Earned Income Tax Credit (EITC) has emerged as a noteworthy public health intervention, positively impacting the economic stability of low-income families and, consequently, their overall health and well-being.

These examples highlight the extensive reach and profound potential of public health interventions to enact meaningful, positive changes in population health. Evidence demonstrates that targeted strategies lead to lasting improvements in health outcomes, reinforcing the need for continued investment and innovation in this field.

The importance of public health and preventive care, detailing funding priorities and public health interventions.

Public health and preventive care are essential components of a well-functioning healthcare system, crucial for promoting and maintaining the overall health and well-being of populations. Emphasizing public health improves the quality of life for individuals and addresses the underlying determinants of health, such as social, economic, and environmental factors (Radicke et al., 2021; Lim, S., 2023; Han, C., 2023). In this regard, funding priorities and public health interventions are instrumental in ensuring the success of preventive measures and achieving optimal health outcomes.

Public health funding should be strategically allocated to support initiatives that significantly impact population health. This involves investing resources in evidence-based programs and interventions targeting key health issues, such as chronic diseases, infectious diseases, mental health, and substance abuse. By prioritizing funding in these areas, public health agencies can effectively address the root causes of health disparities and reduce the burden of preventable illnesses on society.

Public health interventions encompass diverse strategies designed to prevent diseases, promote healthy behaviors, and protect communities from health threats. These interventions include vaccination campaigns, health education programs, screening and early detection initiatives, environmental health regulations, and policy advocacy. By implementing these interventions, public health agencies can proactively address health risks at the population level and create a supportive environment for individuals to make healthier choices.

Preventive care plays a pivotal role in public health by focusing on preemptive measures to prevent the onset of diseases or conditions before they progress to more severe stages. This proactive approach helps individuals maintain their health and well-being while also reducing healthcare costs associated with treating preventable conditions. By promoting regular health screenings, vaccinations, lifestyle modifications, and early interventions, preventive care can significantly impact health outcomes and improve overall quality of life (Brownson et al., 2018; Institute for Health Metrics and Evaluation, 2024; Maciosek et al., 2017; Sharma et al., 2020; Ward & Goldie, 2024; World Health Organization, 2020).

In conclusion, public health and preventive care are indispensable components of a comprehensive healthcare system, emphasizing the importance of investing in proactive strategies to protect and promote population health. By prioritizing funding in key areas and implementing evidence-based interventions, public health agencies can effectively address health disparities, prevent disease outbreaks, and enhance the well-being of individuals and communities. Embracing a preventive care approach not only improves health outcomes but also contributes to a more sustainable and resilient healthcare system.

Bibliography

Abdullah, M.Y., Esmael, E.A., Alqahtani, K.M., Qahl, K.H., Alanazi, N.A., Alshakhs, H.W., Alayyash, F.A., Almalki, Y.A., Alharbi, M.A., Alharbi, A.I., & Alhamdan, M.S. (2023). Diabetes prevention in primary care: a review of lifestyle interventions, screening, and risk reduction. International Journal of Community Medicine and Public Health.

Bartsch, S. M., Ferguson, M. C., McKinnell, J. A., O'Shea, K. J., Wedlock, P. T., Siegmund, S. S., & Lee, B. Y. (2020). The Potential Health Care Costs and Resource Use Associated with Covid 19 in the United States. *Health Affairs (Project Hope)*, *39*(6), 927935. https://doi.org/10.1377/hlthaff.2020.00426

Bichachi, R. (2024). *Healthcare & Hospital Budgeting Guide for 2024.* https://www.netsuite.com/portal/resource/articles/financial-management/healthcare-budgeting.shtml

Brownson, R. C., Fielding, J. E., & Green, L. W. (2018). Building Capacity for Evidence-Based Public Health: Reconciling the Pulls of Practice and the Push of Research. *Annual Review of Public Health*, *39*, 27–53. https://doi.org/10.1146/annurev-publhealth-040617-014746

Cadet, K., Baker, D. R., & Brown, A. (2023). A qualitative assessment of provider satisfaction and experiences with a COVID-19 community mobile health clinic outreach model in underserved Baltimore neighborhoods. *SAGE Open Medicine*, *11*. https://doi.org/10.1177/20503121231152090

Campbell, M., Escobar, O., & Fenton, C. et al. (2018). The impact of participatory budgeting on health and wellbeing. *BMC Public Health, 18*(822). https://doi.org/https://doi.org/10.1186/s12889-018-5735-8

Clark, E. C., Neumann, S., Hopkins, S., Kostopoulos, A., Hagerman, L., & Dobbins, M. (2024). Changes to Public Health Surveillance Methods Due to the COVID-19 Pandemic: Scoping Review. In *JMIR Public Health and Surveillance* (Vol. 10, Issue 1). JMIR Publications Inc. https://doi.org/10.2196/49185

CMS.gov. (n.d.). *Total Cost of Care and Hospital Global Budgets Defining key terms.* https://www.cms.gov/priorities/innovation/key-concepts/total-cost-care-and-hospital-global-budgets

Collins, T., Akselrod, S., Bloomfield, A., Gamkrelidze, A., Jakab, Z., & Placella, E. (2020). Rethinking the COVID-19 pandemic: Back to public health. *Annals of Global Health, 86*(1), 1–7. https://doi.org/10.5334/aogh.3084

Congressional Research Service. (2019). *Federal Grants to State and Local Governments: A Historical Perspective on Contemporary Issues.* https://crsreports.congress.gov

Dabestani, N. M., Leidner, A. J., Seiber, E. E., Kim, H., Graitcer, S. B., Foppa, I. M., & Bridges, C. B. (2019). A review of the cost-effectiveness of adult influenza vaccination and other preventive services. In *Preventive Medicine* (Vol. 126). Academic Press Inc. https://doi.org/10.1016/j.ypmed.2019.05.022

Daniels, N. (2016). Resource Allocation and Priority Setting.

In W. H. Barrett D, Ortmann L, & et al., Dawson A (Eds.), *Public Health Ethics: Cases Spanning the Globe.* Springer.

Fluxa, D., Roussel, B., Hashash, J. G., & Farraye, F. A. (2022). Preventive Care and Health Maintenance in Patients with Inflammatory Bowel Disease. Rhode Island Medical Journal (2013), 105(9), 8–12.

Han, C., J., Tounkara, F., Kalady, M., Noonan, A., Burse, N., Paskett, E., Ah, D., V. (2023) Risk Factors of Health-Related Quality of Life among Gastrointestinal Cancer Survivors in the U.S.: With a Focus on Social and Behavioral Determinants of Health (SBDH) International Journal of Environmental Research and Public Health 20

Institute for Health Metrics and Evaluation. (2024). *Global Burden of Disease 2021 Findings from the GBD 2021 Study.*

Johns M., & Rosenthal J., (2024). *How the Affordable Care Act Improved Access to Preventive Health Services - Center for American Progress.*

Larson, K., Levy, J., Rome, M., Matte, T., Silver, L., Frieden, T. (2006) Public Health Detailing: A Strategy to Improve the Delivery of Clinical Preventive Services in New York City Public Health Reports 121, 228-234

Lim, S., Chan, Y., Gan, W., Y. (2023) Social and Health Determinants of Quality of Life of Community-Dwelling Older Adults in Malaysia International Journal of Environmental Research and Public Health 20

Maciosek, M. V., LaFrance, A. B., Dehmer, S. P., McGree, D. A., Flottemesch, T. J., Xu, Z., & Solberg, L. I. (2017). Updated priorities among effective clinical preventive services. *Annals of Family Medicine*, *15*(1), 14–22. https://doi.org/10.1370/afm.2017

Maciosek, M. V., LaFrance, A. B., St. Claire, A. W., Keller, P. A., Xu, Z., & Schillo, B. A. (2020). The 20-year impact of tobacco price and tobacco control expenditure increases in Minnesota, 1998-2017. In *PLoS ONE* (Vol. 15, Issue 3). Public Library of Science. https://doi.org/10.1371/journal.pone.0230364

Maciosek, M. V., Lafrance, A. B., St Claire, A., Xu, Z., Brown, M., & Schillo, B. A. (2020). Twenty-year health and economic impact of reducing cigarette use: Minnesota 1998-2017. *Tobacco Control*, *29*(5), 564–569. https://doi.org/10.1136/tobaccocontrol-2018-054825

Ng, N. Y., & Ruger, J. P. (2014). Ethics and Social Value Judgments in Public Health. In *Encyclopedia of Health Economics* (pp. 287–291). Elsevier. https://doi.org/10.1016/B978-0-12-375678-7.00415-6

Nicholson, W. K., Silverstein, M., Wong, J. B., Barry, M. J., Chelmow, D., Coker, T. R., Davis, E. M., Jaén, C. R., Krousel-Wood, M., Lee, S., Li, L., Mangione, C. M., Rao, G., Ruiz, J. M., Stevermer, J. J., Tsevat, J., Underwood, S. M., & Wiehe, S. (2024). Screening for Breast Cancer: US Preventive Services Task Force Recommendation Statement. In *JAMA* (Vol. 331, Issue 22, pp. 1918–1930). American Medical Association. https://doi.org/10.1001/jama.2024.5534

Nwobu, O. A. (2021). *Corporate Social Responsibility and the Public Health Imperative: Accounting and Reporting on Public Health.* https://doi.org/http://dx.doi.org/10.5772/intechopen.94356

Nyiramana, M.P. (2024). The Impact of Public Health on

Disease Prevention. RESEARCH INVENTION JOURNAL OF SCIENTIFIC AND EXPERIMENTAL SCIENCES.

O'Connell, J., J., M., S., Judge, C., M., Allen, H., J., S., Koh, H., K. (2005) A public health approach to reducing morbidity and mortality among homeless people in Boston. Journal of public health management and practice: JPHMP 11 4, 311-6

Pavlović, R., Solaković, S., Simeonov, A., Milićević, L., & Radulović, N. (2022). PHYSICAL ACTIVITY AND HEALTH: THE BENEFITS OF PHYSICAL ACTIVITY IN THE PREVENTION OF DIABETES MELLITUS AND CARDIOVASCULAR DISORDERS. European Journal of Physical Education and Sport Science.

Radicke, A., Barkmann, C., Adema, B., Daubmann, A., Wegscheider, K., Wiegand-Grefe, S. (2021) Children of Parents with a Mental Illness: Predictors of Health-Related Quality of Life and Determinants of Child–Parent Agreement International Journal of Environmental Research and Public Health 18

Sharma, K. P., Grosse, S. D., Maciosek, M. V., Joseph, D., Roy, K., Richardson, L. C., Jaffe, H., & Sharma, K. P. (2020). Preventing Breast, Cervical, and Colorectal Cancer Deaths: Assessing the Impact of Increased Screening. *Preventing Chronic Disease*, *17*. https://doi.org/10.5888/pcd17.200039

Sharma, R., Meurk, C., Bell, S., K., Ford, P., G., C. (2018). Australian mental health care practitioners' practices and attitudes for encouraging smoking cessation and tobacco harm reduction in smokers with severe mental illness International Journal of Mental Health Nursing 27, 247–257

Singh, B.R., Gandharva, R., Karthikeyan, R., Singh, S.V., Yadav, A., O.R., V.K., Sinha, D.K., Jayakumar, V., Dhama, K., Kumar, D., & Gandharava, S. (2020). Epidemiological Determinants of Acute Respiratory Syndrome Coronavirus-2 Disease Pandemic and The Role of the Bacille-Calmette-Guerin Vaccine in Reducing Morbidity and Mortality. Journal of Pure and Applied Microbiology.

Sudari, F., Priskilla, I., Febiola, M., & Sinuraya, R. K. (2022). Strategies to improve the vaccine distribution and community awareness of taking the COVID-19 vaccine in rural areas in Indonesia. *Pharmacia*, *69*(2), 543–553. https://doi.org/10.3897/pharmacia.69.e81525

Vollset, S. E., Ababneh, H. S., Abate, Y. H., Abbafati, C., Abbasgholizadeh, R., Abbasian, M., Abbastabar, H., Abd Al Magied, A. H. A., Abd ElHafeez, S., Abdelkader, A., Abdelmasseh, M., Abd-Elsalam, S., Abdi, P., Abdollahi, M., Abdoun, M., Abdullahi, A., Abebe, M., Abiodun, O., Aboagye, R. G., … Murray, C. J. L. (2024). Burden of disease scenarios for 204 countries and territories, 2022–2050: a forecasting analysis for the Global Burden of Disease Study 2021. *The Lancet*, *403*(10440), 2204–2256. https://doi.org/10.1016/S0140-6736(24)00685-8

Ward, Z. J., & Goldie, S. J. (2024). Global Burden of Disease Study 2021 estimates_ implications for health policy and research. *Lancet*, *403*(10440), 1958–1959. https://doi.org/https://doi.org/10.1016/S0140-6736(24)00812-2

World Health Organization. (2020). *WHO methods and data sources for global burden of disease estimates 2000-2019*. http://www.who.int/gho/mortality_burden_disease/en/index.html

Chapter 5: Clinical Care and Universal Health Insurance

Vignette: Clinical Care and Universal Health Insurance

The air in the waiting room was thick with anxiety and the scent of stale coffee. Elena, a young woman with worried eyes and a persistent cough, clutched a worn tissue in her hand. She had not seen a doctor in over two years—not since losing her diner job and health insurance. The cost of seeing a doctor without coverage felt insurmountable, a luxury she could not afford.

Today was different. Today, Elena felt a flicker of hope. Her local clinic, usually overwhelmed with patients, buzzed with excitement. A banner hung proudly on the wall, proclaiming:

"Universal Health Insurance Now Available. Healthcare for All!"

When Elena finally saw Dr. Amina, she could barely contain her relief.

"I haven't been able to sleep," she confessed, her voice raspy. "This cough just will not go away."

Dr. Amina, her face etched with years of witnessing the healthcare struggles of her community, smiled warmly.

"Don't worry, Elena. With the new Universal Health Insurance, you can finally get the care you need without worrying about the cost."

Elena's eyes welled up. She felt seen, heard, and—most importantly—cared for, perhaps for the first time in years. As Dr. Amina listened to her lungs and promised further tests, Elena couldn't help but think of her neighbors, friends, and countless others struggling silently. Universal Health Insurance wasn't just a policy; it was a lifeline.

Discussion Questions:

1. Beyond access to care, what are some other potential benefits of Universal Health Insurance for individuals and communities? (Consider financial security, public health, and economic productivity).
2. The vignette highlights the emotional toll of healthcare insecurity. How might Universal Health Insurance impact the patient-provider relationship? (Think about trust, communication, and shared decision-making).
3. What are some potential challenges in implementing Universal Health Insurance equitably, ensuring everyone has access to

quality care regardless of their background or location? (Consider provider shortages, language barriers, and cultural competency).

4. How might the implementation of Universal Health Insurance impact the roles and responsibilities of healthcare professionals? (Consider patient education, care coordination, and advocacy).
5. The vignette focuses on the positive aspects of Universal Health Insurance. What potential drawbacks or concerns should be considered in discussions about healthcare reform? (Consider different perspectives and potential trade-offs).

Introduction

Universal health insurance represents a healthcare system in which every citizen has the financial protection necessary to access essential healthcare services without experiencing financial hardship. This system is founded on the principles of equity and accessibility, ensuring that clinical care is provided based on patients' needs rather than their ability to pay.

The importance of universal health insurance in promoting public health and well-being cannot be overstated. By striving to reduce disparities in healthcare access, universal health insurance significantly enhances the overall health status of populations. This framework guarantees that individuals can access a full spectrum of necessary medical services—from preventive care to rehabilitation—ultimately fostering a healthier and more productive society.

Clinical care and universal health insurance are integral to a comprehensive healthcare system. Clinical care involves providing medical services and treatments to promote health, prevent illness, and manage existing medical conditions. This includes a wide range of services, such as preventive care, diagnostic testing, therapeutic interventions, and the ongoing management of chronic diseases.

Conversely, universal health insurance ensures that all individuals can access necessary healthcare services without financial barriers. By implementing a universal health insurance system, governments or governing bodies can guarantee that every citizen receives coverage for essential medical needs, regardless of socio-economic status or financial capacity.

The integration of clinical care and universal health insurance is essential for advancing public health and reducing healthcare disparities. Access to high-quality clinical care is critical for improving individual health outcomes and overall quality of life. Meanwhile, universal health insurance alleviates financial burdens that might prevent individuals from seeking medical attention. The synergy between universal health insurance and clinical care is paramount in promoting health equity and improving public health outcomes. Investing in these systems not only safeguards individual well-being but also strengthens the overall fabric of society.

Impact of Universal Health Insurance on Clinical Care

Universal health insurance (UHI) plays a pivotal role in shaping clinical care by delivering numerous benefits that significantly enhance healthcare systems. One of the key advantages is the increased accessibility of healthcare services for all individuals, regardless of socio-economic status. This inclusivity is critical for reducing health disparities and ensuring that everyone receives timely medical attention.

Moreover, UHI is associated with improvements in the quality of clinical care. By ensuring a consistent funding stream, healthcare facilities can maintain high service standards, invest in advanced medical technologies, and attract top-tier healthcare professionals. Universal coverage encourages individuals to seek early medical intervention for diseases, significantly improving disease management and patient outcomes. Expanding preventive services and screenings under UHI facilitates the early detection of severe conditions such as cancer and diabetes. When these conditions are identified and treated promptly, healthcare costs are markedly reduced, and patient prognoses improve substantially.

The discourse surrounding UHI has gained considerable traction within global health policy discussions, particularly regarding its influence on clinical care. UHI's fundamental objective is to provide all individuals with access to health services without imposing financial burdens. This chapter thoroughly examines the existing body of research on UHI's impact on clinical care, focusing on critical dimensions such as access to services, quality of care, and overall health outcomes. Through a comprehensive analysis, it is evident that UHI stands as a transformative solution for fostering equitable and effective healthcare systems. .

Access to Health Services

Access to health services is a fundamental outcome in studies evaluating the effects of Universal Health Insurance (UHI). Substantial evidence indicates that UHI significantly enhances access to medical care, particularly for marginalized populations. For example, the research conducted by Doran et al. (2016) demonstrates a notable increase in healthcare utilization among low-income individuals residing in countries that have adopted UHI. This assertion is further supported by Ginsburg (2018), who posits that UHI effectively mitigates many financial barriers that often deter individuals from seeking necessary medical care. In addition to increasing overall access, UHI substantially improves access to preventive services.

A systematic review by Kutzin (2013) reveals that nations employing UHI models frequently report higher rates of preventive care utilization, including vaccinations and cancer screenings. This is particularly significant in addressing health disparities, as preventive care is crucial for detecting and managing diseases, as noted by Woolhandler and Himmelstein (2016). However, it is essential to acknowledge that while UHI enhances access to medical care, unintended consequences can arise from its implementation. Some studies suggest that increased demand for healthcare services might result in longer wait times for treatment.

A comparative analysis by Marmor et al. (2017) reveals that, although countries with UHI generally report higher levels of satisfaction and improved access, they also face challenges related to resource allocation and service delivery efficiency. These findings underscore the complexity of UHI's impact on healthcare access, highlighting that while increased utilization is a positive indicator, it does not necessarily equate to timely or efficient care.

While UHI undoubtedly plays a pivotal role in enhancing healthcare access and utilization—especially among vulnerable populations—it simultaneously presents challenges that require careful consideration. The relationship between increased access and the timeliness of care underscores the need for ongoing research and policy adjustments to optimize UHI systems and ensure equitable, efficient healthcare delivery for all.

Quality of Care

The impact of Universal Health Insurance (UHI) on the quality of clinical care is a multifaceted issue that warrants meticulous examination. Research consistently shows that UHI can significantly improve the quality of care received by patients. A pivotal study by McKee and Healy (2002) illustrates that UHI systems often implement standardized protocols and guidelines that promote consistent quality across various health services. These well-structured frameworks are essential in providing a baseline for best practices in clinical care, ultimately resulting in improved patient outcomes. Moreover, establishing universal coverage typically correlates with increased investments in essential healthcare infrastructure, staff training, and advanced technology. Bennett and Franco (2014) contend that such investments are crucial for facilitating high-quality healthcare delivery. By fostering an environment where healthcare providers are well-equipped and well-trained, UHI systems can ensure patients receive the best possible care.

However, the relationship between UHI and quality of care is not unequivocally positive. Critics argue that an influx of patients into a more accessible healthcare system may strain existing resources, potentially compromising the quality of care delivered. A study by Sweeney et al. (2017) substantiates this concern, revealing that while UHI enhances healthcare access, it poses significant challenges in maintaining quality, particularly within emergency care settings characterized by surges in demand. This situation underscores the need for careful planning and strategic resource allocation within UHI systems to ensure that access improvements do not come at the expense of care quality.

Furthermore, the governance and management of UHI systems play a critical role in shaping the quality of care provided. The comparative study by Saltman and Figueras (2013) highlights that effective governance structures are vital for realizing UHI's full potential in delivering high-quality care. The authors assert that transparency, accountability, and stakeholder engagement are essential to improving care quality within UHI frameworks.

In conclusion, while UHI has the potential to significantly improve the quality of clinical care, it is crucial to approach its implementation strategically. Ensuring robust governance, adequate resource allocation, and a commitment to continuous improvement will be key to harnessing the benefits of UHI while mitigating the risks associated with increased patient volume and care complexity.

Health Outcomes

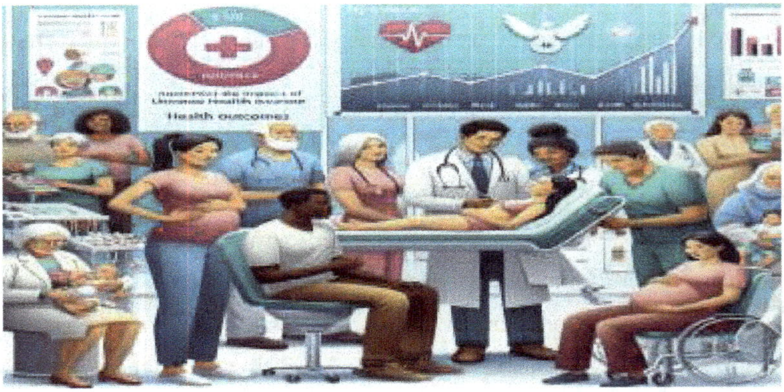

Universal Health Insurance (UHI) is a crucial initiative to ensure everyone can access necessary healthcare services without experiencing financial hardship (World Economic Forum, 2024; American University in Cairo, 2022; Diplomatist, 2024; Patel, P., 2024). Many nations recognize the importance of UHI as a key strategy in pursuing Universal Health Coverage (UHC), which guarantees that all individuals can obtain the healthcare they require without incurring financial distress. Despite these efforts, approximately 4.5 billion people still lack adequate health coverage, and the proportion of households spending over 10% of their budget on out-of-pocket healthcare expenses has risen since 2015 (World Economic Forum, 2024). Alarmingly, the pandemic has placed an additional 1.3 billion people into poverty due to medical expenditures (World Economic Forum, 2024). Empirical studies illustrate a significant correlation between UHI and improved health outcomes, including reduced mortality rates and increased life expectancy (Erlangga, 2019; Yale School of Public Health, 2023; World Bank. n.d.) This improvement appears to stem from enhanced access to timely care and the effective management of chronic conditions. Moreover, UHI has the potential to alleviate the adverse effects of socio-economic disparities on health outcomes by ensuring equitable access to health services (Erlangga, 2019). Importantly, UHI safeguards against catastrophic healthcare costs, a formidable barrier to care, especially in low- and middle-income countries.

Nevertheless, the relationship between UHI and health outcomes is intricate and shaped by several additional factors. A well-functioning healthcare system is paramount for harnessing the full benefits of UHI; this entails adequate infrastructure, a well-trained workforce, and efficient resource allocation. Moreover, individual health choices—particularly those related to diet and exercise—play a critical role in determining overall health outcomes independent of insurance coverage.

The implementation of UHI is not without its challenges. High initial costs, administrative complexities, and potential resistance from various stakeholders can hinder progress. Various funding models exist, including mandatory contributions, taxation, and equity funds, each presenting distinct advantages and disadvantages. Countries adopting UHI employ diverse strategies to suit their unique contexts (World Bank, 2013). Notable examples include Egypt, which enacted the Universal Health Insurance Law in 2018, aiming for comprehensive coverage while separating financing from service provision. Tanzania has also taken significant strides, having passed the UHI Bill in 2023, mandating health insurance for all citizens and creating an equity fund for marginalized populations (American University in Cairo, 2022). Burkina Faso has integrated free healthcare policies into its UHI framework to enhance equity. At the same time, Zanzibar has launched a Health Financing Strategy incorporating UHI and an equity fund for those not eligible for traditional insurance (Bergen Centre for Ethics and Priority Setting, n.d.).

While UHI stands as a formidable instrument for advancing health outcomes and promoting equity, its successful implementation demands meticulous planning, robust funding mechanisms, and a holistic approach that accounts for the broader determinants of health. Continuous monitoring and evaluation will be essential for adapting and enhancing UHI programs, ensuring they effectively meet all individuals' health needs.

Comparative Perspectives

The impact of Universal Health Insurance (UHI) on clinical care is best understood through comparative analyses of various health systems worldwide. Countries such as Canada, the United Kingdom, and Sweden provide compelling insights into the benefits and challenges associated with UHI. A pivotal study by Busse et al. (2017) elucidates that while UHI has significantly enhanced access to healthcare services and improved overall health outcomes in these nations, persistent challenges remain. Notably, issues related to waiting times and equitable resource allocation are prevalent, underscoring the complexities of managing a universal system effectively.

Moreover, the experiences of nations recently embarked on the journey toward UHI, such as Mexico and Thailand, offer invaluable lessons regarding the transitions to universal coverage. According to a comprehensive analysis by Papanicolas et al. (2018), these countries encountered considerable difficulties in guaranteeing both quality and equity during the implementation of UHI. These challenges highlight the intricate balance required to ensure that universal coverage does not compromise the standard of care provided to populations.

However, it is crucial to acknowledge that over time, both Mexico and Thailand displayed significant improvements in access to healthcare services and health outcomes. This progress serves as a testament to the notion that the benefits of UHI can indeed be realized; with the appropriate policy frameworks and strategic investments in health infrastructure, these systems can address the pre-existing challenges. Therefore, while the implementation of UHI is fraught with hurdles, the potential for substantial enhancements in clinical care is achievable and well-documented in the experiences of countries that have successfully navigated this path.

Policy Implications

The literature on universal health insurance (UHI) presents several compelling policy implications for successfully implementing and managing UHI systems.

Firstly, policymakers must prioritize resource allocation strategically. This is essential in mitigating the potential strain on healthcare services that may arise from increased demand as access to care expands. Investment in healthcare infrastructure, workforce training, and advanced technology must be at the forefront of this allocation strategy to ensure the quality of care is maintained and enhanced (Bennett & Franco, 2014).

Secondly, establishing effective governance structures is vital for the success of UHI systems. Policymakers are urged to focus on creating frameworks characterized by transparency and accountability. Engaging stakeholders—from healthcare providers to patients—is critical to ensure that the population's needs are met promptly and efficiently (Saltman & Figueras, 2013). Such governance structures foster an environment where continuous quality improvement is both possible and expected.

Furthermore, a comprehensive approach integrating UHI with broader public health initiatives is essential to maximize health outcomes. This approach must promote healthy behaviors and address the social determinants of health, ensuring the advantages of UHI are equitably accessible across diverse populations (Baker et al., 2016). Failing to consider these aspects risks perpetuating existing health disparities instead of alleviating them.

The current body of literature unequivocally demonstrates that universal health insurance profoundly impacts clinical care, enhancing access to services, improving quality of care, and ultimately leading to better health outcomes for the population. Nevertheless, successfully implementing UHI requires dedicated attention to resource allocation, governance, and comprehensive public health strategies. As nations worldwide continue to explore UHI as a pathway to achieving health equity, the insights derived from existing systems will prove invaluable in informing and shaping effective health policies. The commitment to robust policy frameworks is not merely recommended; it is essential for realizing the transformative potential of UHI.

Challenges in Implementing Universal Health Insurance

The implementation of universal health insurance (UHI) represents a paramount objective for many nations seeking to guarantee equitable access to healthcare services for all individuals, thereby alleviating the financial burdens associated with medical expenses. However, the transition to such a comprehensive system presents many challenges. Foremost among these challenges is the issue of financial sustainability. Governments and policymakers are tasked with devising effective funding mechanisms for expansive insurance programs that do not overextend public resources or compromise the quality of care provided to citizens.

The literature extensively discusses various funding models, including taxation, premiums, and government subsidies. Each model presents distinct advantages and disadvantages, with significant implications for the economy and individuals relying on these services. For instance, while taxation-based models are often perceived as equitable, they may encounter resistance from taxpayers concerned about the overall tax burden. Conversely, premium-based models can introduce barriers for low-income populations, potentially undermining the very principle of universal access. Moreover, integrating universal health insurance can exert considerable pressure on healthcare providers and facilities. An influx of patients resulting from increased coverage can lead to heightened service demand, culminating in longer wait times and concerns regarding the dilution of care quality. If not meticulously managed, these factors could exacerbate existing disparities rather than ameliorate them, posing a significant challenge to the overarching goal of UHI.

In navigating these complexities, it is imperative to strike an appropriate balance among the triad of cost, quality, and accessibility. This balancing act is essential to ensure the effective functioning of a universal health insurance system that satisfies the needs of all stakeholders involved—including patients, healthcare providers, and financial institutions. As illuminated by the research of Mori (2023), Habte et al. (2022), and Hu et al. (2022), these challenges underscore the necessity for thoughtful planning and innovative solutions. While the vision of universal health insurance holds tremendous promise for improving access and equity in healthcare, its realization requires a comprehensive understanding of the financial, structural, political, and social dimensions involved. Addressing these barriers with strategic foresight is not only critical for successful implementation but also essential to ensure the transition to UHI results in tangible enhancements in clinical care, free from unintended negative consequences. Therefore, continued investigation into these dimensions is vital to shaping effective UHI policies that fulfill all citizens' essential right to healthcare.

Universal health insurance (UHI) seeks to provide comprehensive healthcare access to all individuals, irrespective of their financial circumstances. This initiative holds the potential to improve health outcomes across diverse populations. However, several formidable challenges hinder the effective implementation of UHI, necessitating thorough analysis and innovative solutions (Kodali, 2024).

A primary concern centers on financial sustainability. Governments must explore various funding models, including taxation, premiums, and subsidies, while carefully considering their economic impact on individuals, employers, and public resources (American University in Cairo, 2022). A solid financial strategy is imperative for UHI to succeed in the long term. Different tax structures can significantly influence the scope and quality of healthcare coverage (Reeves et al., 2015). Notably, taxes on capital gains and profits correlate positively with increased health spending and coverage, while consumption taxes correlate negatively and may even detrimentally impact health outcomes (Reeves et al., 2015). Therefore, implementing progressive tax systems is vital, especially in countries with limited tax bases.

Structural challenges also present major hurdles. The surge in demand for healthcare services following UHI implementation can overwhelm existing infrastructure and workforce capacity. This situation often results in extended waiting times and may jeopardize the quality of care (Sharma et al., 2023; IOM, 2014). Therefore, substantial investments in infrastructure, workforce expansion, and proactive capacity management are essential. Furthermore, insufficient administrative capacity can impede enrollment procedures, exacerbating the challenges associated with implementation.

Political and social factors are equally important (Ho et al., 2022). Political will and collaborative governance are essential for addressing and mitigating potential opposition from stakeholders vested in existing healthcare systems (Ho et al., 2022). Public perception and acceptance of UHI are vital for success. Effective public awareness campaigns play a vital role in educating communities about the benefits of UHI and fostering a culture that prioritizes equitable healthcare access (Greer et al., 2015).

Strong national ownership and robust political leadership are indispensable for the successful implementation of UHC (Ho et al., 2022). Countries must tailor their approaches to specific contexts, priorities, and infrastructures. This adaptation may require integrating pre-existing systems and gradually shifting toward universal coverage, recognizing the importance of political milestones (The Policy Practice, 2023). Achieving UHC necessitates a comprehensive strategy that addresses financial, structural, political, and social complexities. Successful implementation hinges on strategic planning, innovative solutions, and a steadfast commitment to ensuring that universal coverage manifests meaningful improvements in healthcare for all. While the journey toward UHI is fraught with challenges, decisive and strategic actions can establish a healthcare system that benefits all stakeholders.

Key factors contributing to successful UHC implementation include strong political support, increased pooled health expenditures, economic growth, expanded government fiscal space, and a transition from out-of-pocket spending to risk-sharing mechanisms (The Policy Practice, 2023). Importantly, achieving high coverage alone is not enough; the healthcare system must also provide adequate financial protection and equitable access to quality care. This requires expanding insurance programs to effectively alleviate healthcare's financial burdens and meet the population's diverse needs. Furthermore, funding primary healthcare systems, coordinating financing arrangements, and strategically allocating subsidies according to need are essential to efficient UHC implementation. Finally, addressing service delivery challenges—such as inadequate quality of care, the rising burden of diseases, and healthcare inequities—remains critical for establishing a fully functional UHI system.

Financial Challenges

The financial sustainability of Universal Health Insurance (UHI) systems is a major concern that requires urgent attention. A pivotal challenge lies in allocating adequate funding necessary to meet the healthcare needs of the entire population. Numerous studies underscore that many countries grapple with insufficient financial resources, resulting in the chronic underfunding of essential health services (World Health Organization [WHO], 2010). For example, research conducted by Xu et al. (2018) shows that low-income countries often rely on out-of-pocket expenditures. This reliance exacerbates disparities in healthcare access among different socio-economic groups. The authors assert that establishing a robust taxation framework is crucial for financing UHI; however, many regions encounter significant obstacles related to tax collection and the management of public expenditures. Moreover, the risk of escalating healthcare costs poses another formidable challenge to UHI systems.

Carrin and James (2005) point out that implementing UHI often results in heightened demand for healthcare services, which can potentially outstrip the financial resources available for such services. This issue is particularly pronounced in nations transitioning from predominantly out-of-pocket payment systems to a UHI model. The authors emphasize the need for cost-control measures and efficient resource allocation to alleviate this financial strain. Furthermore, the sustainability of UHI systems is susceptible to economic downturns, as illustrated by the case of Greece during the financial crisis. Significant health spending reductions during this period correlated with drastic healthcare access declines (Karanikolos et al., 2013). Such examples illustrate the precarious nature of UHI systems in the face of adverse economic conditions. In a targeted case study analyzing the financial challenges associated with UHI, a randomized experiment conducted with approximately 6,000 households revealed that time-limited subsidies significantly bolstered enrollment in national health insurance programs. However, the study also identified weak administrative capacity as a critical barrier, leading to a notable number of households failing to enroll despite efforts to facilitate the process (Banerjee et al., 2021).

These findings highlight that poor administrative systems can impede progress toward achieving widespread coverage in developing countries. The financial sustainability of UHI systems is a multifaceted challenge that involves funding allocation, cost management, and administrative efficiency. Addressing these challenges is essential for ensuring equitable access to healthcare and maintaining the integrity of UHI frameworks. Policymakers must prioritize the development of strong financial and administrative structures to enhance the effectiveness and sustainability of health insurance systems globally.

Structural Challenges

Structural challenges are pivotal in determining the successful implementation of Universal Health Insurance (UHI). One of the foremost issues is the pre-existing healthcare infrastructure, which may be inadequately prepared to accommodate the surge in demand for medical services that UHI typically engenders. Kutzin (2013) elucidates that numerous countries face significant deficits in essential resources, including facilities, trained personnel, and medical supplies. This lack of foundational elements can severely undermine the overall effectiveness of UHI. Furthermore, the fragmentation of healthcare services, especially prevalent in nations with diverse insurance schemes, complicates the integration of UHI (Bennett et al., 2015). The authors argue that establishing a unified healthcare system is essential. Such a system mitigates inefficiencies and enhances service delivery, facilitating a more coherent approach to health management. In addition to infrastructural issues, the administrative complexity inherent in UHI implementation poses considerable challenges. As Dussault and Franceschini (2006) noted, establishing effective governance and management structures is crucial for the seamless operation of UHI systems. Countries with weak administrative capacities are at significant risk of struggling with implementing and managing UHI. This struggle can lead to pronounced disparities in both access to and the quality of care provided to citizens, ultimately compromising the goals of UHI. The importance of building robust institutional frameworks cannot be overstated. Additionally, investment in capacity-building initiatives is critical to overcoming the challenges. By prioritizing these strategies, countries can enhance their readiness for UHI, ensuring that it functions effectively and equitably for all population segments. In summary, addressing structural challenges through strategic improvements in infrastructure, service integration, governance, and capacity-building will be instrumental in successfully realizing UHI.

Political Challenges

Implementing Universal Health Insurance (UHI) is profoundly shaped by political factors that can either facilitate or hinder the necessary reforms. Central to the successful rollout of UHI is the political will to reform existing healthcare systems. As highlighted in the research conducted by McKee and Healy (2002), political resistance often arises from entrenched interests within the healthcare sector, particularly from private insurance companies and healthcare providers. These entities frequently perceive proposed changes as threats to their financial stability, leading to opposition against UHI implementation. Engaging stakeholders throughout the reform process is essential to navigating this resistance. Building consensus among various interest groups enhances the likelihood of successful implementation and fosters a more inclusive policy environment. McKee and Healy emphasize that stakeholder engagement is critical in overcoming the challenges vested interests pose. Moreover, the importance of governance and effective policy-making processes cannot be overstated. Gilson et al. (2014) underscore that successful policy-making hinges on a clear vision and unwavering commitment from political leaders. Without decisive leadership, the coherence and effectiveness of reforms can be severely compromised. Political instability and a lack of continuity in leadership present additional challenges that can derail UHI initiatives. A pertinent example of this phenomenon can be observed in countries experiencing political transitions, such as Egypt during the Arab Spring. Healthcare reforms were frequently deprioritized during this tumultuous period to address broader socio-political issues. As Khalil et al. (2015) noted, diverting attention from healthcare reform can result in stagnation and disillusionment, ultimately hindering the progress necessary for UHI implementation. The interplay between political will, stakeholder engagement, consistent governance, and leadership stability plays a pivotal role in the successful implementation of

Universal Health Insurance. Addressing these political factors is essential for overcoming barriers to reform and ensuring that healthcare systems can evolve to meet the population's needs effectively.

Social Challenges

Social determinants of health play a significant role in the successful implementation of UHI. Research indicates that public perceptions and attitudes toward UHI can influence its acceptance and effectiveness (Bennett et al., 2015). For example, Gollust et al. (2009) found that mistrust in government institutions can hinder public support for UHI initiatives. The authors argue that building trust through transparent communication and community engagement is essential for fostering public acceptance. Moreover, disparities in health literacy can pose challenges to UHI implementation. Nutbeam (2000) noted that individuals with lower health literacy may struggle to navigate the healthcare system, leading to underutilization of services. This issue is particularly pronounced in marginalized populations, who may face additional barriers to accessing healthcare (Berkman et al., 2011). Addressing health literacy through targeted educational initiatives is crucial for ensuring all individuals benefit from UHI. These are case studies showcasing Universal Health Insurance's (UHI) challenges.

The expansion of universal health coverage (UHC) has gained momentum globally, with numerous countries implementing programs to enhance healthcare access and mitigate the financial burdens contributing to poverty. A recent study by the World Bank Group, titled *Going Universal: How 24 Countries are Implementing Universal Health Coverage Reforms from the Bottom Up*, examines the initiatives of 24 developing nations as they strive toward UHC, mainly focusing on the inclusion of marginalized populations who historically receive inadequate healthcare services. The urgency of expanding UHC is underscored by alarming statistics from the World Health Organization and the World Bank, which report that 400 million individuals lack access to essential health services and that 6% of the populace in low- and middle-income countries is driven into extreme poverty due to healthcare expenditures. The countries analyzed in this study include Argentina, Brazil, China, India, and South Africa, each undergoing transformative health system reforms. The authors highlight five critical challenges policymakers face: ensuring coverage, expanding benefits, managing financial resources, improving healthcare service delivery, and enhancing accountability. The findings indicate that these initiatives are substantial and innovative, fundamentally altering the operational frameworks of health systems and addressing historical inequalities in financing and service provision (World Bank Group, 2024).

Global Perspectives on UHI Implementation

Implementing Universal Health Insurance (UHI) across various nations yields significant insights into the challenges and potential solutions. A comparative analysis of experiences in different countries elucidates the critical role of political commitment and public support. For instance, countries such as Canada and the United Kingdom exemplify the effectiveness of strong political backing and active community endorsement in establishing and sustaining UHI systems (Marchildon, 2013). Conversely, the United States illustrates the formidable obstacles to navigating a fragmented healthcare system driven by entrenched political interests, underscoring the complexities of achieving UHI (Oberlander, 2017). Furthermore, the research conducted by Timmons et al. (2018) emphasizes the necessity of context-specific strategies for UHI implementation. The authors contend that effective solutions must consider each nation's distinctive socio-economic, cultural, and political landscape. For example, the myriad challenges confronted by countries in sub-Saharan Africa are markedly different from those faced by nations in Europe or North America. This divergence necessitates formulating tailored strategies that effectively address local needs and conditions.

The journey toward implementing universal health insurance is fraught with challenges that demand comprehensive strategies and innovative solutions. Key elements such as financial sustainability, structural integrity, political will, and social acceptance are paramount for the success of UHI initiatives. Therefore, ongoing research must prioritize exploring innovative solutions to overcome these barriers, paying particular attention to cross-country comparisons and identifying best practices. By gaining a deeper understanding of the inherent challenges associated with UHI implementation, policymakers are better equipped to pursue equitable and sustainable healthcare solutions for all citizens. The path forward requires a commitment to addressing these obstacles and an unwavering determination to adapt strategies to fit individual countries' contexts. By fostering this approach, we can collectively move closer to the realization of universal health coverage that meets the diverse needs of populations around the globe.

Case Studies: Success Stories of Universal Health Insurance

The global healthcare landscape has increasingly showcased successful implementations of universal health insurance (UHI), a crucial framework for enhancing clinical care and improving health outcomes. Countries such as Canada and the United Kingdom exemplify the efficacy of publicly funded healthcare systems that ensure universal coverage. These nations have demonstrated that universal access to essential healthcare services not only promotes the well-being of citizens but also leads to significantly improved population health outcomes. The prioritization of primary care and preventive services within these systems has resulted in lower rates of chronic diseases and increased life expectancy, reinforcing the vital role of equitable access to healthcare.

In addition to the examples from Canada and the UK, nations such as Germany and Japan offer compelling cases where health insurance is mandated for all citizens. These countries adopt a dual approach, integrating government funding with private insurance contributions, achieving comprehensive coverage while maintaining commendable standards of clinical care. These case studies serve as exemplary benchmarks for other nations endeavoring to achieve universal health insurance. They emphasize that despite the inherent challenges, the benefits—namely enhanced health outcomes and equal access to healthcare—far outweigh the investments and efforts required for implementation.

Promoting health equity is intertwined with establishing universal health insurance within a healthcare system. Ensuring everyone has access to the necessary healthcare services is paramount for thriving societies. Recognizing the critical importance of clinical care and universal health coverage, policymakers must implement strategies that facilitate integration. By doing so, societies can strive toward the goal of achieving better health outcomes for all members of the population.

The case studies presenting the experiences of 11 countries in implementing Universal Health Coverage (UHC) reveal that UHC is a fundamental global objective aimed at ensuring equitable access to quality health services, safeguarding public health, and providing protection against financial hardships stemming from health-related expenditures. The experiences of nations such as Brazil, France, Japan, Thailand, and Turkey illustrate UHC's potential to enhance public health and welfare and stimulate economic growth through sustainable practices. Access to affordable healthcare transcends mere health concerns; it is crucial in eradicating extreme poverty and fostering shared prosperity. This is particularly relevant in low- and middle-income countries (LMICs) with many impoverished populations.

The Japan–World Bank Partnership Program for UHC identifies 11 countries at varying stages of UHC implementation, categorizing them into four groups based on their progress. This framework highlights key policy messages: the need for strong political leadership, sustained commitment, and adaptive governance. Investing in primary care, public health initiatives, and deliberate policies promoting equitable resource distribution is essential. Furthermore, the political economy heavily influences UHC processes, with historical contexts frequently prompting the adoption of UHC during socio-economic transitions.

Countries face numerous challenges in health financing, necessitating the development of innovative strategies for revenue generation and equitable resource allocation. Crucially, addressing the maldistribution of healthcare workers, particularly in rural and underserved areas, is fundamental to the success of UHC initiatives. While the path to UHC is undeniably complex, nations can learn from each other's experiences, enhancing their policies and strategies. This collective learning reinforces the global commitment to inclusive and sustainable development in healthcare, ultimately driving progress toward universal health coverage for all.

Framework for Clinical Care via Universal Health Insurance

Universal health insurance represents a system where healthcare is accessible to all citizens regardless of their financial status, enabling individuals to receive clinical care without financial hardship. Built on principles of equity, accessibility, and efficiency, it aims to provide comprehensive health coverage, including preventive, curative, rehabilitative, and palliative services. The primary role of universal health insurance in clinical care is to bridge the gaps in healthcare access, fostering a more inclusive health system that caters to the needs of every individual. Eliminating financial barriers ensures that essential clinical services are available to all, significantly improving public health outcomes.

The foundation of clinical care within a universal health insurance system relies on a well-defined framework that incorporates several key components. Basic Principles and Objectives: The core principles include universality, equity, and accessibility, with objectives focused on improving health outcomes, ensuring financial risk protection, and increasing satisfaction among healthcare users. Structural Components: The framework consists of insurance coverage that spans a comprehensive range of services, from preventive care to advanced treatments; a network of healthcare providers ensuring services are delivered efficiently; and mechanisms to facilitate patient access to these services anytime and anywhere. Role of Policy and Regulation: Essential to this framework is a robust policy and regulatory environment that guides the operation of universal health insurance. This includes legislation on funding models, criteria for service inclusion, standards for care delivery, and safeguards for maintaining healthcare quality and patient rights.

Establishing a clear and functional framework is crucial for aligning universal health insurance goals with the operational realities of clinical care, thereby creating a health system that is both responsive and sustainable.

In establishing a framework for clinical care through universal health insurance, a comprehensive system can be developed to ensure access to healthcare services for all individuals, regardless of their socio-economic status. This framework promotes health equity and improves health outcomes and the population's overall well-being. This essay will discuss the benefits and implementation strategy of such a framework.

One of the primary benefits of a universal health insurance system is the equitable access to healthcare services it provides. By eliminating financial barriers to care, individuals are more likely to seek timely medical attention, leading to early detection and management of health conditions. This, in turn, can reduce the disease burden and prevent complications arising from untreated conditions. Additionally, universal health insurance promotes preventive care and wellness initiatives, fostering a culture of health-conscious behavior among the population.

Furthermore, a universal health insurance framework enhances healthcare delivery efficiency by streamlining administrative processes and reducing the fragmentation of care. With a single-payer system, healthcare providers can focus on delivering quality care to patients without the bureaucratic hurdles associated with multiple insurance plans. This promotes continuity of care and patient-centered approaches, ultimately improving the overall patient experience and satisfaction with the healthcare system.

A phased approach is often recommended for transitioning to a universal health insurance model. Initially, a thorough assessment of the existing healthcare system is essential to identify areas for improvement and potential challenges in implementing the new framework. Stakeholder engagement is crucial at this stage to garner support from policymakers, healthcare providers, insurers, and the public.

The next step involves designing a comprehensive benefit package that covers essential health services while ensuring the system's financial sustainability. This may include exploring different financing mechanisms to fund the universal health insurance program, such as taxes, premiums, or a combination. Effective communication and public education campaigns are essential to inform the population about the new system's benefits and address any concerns or misconceptions that may arise. Additionally, investing in healthcare infrastructure and workforce development is vital to meet the increased demand for services under a universal health insurance framework. This may include expanding healthcare facilities, recruiting and training healthcare professionals, and implementing information technology systems to improve care coordination and data management.

The framework for clinical care via universal health insurance has garnered significant attention in the academic community, reflecting a growing recognition of the necessity for equitable health care access. This literature review synthesizes various studies, theories, and frameworks that outline the relationship between universal health insurance and clinical care delivery, emphasizing the implications for health outcomes, healthcare systems, and policy-making.

Theoretical Foundations of Universal Health Insurance

Universal health insurance (UHI) represents a foundational principle in the pursuit of equitable healthcare, asserting that every individual should have unimpeded access to essential health services without encountering financial hardship (World Health Organization [WHO], 2010). This concept is reinforced by established theoretical frameworks, such as the Health Equity Framework (Braveman, 2014) and the Social Determinants of Health (SDH) model (Marmot, 2005), both of which elucidate the mechanisms through which UHI can effectively reduce health disparities across diverse populations. Braveman (2014) asserts that true equity in healthcare transcends mere access to services; it encompasses the quality of care individuals receive and the broader social conditions that influence health outcomes. This perspective underscores the complexity of health equity, emphasizing that factors beyond healthcare access—such as socio-economic status, education, and environmental influences—are critical to understanding health disparities. The implementation of UHI seeks to facilitate access to healthcare, aiming to elevate the standard of care available to all, particularly populations historically facing systemic disadvantages. Moreover, by guaranteeing comprehensive health services to all individuals, UHI has the potential to confront and dismantle the entrenched inequalities that contribute to adverse health outcomes among marginalized groups (Bambra et al., 2010). This is especially salient in contexts where socio-economic disparities are prevalent. UHI can serve as a transformative tool to ensure that all individuals receive adequate healthcare and support regardless of their background. Ultimately, the commitment to UHI recognizes every individual's inherent right to health and acknowledges society's responsibility to address inequities that hinder health and well-being. As we advance toward a more inclusive healthcare paradigm, UHI is a pivotal strategy in fostering healthier populations and a more just society.

UHI and Access to Care

Access to healthcare is undeniably a fundamental element of the Universal Health Insurance (UHI) framework. The significance of this access cannot be overstated, as numerous studies, including one conducted by the Organisation for Economic Co-operation and Development (OECD) in 2020, demonstrate that nations with universal health coverage exhibit markedly higher rates of health service utilization compared to those lacking such coverage. This correlation indicates that UHI not only enhances the overall availability of health services but also promotes a culture of seeking care among the population. A pivotal study by Mossialos et al. (2016) further elucidates this phenomenon through a comparative analysis of various countries. It highlights that nations such as Canada and Sweden, which have implemented UHI systems, report significantly lower rates of unmet medical needs than the United States.

In contrast, the American healthcare system is characterized by access barriers often tied to factors like employment status and income. This stark contrast emphasizes the efficacy of UHI in ensuring that all individuals, regardless of their socio-economic situation, can obtain necessary healthcare services. Moreover, equitable access to healthcare has profound implications. As Buchmueller et al. (2016) argue, UHI facilitates access to routine preventive care and effective management of chronic diseases. Without universal health coverage, many patients may delay seeking medical attention, leading to worsened health outcomes and increased long-term costs for individuals and the healthcare system.

Integrating UHI into a country's healthcare strategy is essential for promoting equitable access to health services, ultimately leading to better health outcomes and improved public health overall. The evidence points unequivocally to the advantages of UHI in fostering an environment where healthcare is accessible to all, thereby diminishing disparities and enhancing the quality of care received by populations across different socio-economic strata.

Quality of Care in UHI Systems

The relationship between Universal Health Insurance (UHI) and the quality of healthcare delivery is complex and multifaceted. Empirical research indicates that UHI systems frequently emphasize the importance of primary care and preventive services, leading to significant improvements in health outcomes (Starfield,

2011). The prioritization of these services is crucial, as they serve as the first point of contact for individuals seeking medical assistance, fostering early intervention and ongoing health management. For instance, a systematic review conducted by Kringos et al. (2013) demonstrates that countries with strong primary care infrastructures, particularly when supported by UHI, tend to experience lower mortality rates and exhibit superior management of chronic illnesses. This correlation highlights the critical role that a robust primary care system plays in extending life expectancy and enhancing the quality of life for patients with long-term health conditions. Moreover, integrating care, a hallmark of UHI systems facilitates a more holistic and coordinated approach to healthcare delivery.

This integrated care model significantly improves patient experiences and clinical outcomes (Bodenheimer & Pham, 2010). By ensuring that patients receive well-coordinated care across various healthcare services, UHI systems can enhance patient satisfaction and adherence to treatment protocols, ultimately leading to better health outcomes. However, it is essential to acknowledge that challenges persist within UHI frameworks, particularly regarding discrepancies in quality across different regions and among various healthcare providers. These variances necessitate ongoing evaluations and policy adaptations to ensure that health services are equitable and consistently high in quality (Hernández-Quevedo et al., 2019).

Without addressing these disparities, the full potential of UHI to improve healthcare quality and access may not be realized. While UHI systems present a promising avenue for enhancing healthcare quality by focusing on primary care and preventive measures, it is crucial to remain vigilant about the underlying challenges. Continuous assessment and policy reform are essential to bridge the gaps in care quality, ensuring that UHI's benefits are accessible to all populations.

Economic Implications of UHI

The economic implications of implementing Universal Health Insurance (UHI) are crucial considerations for policymakers navigating the complexities of healthcare reform. Although there are assertions that introducing UHI might escalate government spending, a growing body of evidence convincingly argues that UHI can ultimately decrease overall healthcare costs. This reduction is primarily achieved through the promotion of preventive care, which significantly diminishes the reliance on expensive emergency interventions (Woolhandler & Himmelstein, 2016).

Research conducted by Tseng et al. (2019) supports this perspective. It provides compelling data indicating that nations with UHI systems exhibit lower per capita health expenditures while simultaneously achieving superior health outcomes compared to countries lacking such systems. This correlation between UHI and enhanced health metrics underscores the potential of UHI to serve as a cost-effective healthcare delivery model.

Furthermore, integrating UHI with comprehensive public health initiatives can amplify its effectiveness. Klein et al. (2019) highlight that a robust support structure accompanying UHI facilitates access to necessary medical services and fosters a healthier population overall. Thus, the evidence reinforces the assertion that UHI is not merely a desirable healthcare framework; it is, in fact, a financially prudent strategy that aligns economic efficiency with improved public health outcomes. As such, policymakers should confidently approach the implementation of UHI, recognizing its potential to transform the healthcare landscape while safeguarding fiscal responsibility.

UHI and Health Outcomes

The relationship between Universal Health Insurance (UHI) and improved health outcomes is well-established in academic literature. A significant meta-analysis by Karanikolos et al. (2013) provides compelling evidence that nations implementing UHI experience marked health benefits. These countries specifically report lower infant mortality rates, increased life expectancy, and superior overall health indicators compared to those without UHI. This indicates a robust healthcare system that facilitates access to essential medical services, ultimately contributing to healthier populations.

The World Health Organization (WHO) corroborates these findings in its 2010 report, emphasizing that UHI is not merely an accessory to health improvements but a critical component for achieving health-related Sustainable Development Goals (SDGs). This assertion underscores the vital role of UHI in fostering equitable health outcomes, particularly in resource-limited settings where disparities can be more pronounced. The significance of UHI has been accentuated in the context of the COVID-19 pandemic, which exposed the vulnerabilities of healthcare systems lacking universal coverage.

Research by Baker et al. (2020) shows that countries with UHI were better positioned to manage the health crisis effectively, demonstrating an enhanced ability to mitigate health disparities among their populations. This evidence further supports the argument that UHI is an indispensable framework for promoting public health and resilience in times of crisis. The literature consistently demonstrates that UHI contributes positively to health outcomes across various metrics. Considering recent global health challenges, the importance of such systems cannot be overstated. The pursuit of UHI must remain a priority for governments worldwide, as its establishment is integral to achieving equitable health access and addressing the diverse needs of populations, especially in the face of future health emergencies.

Challenges and Barriers to Implementation

While Universal Health Insurance (UHI) offers numerous advantages, such as enhanced access to healthcare and improved public health outcomes, its implementation faces significant challenges that must be addressed for successful integration. A primary obstacle is political resistance, particularly pronounced in nations with established private healthcare systems. In these contexts, the entrenched interests and powerful lobbying groups advocating for the status quo can hamper efforts to implement UHI, as evidenced by Stuckler et al. (2017). Moreover, the sustainability of funding for UHI systems has sparked considerable debate among scholars and policymakers alike.

Critics, including Harris et al. (2019), articulate valid concerns regarding the necessity for increased taxation or the reallocation of existing resources to support UHI initiatives. This financial dilemma raises questions about the political will and public support required to sustain such a transformative healthcare model. Furthermore, establishing a robust healthcare infrastructure and a well-trained workforce is imperative for the efficacy of UHI.

The World Health Organization (2010) underscores that providing insurance coverage without sufficient medical services and personnel will not yield the desired improvements in health outcomes. This reinforces the notion that UHI is not merely about access to insurance; it requires a comprehensive approach, including expanding healthcare facilities, training medical professionals, and developing efficient healthcare delivery systems. While the benefits of UHI are evident, overcoming the multifaceted challenges of political resistance, funding sustainability, and infrastructure development is crucial. A concerted effort from policymakers, stakeholders, and the public is needed to navigate these barriers and realize the potential of UHI to transform health systems and improve population health.

Future Directions for Research

Future research in the domain of universal health insurance (UHI) must prioritize longitudinal studies that evaluate the long-term effects of UHI on health outcomes and the performance of healthcare systems. These studies are vital as they will provide comprehensive data regarding the immediate benefits of UHI and its sustained impact over time. Furthermore, qualitative research that delves into the lived experiences of individuals navigating UHI systems can yield invaluable insights. Such studies can illuminate the effectiveness of these frameworks in mitigating health disparities, thus enriching our understanding of UHI's real-world implications. Additionally, comparative studies examining health outcomes and system performance in countries with UHI versus those without can provide crucial evidence on the tangible benefits of such systems.

The work of Bambra et al. (2010) underscores the importance of this comparative analysis, revealing how UHI can fundamentally influence health indicators. The existing literature on UHI emphasizes its transformative potential in clinical care delivery. UHI is heralded for its capacity to enhance access to healthcare, improve the quality of services provided, and promote health equity among diverse populations. Although there are challenges to overcome—such as financing, resource allocation, and political resistance—the compelling evidence supporting UHI as a practical healthcare framework cannot be overlooked. As nations confront the complexities of healthcare reform, the principles guiding UHI will undoubtedly shape ongoing policy discussions and influence the evolution of healthcare systems globally.

In conclusion, adopting a UHI framework for clinical care presents substantial advantages, particularly in equity, efficiency, and quality of care. Countries aiming to achieve universal healthcare coverage must follow a strategic implementation approach, which includes stakeholder engagement, thoughtful benefit design, robust financing mechanisms, and capacity-building initiatives. By adhering to these principles, countries can make meaningful advancements toward improving health outcomes for their populations, ensuring that health equity is not merely an aspiration but a reality.

Bibliography

American University in Cairo. (2022). Health equity in Egypt: Reflections in 2022. American University in Cairo. https://aps.aucegypt.edu/en/articles/786/health-equity-in-egypt-reflections-in-2022

Baker, L. C., Bundorf, M. K., & Kessler, D. P. (2016). The effect of health insurance on health care utilization: A review of the literature. Health Services Research, 51(1), 1-26.

Baker, M. G., Peckham, T. K., & Seixas, N. S. (2020). COVID-19 and the need for health equity. International Journal of Public Health, 65(5), 505-507.

Bambra, C., Riordan, R., Ford, J., & Matthews, S. (2010). The effects of welfare state regimes on health inequalities in the European Union. Journal of Epidemiology and Community Health, 64(12), 1045–1051.

Banerjee, A., Finkelstein, A.N., Hanna, R., Olken, B.A., Ornaghi, A., & Sumarto, S. (2021). The Challenges of Universal Health Insurance in Developing Countries: Experimental Evidence from Indonesia's National Health Insurance. The American Economic Review, 111, 3035-3063.

Bennett, S., & Franco, L. M. (2014). The role of governance in health systems: A review of the literature. Health Policy and Planning, 29(1), 1-12.

Bennett, S., McPake, B., & Mills, A. (2015). Health financing in low-income countries. In Global Health: Diseases, Programs, Systems, and Policies (pp. 175–194). Jones & Bartlett Learning.

Bergen Centre for Ethics and Priority Setting. (n.d.). Universal health coverage (UHC) in Zanzibar. University of Bergen.

https://www.uib.no/en/bceps/130753/universal-health-coverage-uhc-zanzibar

Berkman, N. D., Sheridan, S. L., Donahue, K. E., Halpern, D. J., & Crotty, K. (2011). Health literacy interventions and outcomes: An updated systematic review. Evidence Report/Technology Assessment, (199), 1–941.

Bodenheimer, T., & Pham, H. H. (2010). Primary care: Current problems and proposed solutions. Health Affairs, 29(5), 799-805.

Braveman, P. (2014). What are health disparities and health equity? Public Health Reports, 129(Suppl 2), 5–8.

Buchmueller, T. C., Couffinhal, A., Grignon, M., & Perronnin, M. (2016). Access to health care services: The role of health insurance in the French health care system. Health Economics, 25(3), 251-267.

Busse, R., Geissler, A., & Rütten, A. (2017). Health systems in transition: Learning from the past to improve future health systems. European Observatory on Health Systems and Policies.

Carrin, G., & James, C. (2005). Health financing for universal coverage. Bulletin of the World Health Organization, 83(1), 1–2.

Diplomatist. (2024, June 20). Universal health insurance: Transforming Tanzania's healthcare system. Diplomatist. https://diplomatist.com/2024/06/20/universal-health-insurance-transforming-tanzanias-healthcare-system/

Doran, T., Fullwood, C., & Gravelle, H. (2016). The impact of the introduction of universal health coverage on health care utilization: A systematic review. BMC Health Services Research, 16(1), 1–10.

Dussault, G., & Franceschini, M. C. (2006). Not enough there, too many here: Understanding human resources imbalances in the health sector. Human Resources for Health, 4(1), 1-10.

Erlangga D, Suhrcke M, Bloor K, Ali S (2019). The impact of public health insurance on health care utilization, financial protection, and health status in low- and middle-income countries: A systematic review. PLoS ONE 14(8): e0219731. https://doi.org/10.1371/journal.pone.0219731

Gilson, L., Schneider, H., & Agyepong, I. A. (2014). Building the evidence for health policy: A systematic review of the literature. Health Policy and Planning, 29(5), 585-593.

Ginsburg, P. B. (2018). The effects of universal health insurance on access to care: A review of the evidence. Health Affairs, 37(6), 881–887.

Gollust, S. E., Nagler, R. H., & Fowler, E. F. (2009). The role of public opinion in health policy: A study of the Affordable Care Act. Health Affairs, 28(5), 1404–1413.

Greer, S. L., & Méndez, C. A. (2015). Universal Health Coverage: A Political Struggle and Governance Challenge. American journal of public health, 105 Suppl 5(Suppl 5), S637–S639. https://doi.org/10.2105/AJPH.2015.302733

Habte, A., Tamene, A., Ejajo, T., Dessu, S., Endale, F., Gizachew, A., Sulamo, D. (2022). Towards universal health coverage: The level and determinants of enrollment in the Community-Based Health Insurance (CBHI) scheme in Ethiopia: A systematic review and meta-analysis PLoS ONE 17

Harris, M. F., et al. (2019). The impact of universal health coverage on health outcomes: A systematic review. Health Policy and Planning, 34(1), 1–13.

Hernández-Quevedo, C., et al. (2019). The quality of health care in Europe: A systematic review. Health Policy, 123(5), 430-441.

Ho, C. J., Khalid, H., Skead, K., & Wong, J. (2022). The politics of universal health coverage. The Lancet, 399(10340), 2066-2074. https://doi.org/10.1016/S0140-6736(22)00585-2

Hu, M., Mao, W., Xu, R., Chen, W., & Yip, W.C. (2022). Have Lower-Income Groups Benefited More from Increased Government Health Insurance Subsidies? Benefit Incidence Analysis in Ningxia, China. Health policy and planning.

IOM (Institute of Medicine). 2014. The impacts of the Affordable Care Act on preparedness resources and programs: Workshop summary. Washington, DC: The National Academies Press.

Karanikolos, M., et al. (2013). Health inequalities in the EU: The role of health care systems. European Journal of Public Health, 23(1), 1-5.

Karanikolos, M., Mladovsky, P., & Cylus, J. (2013). Health system responses to financial pressures in four European countries: A comparative study. Health Policy, 113(2-3), 141-151.

Karanikolos, M., Reeves, A., McKee, M., & Stuckler, D. (2013). Financial crisis, austerity, and health in Europe. The Lancet, 381(9874), 1323–1331.

Khalil, H., Moustafa, A., & El-Shafie, M. (2015). The impact of the Arab Spring on health care in Egypt: A qualitative study. BMC Health Services Research, 15(1), 1–9.

Klein, R., et al. (2019). Cost-effectiveness of universal health coverage: A systematic review. Health Economics, 28(1), 1-30.

Kodali, P. B. (2024). Achieving universal health coverage in low- and middle-income countries: Challenges for policy post-pandemic and beyond. Risk Management and Healthcare Policy, 15(5), 336-339. https://doi.org/10.2147/RMHP.S366759

Kringos, D. S., et al. (2013). The importance of primary care in health systems: A systematic review. Health Services Research, 48(4), 1070-1091.

Kutzin, J. (2013). Health financing for universal coverage and health system performance: A comparative analysis. Health Systems & Reform, 3(3), 187–193.

Kutzin, J. (2013). Health financing for universal coverage and health system performance: A comparative analysis. Global Health Action, 6(1), 1–10.

Maeda, A., Cashin, C., Harris, J., Ikegami, N., Reich, M. & World Bank, I. B. (2014). Universal Health Coverage for Inclusive and Sustainable Development: A Synthesis of 11 Country Case Studies. Washington, DC: The World Bank. [Pdf] Retrieved from the Library of Congress, https://www.loc.gov/item/2014020671/.

Marchildon, G. P. (2013). Health systems in transition: Canada. World Health Organization.

Marmor, T. R., Freeman, H. E., & Stano, M. (2017). Universal health care: A global perspective. Health Affairs, 36(3), 408–417.

Marmot, M. (2005). Social determinants of health inequalities. The Lancet, 365(9464), 1099–1104.

McKee, M., & Healy, J. (2002). Hospitals in a changing Europe. European Observatory on Health Systems and Policies.

Mori, A. (2023). Mandatory health insurance for the informal sector in Tanzania—has it worked anywhere! Frontiers in Health Services 3

Mossialos, E., et al. (2016). Universal health coverage in the European Union: An overview of the member states. Health Policy, 120(9), 1014-1022.

Nutbeam, D. (2000). Health literacy as a public health goal: A challenge for contemporary health education and communication strategies into the 21st century. Health Promotion International, 15(3), 259–267.

Oberlander, J. (2017). The political life of Medicare. The New England Journal of Medicine, 376(20), 1967-1974.

OECD. (2020). Health at a glance: Europe 2020. OECD Publishing.

Papanicolas, I., Woskie, L. R., & Jha, A. K. (2018). Health care spending in the United States and other high-income countries. JAMA, 319(10), 1024-1039.

Patel, P. (2024). Universal health insurance for lower-income and lower-middle-income countries: A lesson from India. National Journal of Community Medicine, 15(5), 336–339. https://doi.org/10.55489/njcm.150520244049

Reeves, A., Gourtsoyannis, Y., Basu, S., McCoy, D., McKee, M., & Stuckler, D. (2015). Financing universal health coverage--effects of alternative tax structures on public health systems: cross-national modelling in 89 low-income and middle-income countries. Lancet

(London, England), 386(9990), 274–280. https://doi.org/10.1016/S0140-6736(15)60574-8

Rizvi, S. S., Douglas, R., Williams, O. D., & Hill, P. S. (2020). The political economy of universal health coverage: A systematic narrative review. Health Policy and Planning, 35(3), 364–372. https://doi.org/10.1093/heapol/czz171

Saltman, R. B., & Figueras, J. (2013). Analyzing the evidence on health systems in Europe. European Observatory on Health Systems and Policies.

Sharma, D., & Cotton, M. (2023). Overcoming the barriers between resource constraints and healthcare quality. Tropical Doctor, 53(3), 341–343. https://doi.org/10.1177/00494755231183784

Starfield, B. (2007). The effectiveness of primary care. The New England Journal of Medicine, 357(20), 2084-2092.

Starfield, B. (2011). Is primary care essential? The Lancet, 377(9769), 868–869.

Stuckler, D., et al. (2017). The role of the state in the provision of health care: A comparative analysis. Social Science & Medicine, 188, 1–10.

Sweeney, K., McCarthy, M., & O'Reilly, D. (2017). The impact of universal health insurance on emergency care: A systematic review. Emergency Medicine Journal, 34(6), 345–350.

Tarlov, A. R. (1996). Social determinants of health: The role of health insurance. Journal of Health Politics, Policy and Law, 21(1), 1-14.

The Policy Practice. (2023). Reaching universal health coverage: A political economy review of trends across 49 countries. The Policy Practice. https://thepolicypractice.com/sites/default/files/2023-03/Reaching%20universal%20health%20coverage-%20a%20political%20economy%20review%20of%20trends%20across%2049%20countries.pdf

Timmons, J. C., McHugh, M. L., & Mendez, A. (2018). Universal health coverage: Lessons from the world. Health Affairs, 37(12), 1977-1984.

Tseng, P. Y., et al. (2019). The impact of universal health coverage on health service utilization: A systematic review. International Journal of Health Services, 49(1), 1-22.

WHO. (2010). Health systems financing: The path to universal coverage. World Health Organization.

WHO. (2010). The World Health Report 2010: Health systems financing: The path to universal coverage. World Health Organization.

Woolhandler, S., & Himmelstein, D. U. (2016). The relationship of health insurance and mortality: Is lack of insurance deadly? American Journal of Public Health, 106(2), 269-273.

World Bank Group (2024). Going Universal: How 24 countries are implementing universal health coverage reforms from the bottom up. https://www.worldbank.org/en/topic/universalhealthcoverage/publication/going-universal-how-24-countries-are-implementing-universal-health-coverage-reforms-from-bottom-up

World Bank. (2013). Universal health coverage for inclusive and sustainable development: A synthesis of 11 country case studies.

World Bank.
https://documents1.worldbank.org/curated/ru/349621468158382497/pdf/753260NWP0Box30ewofExistingEvidence.pdf

World Bank. (n.d.). Universal health coverage study series. World Bank.
https://www.worldbank.org/en/topic/health/publication/universal-health-coverage-study-series

World Economic Forum. (2024, December). Universal Health Coverage Day: How to finance global health equity. World Economic Forum.
https://www.weforum.org/stories/2024/12/universal-health-coverage-day-how-to-finance-global-health-equity/

Xu, K., Evans, D. B., Kawabata, K., Zeramdini, R., Klavus, J., & Murray, C. J. (2018). Household catastrophic health expenditure: A multicountry analysis. The Lancet, 362(9378), 111-117.

Yale School of Public Health. (2023, May 10). Study: More than 335,000 lives could have been saved during pandemic if U.S. had universal health care. Yale School of Public Health.
https://ysph.yale.edu/news-article/yale-study-more-than-335000-lives-could-have-been-saved-during-pandemic-if-us-had-universal-health-care/

Chapter 6: The Role of Free Market and Government in Healthcare Funding

Vignette: The Role of the Free Market and Government in Healthcare Funding

In a bustling city, two friends, Alex and Jamie, often found themselves debating the best way to fund healthcare. Alex, a firm believer in the free market, argued that competition among private providers would drive innovation and efficiency. On the other hand, Jamie believed government intervention was essential to ensure equitable access to healthcare for all citizens.

One evening, as they sat in their favorite café, their conversation turned to the recent changes in healthcare policies. Alex pointed out that private hospitals had introduced new technologies and treatments faster than public ones. Jamie countered that these advancements were often out of reach for the average person due to high costs.

Their discussion grew more intense as they delved into the complexities of healthcare funding. Alex emphasized the importance of personal responsibility and choice, while Jamie stressed the need for a safety net to protect the most vulnerable.

Questions:

1. What are the main arguments for and against the free market approach to healthcare funding?
2. How does government intervention in healthcare impact access and quality of care?
3. Can a balance be struck between free market principles and government regulation in healthcare? If so, how?
4. What are some examples of countries successfully integrating free market and government-funded healthcare systems?
5. How do personal experiences and values influence one's perspective on healthcare funding?

Their conversation continued late into the night. There was no clear winner in the debate, but both friends better understood the complexities of funding healthcare.

Introduction

The healthcare funding landscape is shaped significantly by the interplay between free-market mechanisms and government intervention. While the free market relies on competition, supply and demand, and consumer choice to dictate prices and services, government involvement typically aims to ensure accessibility, equity, and public health standards. The role of each in healthcare funding reflects broader economic and social policies and philosophies regarding the extent to which healthcare is considered a market commodity versus a public good. Understanding these roles is crucial for any analysis of healthcare systems, as the balance between them can significantly affect the availability, quality, and cost of healthcare services.

Theoretical Frameworks

A foundational aspect of the literature on healthcare funding is the theoretical framework that distinguishes between market-based and government-led approaches. The free-market model posits that competition among private entities leads to improved efficiency, innovation, and consumer choice (Friedman, 1962). Proponents of this model argue that a deregulated healthcare environment fosters a dynamic system where providers compete for patients, ultimately driving down costs and enhancing service quality (Arrow, 1963).

Conversely, the government intervention model emphasizes the need for regulation and oversight to address market failures that can arise in healthcare systems. For instance, Stiglitz (1989) discusses how asymmetric information can lead to adverse selection and moral hazard, necessitating government involvement to protect consumers and ensure equitable access to care. This perspective is supported by the work of Blumenthal and Hsiao (2005), who argue that without government regulation, disparities in healthcare access and outcomes can widen, particularly among vulnerable populations.

Historical Context

The historical context of healthcare funding in various countries provides critical insights into the evolving roles of the market and government. In the United States, the predominance of a market-oriented system has led to a unique healthcare landscape characterized by high costs and significant disparities in access (Ginsburg, 2010). The introduction of Medicare and Medicaid in the 1960s marked a significant shift toward government involvement in healthcare funding to provide coverage for the elderly and low-income individuals (Oberlander, 2017). However, the coexistence of private insurance has created a hybrid system that often complicates access and affordability (Kaiser Family Foundation, 2021). In contrast, countries with single-payer systems, such as Canada and the United Kingdom, demonstrate a different balance between market forces and government control. These systems prioritize universal access and equity, funded primarily through taxation (Marchildon, 2013). Research by Busse et al. (2017) indicates that while these systems may lack the same level of competition as market-driven models, they often achieve better health outcomes at lower costs, highlighting the potential benefits of government-led funding mechanisms.

Current Trends in Healthcare Funding

Recent trends in healthcare funding reveal a growing recognition of the limitations inherent in both market and government approaches. The rise of value-based care models reflects a shift towards integrating elements of both systems, aiming to incentivize quality and efficiency while maintaining access (Porter & Lee, 2013). This hybrid approach seeks to leverage market competition while ensuring that government policies safeguard against inequities in care delivery.

The Affordable Care Act (ACA) in the United States exemplifies this trend, combining market-driven insurance reforms with expanded government programs to increase coverage (Sommers et al., 2017). Research indicates that the ACA has successfully reduced the uninsured rate and improved access to care, although challenges remain in addressing the underlying costs and quality of services (Collins et al., 2019). This dual approach underscores the potential for collaboration between market mechanisms and government intervention to create a more equitable healthcare system.

Role of the Free Market in Healthcare Funding

The free market approach to healthcare funding is built on the principles of market-driven competition, consumer choice, and the privatization of healthcare services. Proponents argue that a free market can drive innovation, improve service quality, and offer patients a broader range of healthcare options. In such a system, healthcare providers compete for patients, theoretically leading to improvements in efficiency and the development of new medical technologies and treatments. However, this model also presents significant challenges, particularly regarding accessibility and equity. Without adequate regulation, market-driven systems can lead to disparities in healthcare access, with high-quality services often only available to those who can afford to pay. Additionally, emphasizing profit can sometimes result in inefficiencies, with administrative and marketing expenses consuming a significant portion of healthcare spending.

I agree with Pope John Paul II, who stated, "The free market is the most efficient instrument for utilizing resources and effectively responding to needs… there are many human needs which find no place on the market" (Pilote, 2010). I believe in the free market, but markets work well for goods and services that can be easily packaged and sold, which is not the case with healthcare.

Healthcare policy in sub-Saharan Africa should aim to alleviate current healthcare needs based on available resources and equity. Since countries have limited resources for healthcare systems, cost-benefit analysis with quality-adjusted life years [QALY] can help illuminate the trade-offs in making different healthcare investments.

"Free market is the most efficient instrument for utilizing resources and effectively responding to needs, but many human needs find no place in the market." Healthcare, education, infrastructure, and the environment, as well as questions of beneficial and detrimental externalities, must be satisfactorily addressed by the market. The United States government's involvement in healthcare funding (Medicare and Medicaid) was initially predicated on a failure of markets to provide necessary healthcare coverage to the elderly and poor (Brown et al., 2003).

Furthermore, the Affordable Care Act was predicated on the need to address the failure of the free market in the micro-allocation of healthcare funding (Crowley et al., 2019). Before the ACA, many individuals, especially those with pre-existing conditions or low incomes, faced barriers to obtaining affordable health insurance. The market often failed to provide adequate coverage options, leading to high rates of uninsured individuals and significant disparities in healthcare access (Crowley et al., 2019).

Government's Role in Healthcare Funding

The Federal government—or any government—should not be directly involved in providing healthcare services to patients or employers of healthcare practitioners. At all levels, the government should dissociate itself from the direct provision of healthcare services and employment of healthcare providers; the free market should be used to implement this aspect of healthcare delivery. The government's role should be minimal, ensuring that all providers adhere to the principles of justice and morality and follow ethical and medical guidelines when delivering services (Bodenheimer & Grumbach, 2016).

Government intervention in healthcare funding takes various forms, such as single-payer systems, socialized medicine, and mandatory health insurance schemes. The primary goal of such intervention is to ensure that all citizens have access to healthcare services, regardless of their ability to pay (Williams et al., 2009). The benefits of government involvement include universal coverage, greater equity in healthcare access, and the ability to negotiate lower prices for services and pharmaceuticals, leading to overall cost control. However, government-funded healthcare systems may face challenges such as inefficiencies and bureaucracy that hinder innovation and responsiveness. Additionally, the sustainability of public funding models can be a concern in the face of rising healthcare costs and changing demographics.

The free market and government play crucial roles in healthcare funding, shaping the landscape of healthcare delivery and access. The interaction between these two entities often sparks debates about the most effective and efficient way to fund healthcare services. Both the free market and government have distinct roles in healthcare funding, and a balanced integration of their efforts is essential to ensuring comprehensive and accessible healthcare for all individuals.

The Role of Government in Addressing Inequities

A significant body of literature addresses the government's role in mitigating health inequities, particularly among marginalized populations. Studies by Williams and Mohammed (2009) highlight how systemic barriers, such as socio-economic status and race, contribute to disparities in health outcomes.

Government-funded programs, such as community health centers and public health initiatives, play a key role in addressing these inequities by providing targeted services and resources (Bodenheimer & Grumbach, 2016).

Furthermore, the COVID-19 pandemic has illuminated the critical need for government intervention in healthcare funding. Research by Ranney et al. (2020) emphasizes that the pandemic exacerbated existing disparities, underscoring the importance of government action in ensuring equitable access to vaccines and healthcare services. The rapid response of governments worldwide to fund public health measures demonstrates the necessity of a strong governmental role in healthcare, especially in times of crisis.

Market Dynamics and Innovation

While the government plays a vital role in healthcare funding, the free market's influence on innovation and efficiency cannot be overlooked. Evidence from the literature suggests that competition among private firms can drive advancements in medical technology and pharmaceuticals, leading to improved patient outcomes (Hwang & Christensen, 2008). For instance, the development of telemedicine has been accelerated by market demand, providing new avenues for care delivery, especially during the pandemic (Koonin et al., 2020). However, the reliance on market dynamics raises concerns about prioritizing profit over patient care. Research by Himmelstein and Woolhandler (2016) argues that profit-driven motives can lead to increased healthcare costs and reduced access, particularly for low-income individuals. This tension between innovation and equity requires a careful balance between market forces and government regulation to ensure that advancements in healthcare benefit all populations.

The free market plays a significant role in healthcare funding by promoting competition, innovation, and efficiency. In a free-market system, healthcare providers and insurers operate based on market forces such as supply and demand, price competition, and consumer choice. This competitive environment can drive improvements in quality of care, technological advancements, and cost-effective solutions. Additionally, the free market encourages healthcare providers to tailor their services to meet consumer needs and preferences, resulting in a diverse range of healthcare options available in the market.

On the other hand, government intervention in healthcare funding is essential to addressing market failures and ensuring equitable access to healthcare services. Governments are pivotal in funding healthcare through Medicare, Medicaid, and other social insurance schemes. These programs aim to provide healthcare coverage to vulnerable populations, such as low-income individuals, the elderly, and individuals with disabilities, who may face barriers to accessing private healthcare services. Government funding also supports public health initiatives, medical research, and infrastructure development within the healthcare system.

Integrating the free market and government in healthcare funding is essential to balancing efficiency and equity in the healthcare sector. While the free market promotes competition and innovation, government intervention is necessary to address market failures, regulate healthcare providers, and ensure universal access to essential healthcare services. A collaborative approach that leverages the strengths of both the free market and government can create an economically efficient and socially equitable healthcare system.

In conclusion, the roles of the free market and government in healthcare funding are complementary and essential for ensuring the delivery of high-quality and accessible healthcare services. By harnessing the strengths of both entities and fostering collaboration between them, healthcare systems can achieve a balance between market-driven efficiency and government-supported equity.

Government and Free Market Collaboration in Healthcare Funding

In the complex landscape of healthcare funding, collaboration between the government and the free market provides a pathway to harnessing the strengths of both sectors for the common good. This cooperative approach leverages the private sector's innovation and efficiency while ensuring universal access and equity through government oversight and support.

Free Market's Role: The free market drives innovation and quality in healthcare by fostering competition among providers and giving consumers the freedom to choose their healthcare services. This competition incentivizes the development of new treatments, technologies, and care delivery methods, potentially leading to better outcomes and more efficient use of resources. Private entities can rapidly adapt to changes in demand and preferences, embodying flexibility that can be beneficial in responding to health crises or integrating new technologies.

Government's Role: The government's primary responsibility in healthcare is ensuring that all individuals have access to necessary health services, particularly those unable to afford them, in a purely market-driven system. This includes implementing policies that provide a safety net for the most vulnerable populations, regulating the market to prevent abuses and ensure fairness, and investing in public health initiatives that may not be profitable but are essential for the overall health of the population (Sorato et al., 2020). Through subsidies, regulation, and direct healthcare provision, the government can address market failures and disparities in access to care.

Collaboration for Healthcare Funding: The government and the free market can collaborate to create a healthcare funding model that benefits from the efficiency and innovation of the private sector while maintaining the universal coverage and equity facilitated by public funding. This could involve the government subsidizing private insurance for low-income populations, public-private partnerships in healthcare delivery, and leveraging private sector advancements in healthcare technologies while ensuring these innovations are accessible to all through regulation and subsidies (Schwab et al., 2023). When aligned towards common goals, the distinct roles of the government and free market in healthcare funding can create a balanced, dynamic system that delivers high-quality, accessible healthcare services. This synergy requires careful regulation, transparent collaboration, and a commitment to prioritizing public health outcomes over profit.

In healthcare financing, a collaborative approach between the government and the free market offers a harmonious solution that leverages the strengths and expertise of both entities while recognizing their distinct roles in achieving comprehensive coverage and sustainable funding. The government is pivotal in ensuring universal access to healthcare services, particularly for vulnerable populations and those with limited resources. Through policies and programs, the government can provide a safety net for individuals who cannot afford essential medical care. This includes initiatives such as Medicaid and Medicare, which offer health coverage to low-income earners, the elderly, and people with disabilities.

On the other hand, the free market operates on principles of competition, efficiency, and innovation. Private healthcare providers and insurers are crucial in expanding service delivery, improving quality, and driving technological advancements in the healthcare sector. By encouraging competition and entrepreneurship, the free market fosters a dynamic environment that spurs investment in healthcare infrastructure, research, and development.

Effective collaboration between the government and the free market involves recognizing and leveraging each entity's strengths while respecting their distinct roles. The government can set the regulatory framework and standards to ensure the delivery of high-quality and affordable healthcare services, establish cost control and transparency mechanisms, and provide oversight to protect consumer interests. At the same time, the free market contributes by offering a range of healthcare options, promoting efficiency through market mechanisms, and driving innovation in treatments, drugs, and medical technologies.

By embracing a collaborative approach, the government and the free market can work together to address the healthcare system's complex challenges, including rising costs, unequal access to care, and continuous innovation. This partnership can lead to a more resilient and sustainable healthcare financing model that combines the strengths of public oversight and private sector dynamism. Ultimately, by recognizing and respecting the distinct roles of the government and the free market in healthcare financing, we can pave the way for a system that provides quality care for all while promoting economic growth and innovation in the healthcare sector.

Bibliography

Arrow, K. J. (1963). Uncertainty and the welfare economics of medical care. The American Economic Review, 53(5), 941–973.

Blumenthal, D., & Hsiao, W. (2005). Privatization and its discontents—The evolving Chinese health care system. New England Journal of Medicine, 353(11), 1165-1170.

Bodenheimer, T., & Grumbach, K. (2016). Understanding Health Policy: A Clinical Approach (7th ed.). McGraw-Hill Education.

Brown, L. D., & Sparer, M. S. (2003). Poor program's progress: the unanticipated politics of Medicaid policy. Health affairs (Project Hope), 22(1), 31–44. https://doi.org/10.1377/hlthaff.22.1.31

Busse, R., Blumel, M., & Scheller-Kreinsen, D. (2017). Tackling chronic disease in Europe: Strategies, interventions, and challenges. Health Policy, 121(4), 329-335.

Collins, S. R., Gunja, M. Z., & Doty, M. (2019). Health Insurance Coverage Eight Years After the ACA. The Commonwealth Fund. https://www.commonwealthfund.org/publications/issue-briefs/2019/feb/health-insurance-coverage-eight-years-after-aca

Crowley, R. A., Bornstein, S. S., & Health and Public Policy Committee of the American College of Physicians (2019). Improving the patient protection and Affordable Care Act's insurance coverage provisions: A position paper from the American college of physicians. Annals of Internal Medicine, 170(9), 651–653. Web.

Friedman, M. (1962). Capitalism and Freedom. University of Chicago Press.

Ginsburg, P. B. (2010). The role of the private sector in health care. Health Affairs, 29(6), 1005–1008.

Himmelstein, D. U., & Woolhandler, S. (2016). The current and projected taxpayer shares of US health costs. American Journal of Public Health, 106(3), 449-454.

Hwang, J., & Christensen, C. M. (2008). Disruptive innovation in health care delivery: A framework for analyzing the impact of telemedicine. Health Affairs, 27(5), 1334-1345.

Kaiser Family Foundation. (2021). The U.S. healthcare system: A brief overview. KFF.

Koonin, L. M., Hoots, B., & Tsang, C. A. (2020). Trends in the use of telehealth during the emergence of the COVID-19 pandemic—United States, January–March 2020. Morbidity and Mortality Weekly Report, 69(43), 1595-1599.

Marchildon, G. P. (2013). Canada: Health system review. World Health Organization.

Oberlander, J. (2017). The political life of Medicare. The New England Journal of Medicine, 376(11), 1074-1078.

Pilote, A. (2010). Catholic social teaching on capitalism. A journal of Catholic patriots for the Social Credit monetary reform. https://www.michaeljournal.org/articles/roman-catholic-church/item/catholic-social-teaching-on-capitalism

Porter, M. E., & Lee, T. H. (2013). The strategy that will fix health care. Harvard Business Review, 91(10), 50-70.

Rachel Schwab et al., Policy Innovations in the Affordable Care Act Marketplaces (Commonwealth Fund, Nov. 2023). https://doi.org/10.26099/34x2-yj98

Ranney, M. L., Griffeth, V., & Jha, A. K. (2020). Ensuring the safety of health care workers during the COVID-19 pandemic. New England Journal of Medicine, 382(6), 509-511.

Sommers, B. D., Goin, D. E., & Blendon, R. J. (2017). The Affordable Care Act has reduced the number of uninsured adults by 20 million. Health Affairs, 36(6), 1046–1054.

Sorato, M., Davari, M., Asl, A., Soleymani, F. and Kebriaeezadeh, A. (2020), Why healthcare market needs government intervention to improve access to essential medicines and healthcare efficiency: a scoping review from pharmaceutical price regulation perspective. J Pharm Health Serv Res, 11: 321-333. https://doi.org/10.1111/jphs.12379

Stiglitz, J. E. (1989). The economic role of the state. The Economic Journal, 99(397), 1009-1021.

Williams, D. R., & Mohammed, S. A. (2009). Discrimination and racial disparities in health: Evidence and needed research. Journal of Behavioral Medicine, 32(1), 20–47.

Chapter 7: Healthcare Delivery and Priority Setting

Vignette: Navigating Healthcare Delivery and Priority Setting

In a small village in sub-Saharan Africa, the community health center was bustling with activity. The center, a modest building with a tin roof, was the primary healthcare facility for miles around. Healthcare workers were busy attending to patients, administering vaccines, and providing essential medical care.

At the center's heart, a meeting was taking place. The village chief, healthcare workers, and community leaders had gathered to discuss their community's pressing health issues. The room was filled with urgency and determination as they reviewed data on disease prevalence, maternal and child health, and access to clean water and sanitation.

The discussion turned to priority setting. With limited resources, the community needed to decide which health interventions to prioritize. Should they focus on expanding vaccination programs, improving maternal health services, or investing in clean water infrastructure? Each option had its merits, and the decision was not easy.

As the meeting progressed, the participants shared their perspectives and experiences. The healthcare workers emphasized the importance of preventative care and education, while the community leaders highlighted the need for sustainable solutions to benefit future generations. The village chief listened carefully, weighing the options and considering the long-term impact of each decision.

Questions:

1. What criteria should prioritize healthcare interventions in resource-limited settings?
2. How can community involvement and local knowledge be integrated into the decision-making process for healthcare delivery?
3. What are the potential benefits and challenges of focusing on preventative care versus immediate medical needs?
4. How can partnerships with non-governmental organizations and international agencies enhance healthcare delivery in sub-Saharan Africa?
5. What strategies can be implemented to ensure healthcare

interventions' sustainability and long-term impact?

Introduction

"Not everything that counts can be counted, and not everything that can be counted counts"-Albert Einstein.

No country (not even the richest) can afford to carry out all the potentially beneficial procedures now available to everyone who might benefit from them. Hence, "priority setting can no longer be a matter of eliminating ineffective activities, but a matter of allocation efficiency rather than technical efficiency with inevitable equity."

"The nasty secret of healthcare economics is that a lot done for patients is useless or dangerous and costly and that much that could help them at relatively low cost is not done."- Daniel S. Greenberg.

Priority settings mean deciding who gets what at whose expense. "Giving priority to one group of people means taking it away from another group." No nation, even the wealthiest country in the world, can survive a healthcare policy driven by technology rather than healthcare needs in the long run. This is a sure route to everlasting disaster in sub-Saharan African countries with scarce healthcare funding.

Healthcare delivery encompasses the organization, management, and provision of services to prevent disease, promote health, and deliver medical care to populations. It involves a complex network of healthcare professionals, facilities, and resources working collaboratively to meet the health needs of individuals and communities. The primary goal is to achieve optimal health outcomes through efficient and effective care delivery, ensuring access to necessary services for all population segments. This introduction presents an overview of healthcare delivery's role, emphasizing its importance in enhancing overall health and well-being.

Principles of Priority Setting in Healthcare

Healthcare delivery systems are vital in providing medical services and promoting public health. These systems encompass personnel, facilities, resources, and organizational structures, all instrumental in delivering effective and efficient care to individuals and communities. The goal is to improve overall health outcomes across populations (American Institute of Health Care Professionals, 2024; FreeCE, n.d.; Piña, 2015). However, healthcare delivery systems face numerous challenges that hinder their optimal functioning globally. A primary concern is the delicate balance between technological advancements and genuine healthcare needs within constrained budgets. As medical technology progresses, the cost of delivering every potentially beneficial procedure to all who might need it continues to rise. This scenario necessitates difficult decisions regarding resource allocation and priority setting, where prioritizing one patient group invariably diverts resources from another. Such trade-offs raise complex ethical dilemmas, particularly in sub-Saharan Africa, where limited funding makes it unsustainable to prioritize technology-driven healthcare policies over basic, essential needs. Further complicating matters are financial constraints that healthcare providers must navigate (DocResponse, n.d.; Healthcare Communications, n.d.; Brandeau, 2018). Many providers grapple with increasing operational costs, complicated reimbursement structures, and evolving regulations. These financial pressures can lead to restricted services, reduced patient capacity, and potential compromises in the quality of care, disproportionately impacting vulnerable populations. Health inequities represent another significant hurdle in the effective delivery of healthcare services (Healthcare Communications, n.d.).

Disparities in access to healthcare stem from various factors, including financial limitations, lack of insurance, transportation barriers, language differences, and a shortage of providers in certain areas. Marginalized groups often suffer the most from these disparities, resulting in unequal access and poorer health outcomes.

Additionally, navigating the healthcare system can pose challenges for individuals with disabilities, low incomes, or limited knowledge of available resources, exacerbating accessibility issues (Healthcare Communications, n.d.). Workforce burnout is a further complicating factor that cannot be overlooked. Healthcare professionals frequently face increasing workloads, staff shortages, and overwhelming administrative demands, leading to elevated stress levels and burnout. Effectively addressing this issue requires systemic changes to reduce administrative burdens, recognize and value staff contributions, and foster overall well-being (Healthcare Communications, n.d.).

While healthcare delivery systems face substantial challenges, the commitment to enhancing healthcare access and equity remains imperative. Addressing these multi-faceted issues can pave the way for a more effective and equitable healthcare landscape.

Other critical challenges facing healthcare delivery systems include:

Rising Healthcare Costs: Rising healthcare costs present a significant challenge to healthcare systems around the globe. Key factors contributing to this escalation include inflation, aging populations, and evolving government policies. These elements strain existing resources and limit investment opportunities in vital infrastructure and equipment (Healthcare Communications, n.d.). Furthermore, the increasing demand for resource-intensive care amplifies this issue, compounding healthcare funding and resource allocation (Healthcare Communications, n.d.).

Patient Experience: Enhancing patient experience is critical to the efficacy of healthcare delivery. This improvement necessitates focusing on patient-centered care, practical communication, and streamlined processes. Technological advancements, such as telehealth and electronic health records, offer promising avenues to enrich the patient experience. However, implementing these technologies requires careful consideration to ensure clinical staff are not unduly burdened (NetSuite, n.d.).

Data Management and Security: Maintaining continuous operations, patient safety, and data security within healthcare systems is paramount. These responsibilities demand significant investments in personnel, technology, and efficient processes, which adds to the financial burden faced by healthcare providers (NetSuite, n.d.). As such, addressing the challenges of data management and security is essential for operational integrity and maintaining trust in healthcare systems.

Regulatory Changes: The dynamic nature of the healthcare landscape necessitates that providers remain agile in adapting to new regulations and policies. Such adaptations can be complex and costly (NetSuite, n.d.). Achieving a balance between regulatory compliance, financial stability, and high-quality care represents an ongoing challenge for healthcare providers (DocResponse, n.d.; NetSuite, n.d.).

Competition and Disruption: Healthcare providers are increasingly confronted with competition from new entities introducing alternative care models and technologies. Existing providers must actively innovate and adapt to the shifting landscape to maintain their market position.

Cultural and Societal Factors: Cultural traditions, societal expectations, and government policies are critical in healthcare delivery, particularly in low—and middle-income countries. Addressing these multifaceted challenges requires culturally sensitive approaches and effective policies tailored to local contexts.

Multi-faceted solutions are essential to overcoming the myriad challenges facing healthcare systems. These solutions must address financial constraints, promote health equity, enhance patient experience, support healthcare workers, and foster innovation. Collaboration among policymakers, providers, patients, and technology developers is vital for creating sustainable and equitable healthcare systems for all individuals. Though the future of healthcare delivery is laden with challenges, it simultaneously offers significant opportunities to leverage technology, enhance operational efficiency, and improve health outcomes for individuals and communities globally.

Practical Application of Healthcare Priority Setting

Healthcare priority setting operates across multiple levels, from national policy decisions regarding healthcare coverage to individual clinicians making informed choices about patient care (World Health Organization, 2021). This multi-faceted process demands the establishment of clear criteria and systematic methodologies to effectively evaluate diverse needs and potential treatments. Health technology assessments and program budgeting are frequently utilized to support this evaluation. Several critical factors play a pivotal role in the priority-setting process within healthcare. These include the following:

Medical Need: This key factor assesses the urgency of a medical condition, the likelihood of successful treatment, and the expected impact on a patient's quality of life (American Medical

Association, n.d.). Effective prioritization in this context is essential for judiciously allocating limited healthcare resources.

Severity of Illness: Conditions that pose an immediate threat to life or carry the potential for significant disability are generally assigned higher priority. This categorization ensures that interventions address the most pressing health challenges.

Potential Benefit: Treatments that exhibit a higher probability of success and yield substantial positive patient health outcomes should be prioritized. This focus on demonstrable benefits is crucial for optimizing healthcare delivery.

Cost-Effectiveness: It is essential to thoroughly analyze the costs associated with various treatments concerning their expected benefits. This analysis guarantees that healthcare resources are utilized in the most efficient manner possible.

Equity: Ensuring fairness and equal access to healthcare services is imperative, particularly for vulnerable populations and individuals with limited resources. The principle of equity must be woven into the fabric of healthcare decision-making.

Community Values: Incorporating public input and aligning decisions with community priorities are fundamental to practical healthcare priority setting. This alignment fosters trust and ensures that the healthcare system reflects societal values.

Acknowledging that healthcare priority setting is a dynamic process that must adapt to shifting conditions and communities' evolving needs is vital. Continuous evaluation and refinement of priority-setting frameworks are paramount to maintaining effectiveness and fairness. By embracing this adaptable approach, healthcare systems can respond adeptly to the population's needs, ultimately leading to improved health outcomes. In doing so, we affirm our commitment to responsible healthcare delivery and enhance society's overall well-being.

Priority Setting and Justification

Healthcare priority setting is fundamentally important for optimizing the allocation of resources to enhance health outcomes. This process involves several critical components:

Research Priority Setting: Identifying vital areas for research investment is a foundational step in this process (World Health Organization, 2021). As the WHO endorsed, systematic methods, such as Multi-Criteria Decision Analysis (MCDA) evaluate various factors and facilitate informed decision-making. Employing evidence-informed deliberative processes and frameworks like the Child Health Nutrition Research Initiative (CHNRI) method ensures that research priorities align with overarching health goals and community needs and extend beyond mere cost-effectiveness. Prioritization occurs at multiple levels, ranging from individual research groups to expansive organizations, including governmental and non-governmental organizations (NGOs) (World Health Organization, 2021). Continuous flexibility in adapting research priorities to the shifting political and social landscapes is essential.

Resource Allocation and Service Delivery: Policymakers face the intricate challenge of distributing limited healthcare budgets across competing demands. This challenge encompasses balancing primary care with specialized tertiary care, addressing specific health conditions, and equitably distributing resources among diverse population segments. Establishing fair and transparent procedures for resource allocation is imperative. Considerations such as age, health behavior, and social responsibility must guide the prioritization of services.

Guideline Development: Prioritizing the development of clinical guidelines ensures that resources are directed toward addressing the most pressing health needs. This process includes selecting pertinent topics, refining them to tackle specific clinical inquiries, and employing systematic evidence reviews to generate recommendations (Shekelle, 2019). Collaboration among clinicians, patients, and other stakeholders is vital for creating practical guidelines. Important factors—such as available resources, continuity of care, cost, and feasibility—are integral to topic selection. Organizations like the National Institute for Health and Care Excellence (NICE) have established robust methodologies for guideline development, ensuring that these guidelines are evidence-based and relevant to patients and caregivers (National Institute for Health and Care Excellence, n.d.). These guidelines' dissemination, implementation, and evaluation are crucial subsequent steps.

Furthermore, healthcare organizations frequently struggle to prioritize quality improvement initiatives due to the overwhelming data available (Health Catalyst, n.d.). Adopting a strategic approach with an analytical framework is essential for identifying key areas for impactful improvement (Health Catalyst, n.d.). A well-defined three-step process comprises implementing a healthcare-specific data platform, utilizing principles such as the 80-20 rule to identify priorities, and achieving consensus among clinical teams on projects and objectives (Health Catalyst, n.d.). This data-driven methodology enhances resource utilization, saves costs, and significantly improves the quality of care provided (Health Catalyst, n.d.). A strategic focus on healthcare priority setting, encompassing research prioritization, resource allocation, and guideline development, is essential for maximizing health outcomes and efficiently using available resources. In conclusion, healthcare priority setting requires evidence, deliberation, and strategic decision-making to optimize resource utilization and ultimately enhance overall health outcomes. It is a complex yet essential process that influences the effectiveness and efficiency of healthcare systems.

Bibliography

American Institute of Health Care Professionals. (2024, August 2). Health care delivery system: Key components and management strategies. American Institute of Health Care Professionals. https://aihcp.net/2024/08/02/health-care-delivery-system-key-components-and-management-strategies/

American Medical Association. (n.d.). Allocating limited health care resources. American Medical Association. https://code-medical-ethics.ama-assn.org/ethics-opinions/allocating-limited-health-care-resources

Brandeau, M. L., Sainfort, F., & Pierskalla, W. P. (2018). Challenges facing healthcare delivery systems in low-, middle-, and high-income countries. In Advanced systems for improved public healthcare and disease prevention: Emerging research and opportunities (pp. 69-92). IGI Global. https://doi.org/10.4018/978-1-5225-5528-5.ch001

DocResponse. (n.d.). Current issues in healthcare. DocResponse. https://docresponse.com/blog/current-issues-in-healthcare/

FreeCE. (n.d.). Delivery of modern healthcare. FreeCE. https://www.freece.com/blog/delivery-of-modern-healthcare/

Health Catalyst. (n.d.). 3 steps to prioritize clinical quality improvement in healthcare. Health Catalyst. https://www.healthcatalyst.com/learn/insights/3-steps-prioritize-clinical-quality-improvement-healthcare

Healthcare Communications. (n.d.). 4 main challenges impacting global healthcare today. Healthcare Communications. https://healthcare-communications.com/4-main-challenges-impacting-global-healthcare-today/

National Institute for Health and Care Excellence. (n.d.). Contribute to developing clinical guidelines. National Institute for Health and Care Excellence. https://www.nice.org.uk/media/default/About/NICE-Communities/Public-involvement/Developing-NICE-guidance/Factsheet-1-contribute-to-developing-clinical-guidelines.pdf

NetSuite. (n.d.). Healthcare industry challenges. NetSuite. https://www.netsuite.com/portal/resource/articles/erp/healthcare-industry-challenges.shtml

Piña, I. L., Cohen, P. D., Larson, D. B., Marion, L. N., Sills, M. R., Solberg, L. I., & Zerzan, J. (2015). A framework for describing health care delivery organizations and systems. American journal of public health, 105(4), 670–679. https://doi.org/10.2105/AJPH.2014.301926

Shekelle, P. G., Woolf, S. H., Eccles, M., & Grimshaw, J. (1999). Clinical guidelines: developing guidelines. BMJ (Clinical research ed.), 318(7183), 593–596. https://doi.org/10.1136/bmj.318.7183.593

World Health Organization. (2021). Health systems resilience during COVID-19: Lessons for building back better. World Health Organization. https://iris.who.int/bitstream/handle/10665/348006/WHO-EURO-1998-3966-43725-61512-eng.pdf?sequence=1

World Health Organization. (2021). Research methods for health emergency and disaster risk management. World Health Organization. https://extranet.who.int/kobe_centre/sites/default/files/pdf/WHO%20Guidance_Research%20Methods_Health-EDRM_2.7.pdf

Chapter 8: Healthcare Financing and Nutrition Policy in sub-Saharan Africa

Vignette: A Community's Journey to Better Health

A diverse group of community members gathered under the shade of a large acacia tree in a rural village in sub-Saharan Africa. Farmers, community leaders, teachers, and healthcare workers, all dressed in traditional clothing, sat around a wooden table covered with maps, charts, and diagrams. The air was filled with animated discussion, and their faces expressed concern, hope, and determination.

At the center of the table was a poster of a modern clinic, symbolizing the community's dream of accessible healthcare. The discussion revolved around health initiatives and investment opportunities, focusing on nutrition policy and healthcare financing. The community meal of local vegetables, grains, and fruits reminded them of the importance of nutrition in their daily lives. As the meeting progressed, the community members explored various investment concepts, including solar panels, community gardens, and microfinance projects. The presence of children in the background highlighted the future they were striving to protect and improve.

Questions for Discussion:

1. How do rural communities in sub-Saharan Africa face the primary challenges in accessing healthcare financing?
2. How can nutrition policies effectively be integrated into healthcare initiatives to improve community health?
3. What role do community leaders and local organizations play in promoting and implementing health initiatives?
4. How can investment in renewable energy sources, like solar panels, support healthcare facilities in rural areas?
5. What are the potential benefits and challenges of microfinance projects supporting healthcare and nutrition programs?

Introduction

Healthcare financing and nutrition policy are critical components in addressing the health challenges faced by sub-Saharan Africa, a region characterized by a complex interplay of socio-economic factors, public health crises, and nutritional deficiencies. The World Health Organization (WHO) has identified sub-Saharan Africa as a region with some of the highest rates of malnutrition and related health complications, exacerbated by a range of factors, including poverty, inadequate healthcare systems, and limited access to essential services. The nexus between healthcare financing and nutrition policy is particularly significant in this context, as both elements are essential for fostering improved health outcomes and achieving sustainable development goals.

Healthcare financing in sub-Saharan Africa has been historically inadequate, characterized by low public spending, reliance on out-of-pocket payments, and insufficient investment in health infrastructure. According to the WHO, many countries in the region allocate less than 10% of their gross domestic product (GDP) to health, which is far below the recommended threshold for ensuring universal health coverage (WHO, 2017). This underfunding leads to many challenges, including insufficient healthcare facilities, a shortage of trained healthcare professionals, and limited access to essential medicines. The consequences of inadequate healthcare financing are particularly severe for vulnerable populations, including women, children, and the elderly, who often bear the brunt of health disparities (Arhin et al., 2023).

On the other hand, nutrition policy plays a pivotal role in addressing the dual burden of malnutrition that characterizes many sub-Saharan African countries. Malnutrition manifests in various forms, including undernutrition, micronutrient deficiencies such as anemia, and the prevalence of overweight and obesity, each presenting unique challenges to public health (Christian et al., 2021). The region faces a paradox where undernutrition coexists with rising obesity rates and diet-related non-communicable diseases (NCDs). This dual burden necessitates comprehensive nutrition policies that address immediate food security concerns and promote long-term dietary changes and health education (Delisle et al., 2021).

Integrating healthcare financing and nutrition policy is essential for creating a holistic approach to health in sub-Saharan Africa. Effective financing mechanisms can support the implementation of nutrition interventions, such as school feeding programs, community-based nutrition education, and fortifying staple foods with essential vitamins and minerals. Conversely, robust nutrition policies can contribute to reducing healthcare costs by preventing diet-related diseases and improving overall population health. This interdependence highlights the need for coordinated efforts among governments, non-governmental organizations (NGOs), and international agencies to develop and implement integrated healthcare financing and nutrition policies.

One of the critical challenges in addressing healthcare financing and nutrition policy in sub-Saharan Africa is the lack of comprehensive data and evidence-based research (Ifeagwu et al., 2021). Many countries in the region struggle with inadequate health information systems, making it difficult to assess the effectiveness of existing policies and programs. Furthermore, the fragmentation of health services and nutrition interventions often results in inefficiencies and duplication of efforts, hindering progress toward achieving health equity and improved nutritional outcomes (Ifeagwu et al., 2021). Addressing these challenges requires a concerted effort to strengthen data collection, analysis, and dissemination and foster collaboration among stakeholders at all levels.

In recent years, there has been a growing recognition of the importance of nutrition-sensitive interventions within the broader healthcare financing framework (Salam et al., 2019). Nutrition-sensitive approaches aim to address the underlying determinants of malnutrition by integrating nutrition considerations into various sectors, including agriculture, education, and social protection (Habtu et al., 2022). For instance, improving agricultural productivity and food security can enhance access to nutritious foods. At the same time, social protection programs can provide financial support to vulnerable households, enabling them to invest in better nutrition. By adopting a multi-sectoral approach, policymakers can create synergies between healthcare financing and nutrition policy, ultimately leading to improved health outcomes and economic productivity (Arhin et al., 2023).

Moreover, the role of international organizations and partnerships cannot be understated in the context of healthcare financing and nutrition policy in sub-Saharan Africa. Initiatives such as the Scaling Up Nutrition (SUN) Movement and the Global Financing Facility (GFF) for Women, Children, and Adolescents are examples of collaborative efforts to mobilize resources and promote accountability in nutrition and health financing. These initiatives foster a platform for dialogue, knowledge sharing, and best practices among countries, enabling them to learn from each other's experiences and successes.

The COVID-19 pandemic has further underscored the importance of robust healthcare financing and nutrition policy in sub-Saharan Africa. The pandemic has disrupted health services, exacerbated food insecurity, and increased malnutrition and morbidity rates (WHO, 2020). The economic impact of the pandemic has also strained public finances, making it even more challenging for governments to allocate sufficient resources to health and nutrition. In this context, the need for innovative financing mechanisms, such as blended finance and public-private partnerships, has become increasingly apparent. These approaches can leverage additional resources and expertise from the private sector to support health and nutrition initiatives, ultimately contributing to more resilient healthcare systems (Arhin, et al., 2023).

In conclusion, the interrelationship between healthcare financing and nutrition policy is a critical determinant of health outcomes in sub-Saharan Africa. Addressing the region's health challenges requires a multi-faceted approach that considers each country's unique socio-economic and cultural contexts. Policymakers must prioritize the integration of healthcare financing and nutrition policy to create a comprehensive framework that addresses immediate and long-term health needs. sub-Saharan Africa can make significant strides toward achieving health equity and improving nutritional outcomes for its population by fostering collaboration among stakeholders, strengthening data systems, and promoting innovative financing mechanisms.

As we progress, policymakers, researchers, and practitioners must remain committed to understanding and addressing the complex dynamics of healthcare financing and nutrition policy in sub-Saharan Africa. Continued investment in research, capacity building, and multi-sectoral collaboration will be essential to ensure that the region can effectively tackle its health challenges and build a healthier, more resilient future for all its inhabitants.

Healthcare financing and nutrition policy are critical components of health systems, particularly in sub-Saharan Africa, where the dual burden of malnutrition and communicable diseases presents significant challenges. The interplay between these two domains is crucial for improving health outcomes, reducing poverty, and achieving sustainable development goals. This chapter aims to synthesize existing research on healthcare financing and nutrition policy in sub-Saharan Africa, highlighting the current state of knowledge, identifying gaps, and suggesting areas for future research.

Overview of Healthcare Financing Models

Healthcare financing in sub-Saharan Africa exhibits a complex and multi-faceted structure that comprises public, private, and informal mechanisms. Public financing, a cornerstone of healthcare funding in the region, primarily derives from government budgets. These budgets allocate resources for public health services, which are intended to provide accessible healthcare to citizens. However, the effectiveness of public financing is often hampered by limited governmental resources, inefficiencies, and corruption, leading to inadequate service delivery and insufficient infrastructure. Conversely, private funding mechanisms play a significant role in the healthcare landscape of sub-Saharan Africa. These include out-of-pocket expenditures, where individuals pay directly for healthcare services at the point of care, and private health insurance plans. Out-of-pocket payments are particularly prevalent in situations where public healthcare systems cannot meet demand or where individuals seek higher-quality services that may not be available through public options. However, this reliance on out-of-pocket expenditures poses significant risks, especially for vulnerable populations. As the World Bank (2017) highlighted, such a financial model can precipitate severe financial hardship for households, particularly those already in precarious economic situations. The implications of relying heavily on out-of-pocket payments are profound and multi-faceted. Firstly, this funding model exacerbates existing health inequities, disproportionately affecting the poor and marginalized groups in society. Individuals from lower socio-economic backgrounds may forgo necessary medical treatment due to cost, leading to a cycle of deteriorating health and increasing poverty. Moreover, the pressure of unexpected healthcare costs can lead to catastrophic health expenditures that plunge families further into financial distress. To effectively address these challenges, policymakers in sub-Saharan Africa must explore innovative financing strategies prioritizing universal health coverage. Strengthening public healthcare systems, expanding access to affordable private insurance, and introducing mechanisms to reduce out-of-pocket payments are essential to achieving equitable health outcomes. By shifting the focus from a predominantly out-of-pocket financing model to more sustainable and inclusive mechanisms, sub-Saharan African countries can enhance their healthcare capacities, reduce inequalities, and ultimately improve the health and well-being of their populations.

Challenges in Healthcare Financing

The healthcare financing landscape in sub-Saharan Africa is characterized by many challenges that have been thoroughly documented through various studies. A systematic review conducted by Oxfam in 2018 critically analyzes these challenges, identifying inadequate government funding, inefficiencies in resource allocation, and pervasive corruption as prominent barriers to achieving comprehensive healthcare financing in the region (Ifeagwu et al., 2021). These factors collectively hinder the ability of health systems to deliver quality care and meet the growing demands of the populations they serve. Further illuminating the deficiencies in healthcare financing, the African Union's report from 2014 reveals that many countries in sub-Saharan Africa consistently fail to meet the Abuja Declaration target, which stipulates that governments should allocate at least 15% of their national budgets to health. This shortfall in financial commitment has far-reaching implications for the sustainability and effectiveness of health services, particularly in a region grappling with a high disease burden. The onset of the COVID-19 pandemic has exacerbated the challenges in healthcare financing, leading to a substantial increase in demand for health services while simultaneously prompting a reallocation of scarce resources. This shifting focus has often come at the expense of non-communicable diseases and nutrition programs, which are crucial for the overall health and well-being of populations in sub-Saharan Africa (De Foo et al., 2023; Tannor et al., 2023). The prioritization of communicable diseases during the pandemic has created an urgent need for innovative financing solutions to enhance the resilience of health systems throughout the region.

In conclusion, the complexities surrounding healthcare financing in sub-Saharan Africa necessitate a robust and multi-faceted approach. Innovative financing mechanisms that address the immediate challenges posed by the pandemic are imperative, as they lay the groundwork for a more resilient healthcare system capable of meeting the diverse health needs of the population in the long term. Realizing these goals requires concerted efforts from governments, international organizations, and other stakeholders committed to transforming regional healthcare financing.

Innovative Financing Solutions

In recent years, there has been a notable surge in the exploration of innovative financing solutions to address the healthcare challenges faced by sub-Saharan Africa. One prominent approach that has garnered considerable attention is the implementation of social health insurance schemes. These schemes are designed to pool financial resources and significantly reduce out-of-pocket expenditure for individuals seeking healthcare services. According to Dixon et al. (2020), such models enhance access to healthcare and promote financial protection for vulnerable populations, thereby contributing to overall societal health improvements. Moreover, public-private partnerships (PPPs) have emerged as a compelling strategy to harness private sector investments for enhancing healthcare infrastructure and service delivery. The value of these partnerships lies in their ability to leverage additional resources and expertise from the private sector, which can complement limited public funds. Kumar & Sood (2019), along with Hellowell (2019) and Frimpong et al. (2022), underscore the importance of these collaborative arrangements in expanding healthcare access, improving service quality, and promoting efficiency within health systems in sub-Saharan Africa. Another critical facet of healthcare financing in this region is the role of international aid. McCoy et al. (2016) emphasize the significance of donor funding in sustaining vital health initiatives within low-income countries. Such support is instrumental in addressing immediate healthcare needs, particularly in the face of overwhelming challenges such as disease outbreaks and inadequate healthcare infrastructure. However, it is essential to recognize the potential drawbacks of reliance on international aid. As highlighted by Aslam et al. (2022), while external funding can provide short-term solutions, it may also lead to dependency and create misalignments with national priorities. This emphasizes the need for a balanced approach incorporating domestic and international financing mechanisms. Integrating diverse funding sources effectively is imperative to establish a sustainable healthcare environment, particularly in low- and middle-income countries. This integration enhances resilience against fluctuations in funding availability and strengthens the alignment of healthcare initiatives with local needs and priorities. A comprehensive strategy that blends domestic resource mobilization with international aid can pave the way for developing robust healthcare systems that respond effectively to the evolving healthcare needs of sub-Saharan Africa. Exploring innovative financing solutions, such as social health insurance schemes and public-private partnerships, alongside a judicious approach to international aid, represents a promising pathway toward sustainable healthcare in sub-Saharan Africa. A balanced financing strategy that prioritizes both domestic and external resources will be crucial in building resilient healthcare systems capable of delivering equitable and quality care for all.

Nutrition Policy in Sub-Saharan Africa

Nutrition policy in sub-Saharan Africa is a critical area of focus due to the region's high rates of malnutrition, which include undernutrition, micronutrient deficiencies, and, increasingly, obesity and diet-related non-communicable diseases. Given the diverse socio-economic contexts across countries in sub-Saharan Africa, nutrition policies vary significantly but generally aim to improve the nutritional status of populations and address the dual burden of malnutrition.

The Burden of Malnutrition

Malnutrition is an urgent and critical public health concern in sub-Saharan Africa, characterized by alarmingly high rates of stunting, wasting, and deficiencies in essential micronutrients. According to UNICEF (2020), these conditions impact individual health and hinder broader socio-economic development in the region. The Global Nutrition Report (2021) highlights a particularly alarming statistic: nearly one in three children under five in sub-Saharan Africa suffers from stunting. This condition, which results from inadequate nutrition during the crucial early years of life, has profound and lasting consequences. Stunting is predominantly a manifestation of chronic malnutrition, which limits physical growth and has been conclusively linked to adverse cognitive outcomes. Children who experience stunting during their formative years exhibit reduced cognitive abilities and poorer educational performance, jeopardizing their future economic productivity. This creates a cyclical pattern of poverty and malnutrition that is difficult to break. As these children grow into adults, the cognitive deficits they have experienced can lead to lower earnings, reduced labor market participation, and a decreased capacity to contribute effectively to their communities and economies. In addition to stunting, the region grapples with issues of wasting, which reflects acute malnutrition, typically associated with a sudden drop in food intake or severe illness.

Furthermore, micronutrient deficiencies—such as iron, vitamin A, and iodine—contribute to various health problems, including anemia, compromised immune function, and vision impairment. The ramifications extend beyond individual health, as malnutrition can hinder a country's development, diminish productivity, and strain healthcare systems. Given the multi-faceted nature of malnutrition and its long-term implications for individuals and society, targeted interventions must be implemented. These may include enhanced nutritional programs, food security measures, and comprehensive educational initiatives to foster better dietary practices. Addressing malnutrition in sub-Saharan Africa is not merely a health issue; it is a prerequisite for achieving sustainable development and economic growth in the region. The insights from UNICEF and the Global Nutrition Report underscore the need for immediate and concerted action to combat this pressing issue and safeguard the health and future of future generations.

Policy Frameworks and Strategies

The issue of malnutrition in sub-Saharan Africa has garnered significant attention in recent years, leading to various policy frameworks and strategies to address this complex challenge. One pivotal initiative is the African Union's Agenda 2063, which underscores the crucial role of nutrition in achieving sustainable development across the continent. This agenda has called for comprehensive nutrition policies, recognizing that addressing malnutrition is integral to enhancing economic growth, health, and overall quality of life for African populations (African Union, 2015). In addition to these regional efforts, the Scaling Up Nutrition (SUN) Movement has emerged as a vital global initiative that mobilizes international and national stakeholders to prioritize nutrition within their development agendas. Launched in 2010, the SUN Movement has successfully fostered collaboration among governments, civil society, and the private sector, emphasizing the urgent need for a unified approach to combat malnutrition and elevate nutrition as a fundamental component of public policy (SUN Movement, 2019). Despite these commendable efforts, significant challenges persist in the effective implementation of nutrition policies. Ruel et al. (2018) research highlights the necessity for multi-sectoral approaches that integrate nutrition with critical sectors such as agriculture, education, and health. This perspective advocates for coordinated strategies that address the broader determinants of nutrition, recognizing that malnutrition is not solely a health issue but also deeply intertwined with socio-economic factors.

Furthermore, the lack of robust data on nutrition outcomes poses a significant barrier to effective policy implementation and program evaluation. As Gillespie et al. (2019) and the World Health Organization (2020) noted, inadequate monitoring and evaluation frameworks hinder the ability to assess nutrition interventions' impact and make necessary informed adjustments. This lack of data impairs accountability and diminishes the potential for learning and scaling successful initiatives. While substantial frameworks and strategies to combat malnutrition in sub-Saharan Africa have been established, realizing their full potential necessitates a concerted effort to address implementation challenges. Embracing multi-sectoral approaches and investing in robust data systems are essential steps toward achieving meaningful progress in the fight against malnutrition. With continued commitment and collaboration among all stakeholders, sub-Saharan Africa can pave the way towards a healthier, more nourished future.

Financing Nutrition Interventions

The financing of nutrition interventions is critical for their success. According to the Global Financing Facility (2020), investments in nutrition can yield significant economic returns, yet funding remains insufficient. The World Bank (2019) emphasizes the need for increased domestic financing for nutrition programs, particularly in the context of rising food insecurity exacerbated by climate change and economic shocks. Innovative financing mechanisms, such as results-based financing and social impact bonds, have been proposed to enhance funding for nutrition interventions (Stenberg et al., 2019). These approaches can incentivize performance and ensure resources are allocated to effective programs. However, as the International Food Policy

Research Institute (2021) highlighted, implementing such mechanisms requires careful consideration of local contexts and stakeholder engagement. Funding nutrition interventions is a crucial determinant of their effectiveness and sustainability. According to the Global Financing Facility (2020), strategic nutrition investments foster better health outcomes and yield substantial economic returns, thereby underscoring the need for comprehensive funding mechanisms. Despite the clear benefits, the current level of funding allocated to nutrition initiatives remains insufficient, leading to a significant gap between available financial resources and the required investment to effectively combat malnutrition and food insecurity. The World Bank (2019) has articulated the urgent need for increased domestic financing for nutrition programs, particularly considering the escalating challenges posed by food insecurity exacerbated by climate change and economic shocks. As traditional funding sources become increasingly strained, exploring innovative financing mechanisms that can drive the necessary capital into the nutrition sector is imperative. Innovative approaches such as results-based financing and social impact bonds have been suggested as viable strategies to enhance funding for nutrition interventions (Stenberg et al., 2019). These mechanisms provide financial resources and create incentives for performance, thus ensuring that funding is directed toward programs that demonstrate effectiveness and measurable outcomes. These models can mobilize additional resources and promote accountability within nutrition initiatives by aligning financial incentives with health objectives.

Nevertheless, implementing such mechanisms is not without challenges. The International Food Policy Research Institute (2021) emphasizes that successfully deploying innovative financing approaches necessitates thorough consideration of local contexts and robust stakeholder engagement. Each community possesses unique socio-economic dynamics, cultural practices, and health needs that must be understood and integrated into the design and application of these financing strategies. While the potential for innovative financing mechanisms to enhance nutrition interventions is clear, their successful implementation will rely on a nuanced understanding of local environments and engagement with stakeholders. The financial commitment to nutrition is not merely a matter of funding but a strategic investment in populations' global well-being and economic stability. As such, it is essential to prioritize the mobilization of resources and the design of effective financing strategies to ensure the success of nutrition programs in combating malnutrition and promoting food security.

The Interplay Between Healthcare Financing and Nutrition Policy

Integrated Approaches

In sub-Saharan Africa, the intersection of healthcare financing and nutrition policy emerges as a pivotal strategy for addressing malnutrition's complex and multi-faceted challenges and associated health outcomes. The region is characterized by high rates of both undernutrition and obesity, which contribute significantly to the burden of disease and hinder economic development. Malnutrition, comprising a spectrum of conditions including undernutrition and micronutrient deficiencies, alongside the increasing prevalence of diet-related non-communicable diseases, necessitates a holistic approach that integrates health and nutrition initiatives. A growing body of literature underscores the critical importance of cross-sectoral collaboration in this context. For instance, Benson et al. (2020) highlight how initiatives that bridge health and nutrition sectors can create synergistic effects, fostering better health outcomes and more efficient resource utilization. This perspective is essential, as isolated interventions in either industry often fail to address the underlying determinants of malnutrition and health disparities. The World Health Organization (2021) further reinforces this viewpoint by advocating for re-envisioning health systems to incorporate nutrition as an integral component of primary healthcare. This recommendation recognizes that adequate healthcare financing must extend beyond traditional medical services to encompass nutritional support and interventions. By prioritizing nutrition within primary healthcare frameworks, health systems can enhance their capacity to address the root causes of malnutrition, improve health outcomes, and create sustainable pathways to overall well-being. Integrating healthcare financing with nutrition policy is not merely advantageous; it is essential for fostering resilient health systems capable of tackling the intricate challenges of malnutrition in sub-Saharan Africa. By promoting collaboration across sectors and prioritizing nutrition within healthcare delivery, stakeholders can achieve meaningful progress in improving public health outcomes and addressing the profound implications of malnutrition in this region.

Evidence of Successful Integration

Integrating healthcare financing and nutrition policies is critical for improving public health outcomes, and several case studies effectively demonstrate this synergy. One prominent example is the implementation of the National Health Insurance Scheme (NHIS) in Ghana. This initiative has been associated with significant improvements in access to nutrition services, which, in turn, has positively impacted maternal and child health outcomes. Ameyaw et al. (2021) provide evidence that the NHIS alleviates financial burdens for families seeking healthcare and facilitates greater utilization of essential nutrition programs. As a result, mothers and children benefit from enhanced access to a spectrum of health services, including prenatal care, nutritional counseling, and childhood vaccinations. This connection between healthcare financing and nutrition services underscores the importance of comprehensive policies promoting vulnerable populations' well-being. Similarly, Ethiopia's Health Extension Program exemplifies the effectiveness of integrated health and nutrition strategies. As Assefa et al. (2019) detailed, this program encompasses various activities, including nutrition education and direct nutritional services that trained community health workers deliver. By embedding nutrition within the healthcare framework, Ethiopia addresses immediate dietary needs and fosters long-term health by promoting healthy eating practices and preventative care among communities. This model highlights the value of integrating nutrition into public health initiatives, demonstrating that such approaches can significantly enhance overall health outcomes and reduce the prevalence of malnutrition. Together, these case studies illustrate a compelling narrative: successfully integrating healthcare financing and nutrition policies is foundational for improving health outcomes. By ensuring that nutrition services are accessible and well-funded, countries can make substantial strides toward achieving better maternal and child health results. The evidence from Ghana and Ethiopia supports the argument for policymakers to prioritize such integrative strategies, as they offer a viable pathway to enhancing individual and population health.

Barriers to Integration

The text highlights the complexities associated with integrating various approaches in nutrition and health services despite the clear advantages that such integration may offer. Integrated approaches are designed to create a more cohesive system that enhances service delivery, improves outcomes, and effectively utilizes resources. However, several formidable barriers hinder the realization of these benefits. Branca et al. (2019) identified key impediments that limit the effectiveness of integrated approaches.

One of the primary challenges is the existence of institutional silos, whereby different organizations and departments operate independently without sufficient collaboration. These silos can result in fragmented service delivery, where efforts are duplicated and potential synergies are lost.

Furthermore, a lack of coordination among various stakeholders prevents the establishment of a unified approach to address shared goals. This disjointedness can stifle innovation and reduce the overall impact of interventions designed to improve nutritional and health outcomes. In addition to structural issues, funding presents another significant obstacle. Insufficient financial resources often lead to the inadequacy of integrated programs and create competition among various health and nutrition initiatives, which subsequently undermines their effectiveness. Relying on sporadic or short-term funding can create an unstable environment that discourages long-term planning and implementation. Cultural factors and community perceptions also play a crucial role in shaping the effectiveness of integrated interventions. Lassi et al. (2020) emphasize that the successful uptake of health and nutrition services is often contingent upon the community's understanding and acceptance of these services. Engagement and participation are likely to decline if the population perceives these interventions as misaligned with their cultural values or needs. Therefore, it is imperative to consider local contexts, values, and perceptions when designing and promoting integrated approaches. While the potential benefits of integrated approaches in nutrition and health are substantial, various barriers—such as institutional silos, lack of stakeholder coordination, insufficient funding, and cultural perceptions—must be addressed to realize these benefits fully. For integrated interventions to succeed, concerted efforts are required to dismantle these barriers, foster collaboration among stakeholders, secure sustainable funding, and engage communities in a culturally sensitive manner. Only by overcoming these challenges can integrated approaches lead to meaningful improvements in health and nutrition outcomes.

Conclusion

Sub-Saharan Africa's healthcare financing and nutrition policy landscape presents many challenges and opportunities. While progress has been achieved in developing targeted policies to combat malnutrition and health disparities, substantial obstacles remain. Recognizing that malnutrition is intricately linked to socio-economic factors, cultural practices, and systemic inequities is crucial. Therefore, a comprehensive and integrated approach that aligns healthcare financing with nutrition policies is essential for sustainable public health improvements. Future research must prioritize evaluating integrated strategies that effectively combine healthcare and nutrition initiatives.

Additionally, innovative financing models, such as public-private partnerships and community-based initiatives, are vital to addressing the region's unique financial challenges. These models can enhance resource mobilization and ensure funding is adaptable to regional requirements.

Furthermore, strengthening data collection and monitoring systems is imperative for informed policy-making. Reliable data enables policymakers to design tailored interventions based on specific community needs, thus addressing health outcomes and the socio-economic factors contributing to malnutrition. In summary, while notable advancements have been made, advancing an integrated approach, fostering innovative financing solutions, and enhancing data systems will critically enable stakeholders to achieve sustainable improvements in nutrition and overall health outcomes in sub-Saharan Africa.

Bibliography

African Union. (2015). Agenda 2063: The Africa we want. Addis Ababa: African Union.

Ameyaw, E. K., Ahinkorah, B. O., Baatiema, L., & Seidu, A. (2021). Is the National Health Insurance Scheme helping pregnant women in accessing health services? Analysis of the 2014 Ghana demographic and Health survey. BMC Pregnancy and Childbirth, 21(1). https://doi.org/10.1186/s12884-021-03651-6

Aslam, M. Z., Trail, M., Cassell, A. K., 3rd, Khan, A. B., & Payne, S. (2022). Establishing a sustainable healthcare environment in low- and middle-income countries. BJU international, 129(2), 134–142. https://doi.org/10.1111/bju.15659

Assefa, Y., Gelaw, Y. A., Hill, P. S., Taye, B. W., & Van Damme, W. (2019). Community health extension program of Ethiopia, 2003-2018: Successes and challenges toward universal coverage for primary healthcare services. Globalization and health, 15(1), 24. https://doi.org/10.1186/s12992-019-0470-1

Arhin, K., Oteng-Agbayie, E.F., (2023). Effects of healthcare financing policy tools on health system efficiency: Evidence from sub-Saharan Africa. Heliyon, Volume 9, Issue 10, e20573. DOI 10.1016/j.heliyon.2023.e20573

Benson, T., Shekar, M., & DiGiuseppe, S. (2020). The role of agriculture in improving nutrition in Africa. Food Policy, 95, 101840.

Branca, F., Lartey, A., & Oenema, S. (2019). The role of nutrition in health systems: A framework for action. The Lancet, 393(10171), 1497-1499.

Christian, A., Dake, F., A., A. (2021) Profiling household double and triple burden of malnutrition in sub-Saharan Africa: prevalence and influencing household factors Public Health Nutrition 25, 1563-1576

De Foo, C., Verma, M., Tan, S. Y., Hamer, J., van der Mark, N., Pholpark, A., Hanvoravongchai, P., Cheh, P. L. J., Marthias, T., Mahendradhata, Y., Putri, L. P., Hafidz, F., Giang, K. B., Khuc, T. H. H., Van Minh, H., Wu, S., Caamal-Olvera, C. G., Orive, G., Wang, H., Nachuk, S., … Legido-Quigley, H. (2023). Health financing policies during the COVID-19 pandemic and implications for universal health care: a case study of 15 countries. The Lancet. Global health, 11(12), e1964–e1977. https://doi.org/10.1016/S2214-109X(23)00448-5

Delisle, H., Faber, M., Revault, P. (2021) Evidence-based strategies needed to combat malnutrition in Sub-Saharan countries facing different stages of nutrition transition Public Health Nutrition 24, 3577-3580

Dixon, J., Tey, D. J., & Vickers, M. (2020). The role of social health insurance in improving health outcomes in low- and middle-income countries. Health Policy and Planning, 35(5), 669-675.

Feleke, T. A., Berhane, Y., & Worku, A. (2020). The Health Extension Program in Ethiopia: A review of its achievements and challenges. Ethiopian Journal of Health Sciences, 30(2), 235-246.

Frimpong, A. O., Amporfu, E., & Arthur, E. (2022). Effects of public and external health spending on out-of-pocket payments for healthcare in sub-Saharan Africa. Health policy and planning, 37(9), 1129–1137. https://doi.org/10.1093/heapol/czac068

Gillespie, S., van den Bold, M., & Hodge, J. (2019). Nutrition and the governance of agri-food systems in South Asia: A systematic review. Global Food Security, 82, 13–27. https://doi.org/10.1016/j.foodpol.2018.10.013

Global Financing Facility. (2020). Investing in nutrition: The case for financing. Washington, DC: Global Financing Facility.

Global Nutrition Report. (2021). Global nutrition report 2021: The state of global nutrition. Bristol: Development Initiatives.

Habtu, M., Agena, A. G., Umugwaneza, M., Mochama, M., & Munyanshongore, C. (2022). Effect of integrated nutrition-sensitive and nutrition-specific intervention package on maternal malnutrition among pregnant women in Rwanda. Maternal & child nutrition, 18(3), e13367. https://doi.org/10.1111/mcn.13367

Hellowell, M. (2019). Are public–private partnerships the future of healthcare delivery in sub-Saharan Africa? Lessons from Lesotho BMJ Global Health 4

Ifeagwu, S. C., Yang, J. C., Parkes-Ratanshi, R., & Brayne, C. (2021). Health financing for universal health coverage in Sub-Saharan Africa: a systematic review. Global health research and policy, 6(1), 8. https://doi.org/10.1186/s41256-021-00190-7

Kumar, S., & Sood, A. (2019). Public-private partnerships in healthcare: A review of their impact on healthcare delivery in low-income countries. International Journal of Health Planning and Management, 34(4), e1380-e1395.

Lassi, Z. S., Kumar, N., & Bhutta, Z. A. (2020). Community-based interventions for improving maternal and neonatal health outcomes in low- and middle-income countries: A systematic review. BMC Pregnancy and Childbirth, 20(1), 1–12.

McCoy, D., Hall, J., & Ridge, M. (2016). The role of international aid in health financing: A review of the evidence. Health Policy and Planning, 31(1), 1–10.

Oxfam. (2018). A cure for the health financing crisis: How to make health financing work for the poorest. Oxford: Oxfam International.

Ruel, M. T., Alderman, H., & Ruel, M. (2018). Nutrition-sensitive interventions and programs: How can they help to accelerate progress in improving maternal and child nutrition? The Lancet, 391(10125), 2402–2414.

Salam, R. A., Das, J. K., & Bhutta, Z. A. (2019). Integrating nutrition into health systems: What the evidence advocates. Maternal & child nutrition, 15 Suppl 1(Suppl 1), e12738. https://doi.org/10.1111/mcn.12738

Stenberg, K., Hanssen, O. B., & Edejer, T. (2019). Financing the health-related Sustainable Development Goals in low-income and middle-income countries: A systematic analysis. The Lancet Global Health, 7(9), e1247-e1256.

SUN Movement. (2019). Scaling Up Nutrition: Annual Progress Report 2019. Geneva: SUN Movement.

Tannor, E., Quentin, W., Busse, R., Opoku, D., & Amuasi, J. H. (2023). The impact of COVID-19 on health service utilization in sub-Saharan Africa: a scoping review. The European Journal of Public Health, 33(Suppl 2), ckad160.018. https://doi.org/10.1093/eurpub/ckad160.018

UNICEF. (2020). The state of the world's children 2020: Children, food and nutrition. New York: UNICEF.

World Bank. (2017). Health financing in Africa: A review of the evidence. Washington, DC: World Bank.

World Bank. (2019). The cost of malnutrition: The economic impact of malnutrition in Africa. Washington, DC: World Bank.

World Health Organization. (2010). The World Health Report 2010: Health systems financing: The path to universal coverage. Geneva: WHO.

World Health Organization (2017). World Bank and WHO: Half the world lacks access to essential health services, 100 million still pushed into extreme poverty because of health expenses. https://www.who.int/news/item/13-12-2017-world-bank-and-who-half-the-world-lacks-access-to-essential-health-services-100-million-still-pushed-into-extreme-poverty-because-of-health-expenses

World Health Organization (2020). Impact of COVID-19 on people's livelihoods, their health, and our food systems. Joint statement by ILO, FAO, IFAD, and WHO. https://www.who.int/news/item/13-10-2020-impact-of-covid-19-on-people's-livelihoods-their-health-and-our-food-systems

World Health Organization (2020). Use of Nutrition Data in Decision Making: A Review Paper Conducted on behalf of the Research Priority Working Group of the WHO-UNICEF Technical Expert Advisory Group on nutrition Monitoring (TEAM). https://cdn.who.int/media/docs/default-source/nutritionlibrary/team---technical-expert-advisory-group-on-nutrition-monitoring/team-nutrition-data-decisionmaking-reviewpaper.pdf?sfvrsn=43b43e17_2&download=true

World Health Organization. (2021). Nutrition in health systems: A framework for action. Geneva: WHO.

Chapter 9: Healthcare Financing and Disease Surveillance in sub-Saharan Africa

Sayo Awosika-Olumo MD., MPH., PhD and Debo Awosika-Olumo MD., MS., MPH, PhD., FACE

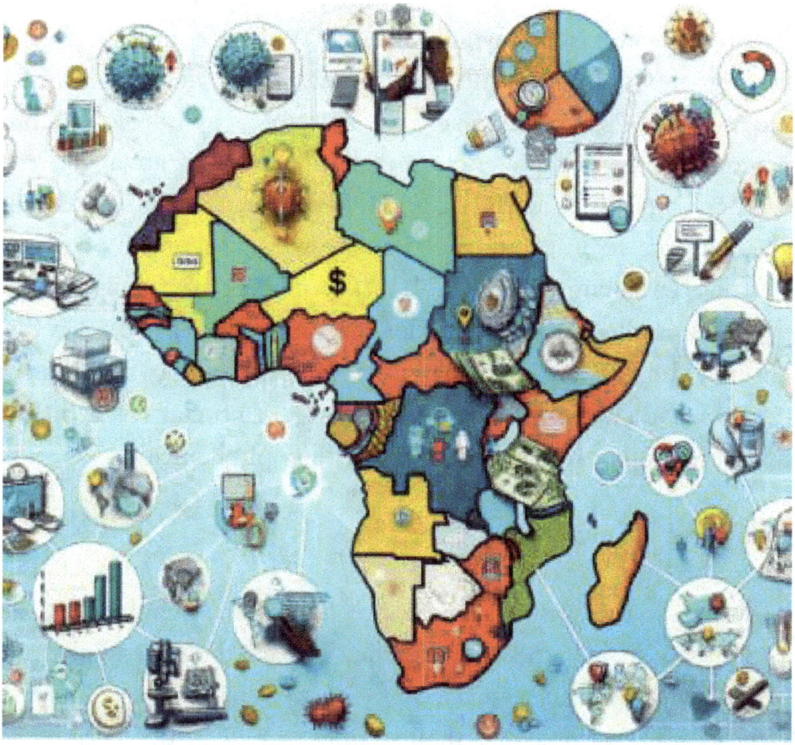

Vignette: Exploring healthcare financing and disease surveillance in sub-Saharan Africa

In the bustling city of Nairobi, Kenya, Dr. Amina Mwangi works tirelessly at a local clinic, providing essential healthcare services to her community. Despite her dedication, she faces numerous challenges, particularly securing adequate funding for the clinic's operations. Healthcare financing in sub-Saharan Africa remains a critical issue, with many countries relying heavily on out-of-pocket payments and donor funding (Ifeagwu, 2021). This often leaves healthcare facilities under-resourced and unable to meet the growing demands of their populations.

Meanwhile, across the continent in Lagos, Nigeria, Dr. Chinedu Okeke is at the forefront of disease surveillance efforts. The Integrated Disease Surveillance and Response (IDSR) strategy, adopted by many sub-Saharan African countries, aims to enhance the detection and management of infectious diseases (Mremi, et al 2021). However, the system faces hurdles such as inadequate data completeness and limited use of advanced data analytics (Mremi, et al 2021). Dr. Okeke's team is integrating big data analytics to improve the timeliness and accuracy of disease reporting (Achieng et al., 2024). As both doctors navigate their respective challenges, they ponder the future of healthcare in their regions. They understand that innovative financing mechanisms and robust disease surveillance systems are crucial for achieving universal health coverage and safeguarding public health.

Questions:

1. What are the primary sources of healthcare financing in sub-Saharan Africa, and how do they impact the accessibility and quality of healthcare services?
2. How can national health insurance schemes be designed to provide equitable and sustainable healthcare financing in sub-Saharan Africa?
3. What are the main challenges faced by the Integrated Disease Surveillance and Response (IDSR) strategy in sub-Saharan Africa, and how can these be addressed?
4. How can big data analytics enhance disease surveillance and

response in sub-Saharan Africa, and what barriers must be overcome for its successful implementation?
5. How can international partnerships and donor funding be leveraged to improve sub-Saharan Africa's healthcare financing and disease surveillance systems?

Introduction

Healthcare financing and disease surveillance are critical areas of study and intervention in sub-Saharan Africa, a region characterized by diverse health challenges, economic disparities, and varying degrees of governance. As the global community grapples with the repercussions of pandemics, endemic diseases, and emerging health threats, the need for robust healthcare systems that can efficiently allocate resources and monitor disease patterns has never been more pressing. This region faces significant obstacles, such as underfunded health systems, reliance on external aid, limited capacity for disease monitoring, and inadequate integration of non-communicable diseases (NCDs) into surveillance systems. These constraints hinder effective responses to infectious and emerging diseases, emphasizing the need for innovative financing mechanisms and robust surveillance frameworks.

This chapter aims to elucidate the intricate dynamics of healthcare financing and disease surveillance in sub-Saharan Africa, examining how these two components interact to shape health outcomes and inform policy decisions.

Healthcare financing refers to the methods and mechanisms through which funds are mobilized, allocated, and utilized to support health services. In sub-Saharan Africa, the financing landscape is multi-faceted, encompassing public funding from government budgets, private expenditures, international aid, and innovative financing mechanisms. The World Health Organization

(WHO) has emphasized the importance of adequate healthcare financing as a cornerstone for achieving universal health coverage (UHC) and the Sustainable Development Goals (SDGs). However, the region faces significant challenges, including limited government revenue, reliance on donor funding, and inefficiencies in resource allocation. These challenges are exacerbated by the dual burden of communicable and non-communicable diseases, necessitating a comprehensive approach to health financing that adapts to evolving health needs.

Disease surveillance, on the other hand, is the systematic collection, analysis, and interpretation of health data to monitor and respond to public health threats. Effective disease surveillance is essential for early detection of outbreaks, understanding disease patterns, and informing public health interventions. In sub-Saharan Africa, the capacity for disease surveillance varies widely, influenced by factors such as infrastructure, human resources, and technological advancements. The region has made strides in enhancing surveillance systems, particularly in response to high-profile outbreaks such as Ebola and COVID-19; however, significant gaps remain, particularly in rural and underserved areas. Integrating healthcare financing and disease surveillance is crucial for building resilient health systems that respond to current and future health challenges.

Socio-political factors, including governance, corruption, and community engagement, further complicate the interplay between healthcare financing and disease surveillance in sub-Saharan Africa. Political stability and effective governance are vital for creating an enabling environment for health financing and effective surveillance. Countries with strong governance structures are more likely to implement transparent financing mechanisms, promote accountability, and foster public trust in health systems. Conversely, weak governance can lead to misallocation of resources, lack of investment in health infrastructure, and diminished capacity for disease surveillance. Furthermore, community engagement is essential for financing and surveillance efforts, as local populations must be involved in decision-making processes to ensure that health interventions are culturally appropriate and effectively address their needs.

In addition to these socio-political dimensions, the role of technology in enhancing healthcare financing and disease surveillance cannot be overstated. The advent of digital health technologies, such as mobile health applications and electronic health records, presents new opportunities for improving data collection, analysis, and dissemination. These technologies can facilitate real-time surveillance of disease outbreaks, streamline financing processes, and enhance the overall efficiency of health systems. However, the digital divide in sub-Saharan Africa poses significant challenges, as access to technology and internet connectivity remains uneven, particularly in rural areas. Ensuring equitable access to digital health solutions is essential for maximizing the benefits of technology in healthcare financing and disease surveillance.

Moreover, the COVID-19 pandemic has underscored the critical need for integrated healthcare financing and disease surveillance approaches. The pandemic exposed vulnerabilities in health systems across the globe, particularly in sub-Saharan Africa, where existing health challenges were compounded by the sudden influx of cases and the strain on healthcare resources. The pandemic prompted governments and international organizations to rethink financing strategies, emphasizing the need for sustainable funding mechanisms that can withstand future shocks. Additionally, the lessons learned from the pandemic have highlighted the importance of strengthening disease surveillance systems to ensure timely detection and response to emerging health threats. Integrating financing and surveillance efforts is essential for building resilient health systems that adapt to changing epidemiological landscapes.

In conclusion, the relationship between healthcare financing and disease surveillance in sub-Saharan Africa is a complex and multi-faceted issue that requires ongoing research, policy attention, and collaborative action. As the region continues to confront myriad health challenges, understanding the interplay between these two components is essential for developing effective strategies that promote health equity and improve health outcomes. Future research should focus on identifying innovative financing models, enhancing surveillance capacities, and fostering partnerships between governments, international organizations, and local communities. By addressing the challenges and leveraging the opportunities presented by healthcare financing and disease surveillance, sub-Saharan Africa can move closer to achieving its health goals and ensuring the well-being of its populations.

Healthcare financing and disease surveillance are critical components of health systems, particularly in sub-Saharan Africa, where the disease burden and resources are limited. This examines the existing body of research on healthcare financing mechanisms and disease surveillance systems in sub-Saharan Africa, exploring the interplay between these two domains, the challenges faced, and potential strategies for improvement. The review is structured to discuss healthcare financing first, followed by an examination of disease surveillance, and finally, the integration of these systems.

Healthcare Financing in Sub-Saharan Africa

Overview of Healthcare Financing Models

A mix of public, private, and informal funding mechanisms characterizes healthcare financing in sub-Saharan Africa. This region faces significant obstacles, such as underfunded health systems, reliance on external aid, limited capacity for disease monitoring, and inadequate integration of non-communicable diseases (NCDs) into surveillance systems. These constraints hinder effective responses to infectious and emerging diseases, emphasizing the need for innovative financing mechanisms and robust surveillance frameworks. The World Health Organization (WHO) emphasizes that adequate healthcare financing is essential for achieving universal health coverage (UHC) (WHO, 2010). The region has implemented various models, including tax-based systems, social health insurance, and out-of-pocket payments. Each model presents unique challenges and opportunities. A considerable portion of health financing comes from international donors. The Global Fund and Gavi have provided substantial funding for HIV, tuberculosis, and malaria programs. However, donor funding is often disease-specific, undermining broader health systems' sustainability (Dieleman et al., 2019).

Public Financing

Public financing through government budgets is a predominant model in several sub-Saharan African countries. According to Mtei et al. (2014), public financing is often inadequate, resulting in limited access to essential health services. The WHO (2010) highlights that many governments allocate less than the recommended 15% of their national budgets to health, leading to significant gaps in service delivery.

Private and Informal Financing

Private financing, including out-of-pocket expenditures, is another critical aspect of healthcare financing in the region. A study by Woldemariam et al. (2017) indicates that high out-of-pocket costs can deter individuals from seeking necessary medical care, exacerbating health disparities. Informal financing mechanisms, such as community-based health insurance schemes, have emerged as alternatives, but their sustainability and coverage remain concerns (Bennett et al., 2018). Challenges in Healthcare Financing

The healthcare financing landscape in sub-Saharan Africa is fraught with challenges, including inefficiencies, corruption, and inequitable resource distribution. A review by Kutzin (2013) identifies fragmentation in funding sources as a significant barrier to effective healthcare delivery. Moreover, the reliance on external funding, particularly from international donors, creates vulnerabilities in health systems (Biesma et al., 2009). The key barriers to adequate healthcare financing include low domestic revenue mobilization. Most SSA countries allocate less than 15% of their budgets to health care, falling short of the Abuja Declaration target. Fragmentation of Funds due to poor coordination among donors, governments, and private entities leads to inefficiencies in resource allocation. Equity concerns regarding marginalized groups, particularly in rural areas, often lack access to affordable care due to weak coverage of health financing mechanisms. A significant proportion of healthcare financing in SSA relies on out-of-pocket payments and donor funds, leaving many vulnerable to catastrophic health expenditures (McIntyre et al., 2018). Public spending on health is insufficient, leading to disparities in access and financial protection. Novignon and Nonvignon (2012) highlight the reliance on donor funds, which introduces volatility and uncertainty in health financing. This dependency complicates long-term planning and investment in health infrastructure. In the context of diabetes care, Beran and Yudkin (2006) underscore the challenges posed by inadequate financing and competing health priorities, which affect disease management and outcomes.

Equity and Access

Equity in healthcare financing is a pressing issue in sub-Saharan Africa. Research by O'Donnell et al. (2008) reveals that marginalized populations often bear a disproportionate burden of healthcare costs, leading to increased inequities in access to health services. Some challenges include inadequate human resources, inadequate budgetary allocation to health, and poor leadership and management (Oleribe et al., 2019). The challenge of ensuring equitable access is compounded by socio-economic factors and geographic disparities (Marmot et al., 2008).

Innovations in Healthcare Financing

Innovative financing mechanisms are being explored to enhance healthcare funding in sub-Saharan Africa. For instance, results-based financing (RBF) has gained traction as a strategy to improve health outcomes by linking funding to performance indicators (Witter et al., 2017). Additionally, the use of mobile technology for health financing, such as mobile money platforms, has shown promise in increasing access to healthcare services (Peters et al., 2016). Mechanisms like health insurance schemes and public-private partnerships (PPPs) are emerging across the region. Rwanda's Mutuelles de Santé is a success story, achieving over 90% health insurance coverage through community-based schemes (Lu et al., 2018).

Disease Surveillance in Sub-Saharan Africa

Importance of Disease Surveillance

Disease surveillance is indispensable in public health, particularly in sub-Saharan Africa (SSA), where the burden of communicable diseases remains acutely high. Effective surveillance systems are paramount for the timely detection, monitoring, and response to infectious disease outbreaks, often exacerbated by various socio-economic and environmental factors in the region. The World Health Organization (WHO) defines disease surveillance as the continuous and systematic collection, analysis, and interpretation of health-related data, underscoring its vital function in public health management (WHO, 2017). Surveillance is critical for a variety of reasons. It serves as the foundation for detecting outbreaks, enabling health authorities to identify unusual patterns that may signal the emergence of a contagious disease.

Furthermore, it allows for monitoring disease trends over time, offering invaluable insights into the effectiveness of existing public health interventions and guiding future policy decisions. In SSA, the susceptibility to epidemics, including but not limited to Ebola, malaria, and COVID-19, accentuates the urgent need for robust and responsive surveillance systems. The frequency and severity of these outbreaks highlight the potential consequences of inadequate surveillance, which can lead to widespread morbidity and mortality. The WHO's Integrated Disease Surveillance and Response (IDSR) strategy has emerged as a cornerstone for addressing the myriad public health challenges faced by countries within the region. IDSR aims to strengthen local and national capacities for disease detection and response by streamlining the collection and analysis of health data across various diseases. This integrated approach facilitates a more coordinated response to outbreaks, effectively mobilizing resources and ensuring that interventions are targeted and timely.

In conclusion, the importance of disease surveillance in sub-Saharan Africa cannot be overstated. It is a critical determinant of public health success, enabling a proactive stance against infectious disease threats. The ongoing development and refinement of surveillance systems, particularly through initiatives like IDSR, are essential to mitigate the profound impact of communicable diseases in the region and safeguard its populations' health. As such, investment in these systems should be a priority for governments and health organizations, as they are integral to achieving health security and improving health outcomes in sub-Saharan Africa.

Current State of Disease Surveillance

The current state of disease surveillance in sub-Saharan Africa presents a heterogeneous landscape, reflecting substantial disparities among the various nations within the region. Some countries have successfully established robust disease surveillance systems that effectively monitor and respond to health threats. In contrast, others grapple with significant deficiencies, primarily rooted in limited resources and inadequate infrastructure. A pivotal study by Otu et al. (2020) underscores a critical challenge within this landscape, revealing that many sub-Saharan African nations lack the essential human resources and technological capabilities required to implement effective surveillance programs. This inadequacy hampers their ability to detect and respond to infectious diseases promptly, thereby escalating public health risks. One noteworthy initiative in the region is the Integrated Disease Surveillance and Response (IDSR), adopted in 1998. IDSR has sought to standardize data collection and reporting processes across member states, facilitating a more cohesive approach to disease monitoring. For instance, Uganda has made significant strides by incorporating community-based surveillance into its IDSR framework, which has proven invaluable in achieving real-time detection of diseases (Nsubuga et al., 2016). This integration of community engagement enhances surveillance efficacy and empowers local populations to take an active role in disease response. Moreover, digital innovations have heralded a transformative shift in disease surveillance. The utilization of mobile technologies and eHealth platforms is gaining momentum to strengthen surveillance systems across the region. A prominent example is the mHealth initiative in Kenya, which leverages SMS alerts to report outbreaks rapidly. Such digital solutions streamline communication and foster timely responses to emerging health threats. While there are notable advancements in disease surveillance systems within sub-Saharan Africa, substantial challenges persist, particularly regarding resources and technology. Initiatives like IDSR and the integration of digital innovations exemplify a proactive approach to overcoming these obstacles, indicating a promising trajectory for enhancing public health surveillance in the region.

Challenges in Disease Surveillance

The effectiveness of disease surveillance in sub-Saharan Africa (SSA) faces many challenges that significantly impede its operational capacity and overall efficacy. A critical issue is the lack of coordination among various health agencies, which often leads to fragmented approaches to surveillance and response efforts. This disorganization is compounded by insufficient funding, which restricts the ability of health systems to develop robust surveillance infrastructures. Furthermore, inadequate personnel training limits the capabilities needed to adeptly manage and respond to disease outbreaks (Kumar et al., 2016). The burden of endemic diseases, such as malaria and HIV/AIDS, further complicates the landscape of disease surveillance in the region. These longstanding health challenges often precede resource allocation and public health focus, thereby overshadowing the essential need for systematic surveillance of emerging infectious diseases (EIDs) (Kumar et al., 2016). As such, public health initiatives often overlook the threats posed by EIDs, undermining the ability to detect and respond to potential outbreaks promptly. Data gaps present another formidable challenge in SSA's disease surveillance efforts. The existing infrastructure is notably poor, and trained human resources are scarce. These limitations result in delayed data collection and analysis, which is crucial for effective public health decision-making. Moreover, the porous borders characteristic of SSA facilitate the rapid spread of infectious diseases, complicating surveillance operations. The Ebola outbreaks in West Africa serve as a stark reminder of the dire need for regional cooperation and cohesive surveillance strategies that transcend national boundaries. Funding constraints persist as a significant barrier to effective disease surveillance in SSA. The reliance on external funding sources renders surveillance efforts vulnerable to shifts in donor priorities. This dependence often implies that critical health issues may not receive the necessary support if they do not align with the current focus of external funders. Although disease surveillance in the region predominantly concentrates on infectious diseases such as tuberculosis and HIV, there remains a concerning lack of integration of non-communicable diseases (NCDs) into routine monitoring systems. This oversight diminishes the potential to effectively address the growing burden of chronic diseases, which are increasingly becoming a public health concern (Nyaaba et al., 2020). Despite these challenges, mobile health (mHealth) initiatives represent a promising avenue for enhancing disease surveillance in resource-limited settings. As Brinkel et al. (2014) noted, mHealth tools can significantly improve data collection and disease monitoring, providing an innovative solution to some of the limitations currently experienced in SSA. The implementation of such technologies has the potential to streamline data acquisition and empower local health workers with the necessary tools to monitor and respond to health threats effectively. Overall, while the challenges facing disease surveillance in sub-Saharan Africa are significant, integrating strategic practices and mHealth technologies can foster improvements that ultimately enhance public health outcomes in the region.

Innovations in Disease Surveillance

The disease surveillance landscape is evolving in response to myriad challenges, necessitating innovative methodologies that leverage modern technology. Emerging digital health technologies, including mobile applications and sophisticated data analytics, have the potential to bolster surveillance capabilities significantly (Fitzgerald et al., 2017). These tools facilitate real-time data collection and analysis, enhancing the overall effectiveness and responsiveness of surveillance efforts. Moreover, community-based surveillance initiatives represent a promising shift toward localized health monitoring. By engaging community members in the data collection process, these initiatives have demonstrated notable improvements in the quality of data gathered and the speed with which public health responses are initiated (Sullivan et al., 2017). This approach empowers communities and creates a more intricate understanding of the health dynamics within specific populations. In an integrated effort to tackle health challenges, the "One Health" approach proposed by Fasina et al. (2021) underscores the importance of cross-sector collaboration. By merging human, animal, and environmental health initiatives, this framework encourages a multi-faceted funding model to strengthen interventions, particularly in zoonotic disease surveillance. The holistic nature of this strategy ensures that resources are utilized more efficiently, ultimately leading to enhanced public health outcomes. Parallel to these developments, Reid et al. (2012) highlight the financial obstacles present within correctional facilities, where constraints severely impede the management of tuberculosis and HIV. Their analysis emphasizes the critical need for innovative financing models tailored to such environments' unique contexts. Addressing these issues is paramount, as effective health interventions in these settings can have far-reaching implications for public health. Further exploring the funding landscape, Kaburi et al. (2024) provide an insightful evaluation of digital disease surveillance financing trends. Their findings reveal a significant disparity in investment levels, drawing attention to the pivotal roles of international foundations and bilateral agreements in promoting digital health projects. This trend illustrates the transformative potential of digital tools to rectify systemic inefficiencies inherent in traditional surveillance methods. The convergence of digital health technologies, community engagement, collaborative frameworks, and innovative financing models presents a robust foundation for advancing disease surveillance. The collective impact of these strategies is poised to significantly enhance public health preparedness and response, thereby safeguarding communities against the ever-evolving challenges posed by infectious diseases.

Integration of Healthcare Financing and Disease Surveillance

Integrating healthcare financing with disease surveillance represents a pivotal strategy for the effective functioning of health systems in sub-Saharan Africa. This region faces unique health challenges, and the interplay between robust funding mechanisms and efficient surveillance systems is beneficial and essential for public health management. Research conducted by Duran et al. (2017) underscores the necessity of adequate funding for surveillance systems, asserting that such financial support is critical for the timely detection and response to infectious disease outbreaks. The ability to rapidly identify and address health threats is considerably enhanced when surveillance is sufficiently funded, thereby mitigating the potential impact of disease spread on communities. Furthermore, effective surveillance is a two-way street; it can optimize resource allocation by identifying and prioritizing funding for high-burden diseases. As Duran et al. (2017) articulate, targeted funding allocations based on surveillance data allow health authorities to focus on the most pressing health challenges, thereby improving health outcomes and ensuring the efficient use of limited resources. Integrating disease surveillance within the broader context of health system strengthening is, therefore, a critical endeavor. Onasanya et al. (2021) highlight the necessity of addressing systemic gaps in both funding and surveillance, particularly concerning neglected tropical diseases (NTDs). Their advocacy for a bottom-up approach is particularly relevant, as it emphasizes the involvement of local health stakeholders in decision-making processes to ensure that funding and surveillance needs are met at the grassroots level. Such inclusivity fosters a more responsive health system that can better meet the needs of the populations it serves. Moreover, the examination by Nonvignon et al. (2024) adds another layer of complexity by addressing the role of inequitable financial arrangements as barriers to effective care delivery in managing NTDs. Identifying these inequities is critical, as they hinder the optimal functioning of health systems and perpetuate health disparities within sub-Saharan Africa. By focusing on equitable financial strategies and enhancing surveillance capabilities, health systems can be more effectively mobilized to respond to NTDs and other public health challenges. Integrating healthcare financing and disease surveillance is not merely beneficial but imperative for effectively managing health systems in sub-Saharan Africa. By ensuring adequate funding for surveillance, prioritizing disease burden in resource allocation, addressing systemic gaps, and advocating for equitable financial arrangements, stakeholders can create a framework that supports resilient health systems capable of effectively addressing current and emerging health threats.

Challenges to Integration

Integrating healthcare financing and disease surveillance presents a promising opportunity for enhancing public health systems; however, several significant challenges impede progress in these areas. One primary obstacle is the existence of fragmented funding streams, which create inefficiencies and disjointed efforts between health financing and surveillance initiatives (Biesma et al., 2009). The lack of coordination complicates the operational aspects of managing health resources and undermines the effectiveness of disease monitoring efforts, which are essential for timely public health responses.

Moreover, there is a pervasive tendency to prioritize immediate health needs over long-term investments in surveillance systems (Kutzin, 2013). This short-sighted approach results in insufficient allocation of resources to strengthen surveillance capabilities, which are critical for identifying health threats and managing disease outbreaks. The COVID-19 pandemic has notably intensified these vulnerabilities, revealing critical gaps in healthcare financing and surveillance frameworks. Bastagli et al. (2020) elucidate how the pandemic placed unprecedented strain on already underfunded health systems, emphasizing the urgent necessity of developing sustainable health financing models that can withstand future public health emergencies.

Furthermore, specialized areas of healthcare, such as antimicrobial resistance (AMR), require focused attention and dedicated funding. Kariuki et al. (2022) stress the necessity of integrating AMR surveillance into national health strategies, reinforcing that a dedicated funding mechanism is vital for effectively monitoring and addressing the threat of antibiotic resistance. This integration is beneficial and essential for crafting a robust health response framework to address current health challenges while also anticipating and mitigating future threats.

While the potential benefits of integrating healthcare financing and disease surveillance are substantial, addressing the challenges of fragmented funding, prioritizing immediate needs over long-term investment, and the need for specialized surveillance is critical. The insights provided by these studies underscore the necessity of comprehensive and coordinated approaches to ensure resilience and effectiveness in our healthcare systems. The call for sustainable models and dedicated funding strategies must be acknowledged and acted upon with urgency and resolve.

Strategies for Improved Integration

Integrating healthcare financing and disease surveillance is a multi-faceted endeavor that requires a strategic and collaborative approach. Several key strategies can be employed to enhance this integration effectively.

Firstly, strengthening partnerships among government agencies, non-governmental organizations (NGOs), and international partners is essential for fostering coordinated efforts in health systems. A collaborative framework between various stakeholders ensures that knowledge, resources, and expertise are shared, ultimately leading to more effective healthcare delivery and robust disease surveillance (Witter et al., 2017). Such partnerships facilitate comprehensive responses to health challenges and enable the pooling of financial resources necessary for sustainable health initiatives.

Moreover, developing comprehensive funding frameworks that prioritize healthcare delivery and surveillance is critical. These frameworks are instrumental in ensuring sustained investments that support health systems over time. By establishing clear priorities and allocating resources effectively, countries can develop robust healthcare infrastructures that are better equipped to respond to public health threats, as articulated by Mtei et al. (2014).

In addition to these strategies, strengthening domestic financing is indispensable. Increased allocation of government budgets to health, coupled with a strategic reduction in dependence on donor funding, can enhance the resilience of health systems. Domestic financing empowers countries to prioritize their health needs and fosters a sense of ownership over health outcomes.

Technology integration is another pivotal aspect of enhancing disease surveillance. Leveraging digital tools such as mobile health (mHealth) platforms can provide cost-effective solutions for monitoring and tracking diseases. These technological interventions have the potential to streamline data collection and improve real-time surveillance capabilities, ultimately leading to more effective public health responses.

Furthermore, incorporating surveillance for non-communicable diseases (NCDs) into routine disease surveillance frameworks is critical. The rising prevalence of NCDs necessitates a comprehensive approach to monitoring both infectious and non-communicable diseases. By integrating NCD surveillance, health systems can effectively manage the dual burden of disease that many countries face today.

Promoting public-private partnerships (PPPs) is another strategy that can significantly enhance health financing and surveillance resources. Collaborative efforts between the public and private sectors can mobilize additional funding, share innovative practices, and enhance the overall effectiveness of health interventions.

Lastly, the development of context-specific interventions is crucial. Tailoring financing and surveillance strategies to the distinct challenges faced by individual countries or regions allows for greater relevance and effectiveness. This localized approach ensures that strategies are practical and resonate with the specific needs and capacities of the health systems being addressed.

In conclusion, integrating healthcare financing and disease surveillance is paramount for improving health outcomes. By implementing these strategies—strengthening partnerships, developing comprehensive funding frameworks, enhancing domestic financing, leveraging technology, integrating NCD surveillance, promoting public-private partnerships, and crafting context-specific interventions—health systems can become more resilient and responsive to the challenges of both communicable and non-communicable diseases.

Case Studies and Regional Perspectives

Country-specific analyses of health issues, exemplified by studies on diabetes management in Ghana (Hall et al., 2011) and schistosomiasis control in Nigeria (Onasanya et al., 2021), offer critical insights into the unique challenges and innovative practices that arise within distinct regional contexts. These scholarly investigations highlight the necessity of customizing health interventions to fit a country's or region's specific circumstances and cultural frameworks.

The study conducted by Hall et al. (2011) on diabetes management in Ghana reveals a multi-faceted approach to addressing this chronic disease, influenced by local dietary habits, healthcare infrastructure, and socio-economic factors. The authors identify barriers such as insufficient access to healthcare resources and a lack of awareness about diabetes among the population. Their findings advocate for tailored educational initiatives and the incorporation of traditional health practices alongside modern medical interventions to enhance the effectiveness of diabetes management in Ghana.

Similarly, Onasanya et al. (2021) comprehensively analyze schistosomiasis control in Nigeria, emphasizing the disease's prevalence in specific geographic areas and among vulnerable populations. Their research demonstrates the need for targeted campaigns that engage local communities in water management and sanitation practices, which are critical for reducing transmission rates. By outlining successful localized interventions, such as community health worker training and environmental modifications, the authors reinforce the idea that effective disease control must align with the socio-cultural dynamics of the affected populations.

These studies articulate a broader need for evidence-based and contextually relevant public health interventions. The stark contrast between the general public health policies often adopted on a broader scale and the specific needs of individual communities underscores the importance of tailoring strategies to localized challenges. Such disparities can lead to inadequate or inefficient responses to health issues, ultimately compromising the effectiveness of public health initiatives.

In conclusion, the analyses of diabetes management in Ghana and schistosomiasis control in Nigeria serve as potent reminders of the context's critical role in health interventions. They convincingly argue for the implementation of localized strategies that cater to the unique circumstances of each region, thereby enhancing the sustainability and impact of health initiatives. As global health efforts progress, prioritizing context-specific approaches will undoubtedly be central to achieving equitable health outcomes across diverse populations.

COVID-19 Surveillance in Africa

Case Study: Democratic Republic of Congo, Nigeria, Senegal, and Uganda

During the COVID-19 pandemic, the need for effective management responses became paramount, particularly in regions heavily impacted by the virus. In this regard, the implementation of comprehensive surveillance strategies by several African countries—including the Democratic Republic of Congo (DRC), Nigeria, Senegal, and Uganda—serves as a significant case study in crisis response and public health management. The case investigation strategy played a crucial role in identifying and understanding the spread of COVID-19. By systematically collecting data on confirmed cases, health authorities were able to identify transmission patterns and the demographics of affected populations. This targeted approach was instrumental in allocating resources effectively and tailoring public health responses to meet the unique needs of various communities.

Contact tracing emerged as another pivotal strategy in combating the virus. This process involves tracking and notifying individuals in close contact with confirmed cases, enabling timely intervention to prevent further spread. In countries such as Nigeria and Uganda, robust contact tracing protocols were established, leveraging technology and community networks to enhance efficiency and accuracy.

Community-based surveillance also proved to be an indispensable tool. By engaging local populations and utilizing their knowledge of community dynamics, health officials in DRC and Senegal were able to gather critical information on potential outbreaks and suspicious cases. This grassroots approach facilitated early detection and fostered trust and collaboration between health authorities and community members.

Furthermore, laboratory-based sentinel surveillance was employed to monitor and assess trends in COVID-19 cases. Public health officials gained a better understanding of epidemiological patterns by strategically positioning laboratories to collect samples from specific locations. This method ensured that data reflected the realities of virus spread across diverse geographical areas, informing decision-making processes.

To complement these methodologies, serological surveys were conducted to assess the prevalence of antibodies against the virus within populations. These surveys provided invaluable insights into the extent of infection and immunity—information critical for guiding public health policies and vaccination efforts.

In addition to these strategies, effective communication channels were established via telephone hotlines, enhancing public access to information and guidance regarding COVID-19. This proactive measure ensured that communities were informed about health protocols, testing locations, and vaccination services, thus empowering individuals to take charge of their health and safety.

Lastly, the adoption of genomic sequencing facilitated a deeper understanding of the virus. Researchers could identify variants, track mutations, and assess their transmission and vaccine efficacy implications by analyzing viral genomes. This scientific rigor underpinned the overall response, providing the data necessary to adapt strategies to counter emerging challenges.

The multi-faceted surveillance strategies implemented by the DRC, Nigeria, Senegal, and Uganda during the COVID-19 outbreak exemplify proactive public health management. By integrating case investigation, contact tracing, community engagement, laboratory monitoring, serological assessments, effective communication, and genomic analysis, these nations not only aimed to mitigate the impact of the pandemic but also laid the groundwork for enhanced health security in the future. The lessons learned from these experiences will undoubtedly inform and strengthen responses to future regional health crises and beyond.

Strengths:

The onset of the COVID-19 pandemic necessitated a swift transformation in global health surveillance systems. Countries worldwide exhibited remarkable agility by rapidly adapting their frameworks to incorporate COVID-19-specific measures. This rapid response was not merely an act of urgency but a strategic imperative aimed at effectively tracking the spread of the virus and mitigating its impact on public health.

In parallel with the adaptation of surveillance systems, substantial investments were made in training health workers and augmenting laboratory resources. This concerted effort led to significant improvements in data management and the overall capacity for surveillance. Health professionals were equipped with the necessary skills to identify, report, and manage COVID-19 cases amidst an evolving understanding of the disease. Furthermore, laboratories received enhancements in capacity, allowing for increased testing and more reliable data collection. These initiatives collectively strengthened the backbone of health systems, enabling a more coherent and precise response to the pandemic.

Innovative approaches played a crucial role in this transformation. Integrating digital technologies into surveillance practices facilitated timely data collection and analysis, allowing health authorities to make informed decisions based on real-time information. Such technologies included mobile health applications, telemedicine platforms, and data analytics tools that enhanced the ability to monitor trends in infection rates and respond accordingly. Additionally, decentralized surveillance systems enabled local health authorities to collect and analyze data pertinent to their regions, fostering a more adaptive and localized response to the pandemic.

In summary, the response to COVID-19 exemplifies the capacity of health systems to evolve in the face of unprecedented challenges. Rapid adaptation of surveillance systems, training health workers, and integrating innovative technologies laid a solid foundation for more effective public health measures. As a result, these initiatives addressed immediate pandemic needs and set a precedent for future health emergencies, demonstrating the importance of agility and innovation in health surveillance.

Weaknesses:

The case studies address several critical issues that emerged during public health crises, particularly pandemics. Each challenge—staffing issues, data integration, and genomic surveillance—underscores the complexities of managing health emergencies effectively.

Staffing Issues: The mention of inadequate staffing indicates significant challenges health systems face in responding to urgent public health needs. Capacity gaps among health workers often hinder the ability to provide timely and effective care to those affected. Insufficient personnel exacerbated the strain on existing medical staff and reflected a systemic failure to prepare for public health emergencies. The ramifications of these staffing shortages were far-reaching, causing delays in patient care, increasing burnout among healthcare providers, and, ultimately, leading to a deterioration in health outcomes during critical periods of the pandemic.

Data Integration: The lack of full integration of data sources is another crucial failure highlighted in the text. Effective public health responses depend heavily on accurate and timely data; without comprehensive integration, the ability to detect and respond to emerging cases diminishes significantly. Under-detection of cases can lead to unmitigated community spread and place a greater burden on healthcare systems. The absence of a unified data framework stymies targeted interventions and highlights the need for investing in cohesive data management systems that facilitate effective communication across various health entities.

Challenges in Genomic Surveillance: Gaps in genomic and postmortem surveillance, as well as community-level seroprevalence studies, further complicate the public health landscape. Genomic surveillance is essential for tracking virus mutations and informing vaccine development, while seroprevalence studies provide invaluable insights into population immunity levels. Insufficient investment and focus on these areas reveal vulnerabilities in healthcare infrastructure, underscoring the need to prioritize genomic surveillance as an integral part of pandemic preparedness and response strategies.

The discussion also emphasizes the importance of integrating financing with effective surveillance systems. Countries such as South Africa, which boasted more robust surveillance mechanisms, were better positioned to allocate resources effectively and manage outbreaks. This example underscores the critical interplay between financial support and operational readiness; robust funding strategies must accompany comprehensive surveillance systems to facilitate timely responses to health emergencies.

However, reliance on donor funding has exposed significant vulnerabilities within lower-income countries, often facing funding gaps that jeopardize public health efforts. Delays in vaccine distribution, resulting from these financial inconsistencies, illustrate a perilous dependency on external resources, which can lead to inequities in health outcomes globally. Consequently, countries must develop sustainable funding models that do not solely rely on external donors but instead foster self-sufficiency and resilience within their health systems.

Addressing these interconnected issues—staffing shortfalls, data integration challenges, and genomic surveillance gaps—is critical for enhancing global health security. The pandemic has made it abundantly clear that investing in health workforce capacity, robust data systems, and sustainable financing is not merely advantageous but essential for effective public health response. Failure to address these areas will only perpetuate vulnerabilities and undermine collective efforts to combat future health crises.

Case Study Ebola Surveillance in Africa

The Ebola outbreak that ravaged West Africa between 2014 and 2016 serves as a critical case study for understanding the multi-faceted challenges that countries like Guinea, Liberia, and Sierra Leone encountered in establishing effective surveillance systems. Central to these challenges was the pre-existing limited public health infrastructure, which hindered the ability of these nations to respond to and control the outbreak effectively (McNamara et al., 2016). To comprehend the implications of this scenario, it is essential to recognize the structural deficiencies in the healthcare systems of the affected countries. Before the epidemic, Guinea, Liberia, and Sierra Leone had been grappling with various health system weaknesses, including inadequate healthcare facilities, insufficient workforce capacity, and a lack of essential medical supplies (McNamara et al., 2016). These systemic issues created a precarious foundation upon which to build an effective surveillance mechanism capable of detecting and responding to emerging infectious diseases promptly.

The ineffectiveness of the surveillance systems in these

nations during the Ebola crisis was further exacerbated by socio-political factors, including limited community trust in governmental health responses, the stigma associated with the disease, and a pervasive sense of fear that led to poorly coordinated efforts to report cases or seek medical assistance (McNamara et al., 2016). This environment undermined public confidence and resulted in a lack of community engagement with health authorities, which is critical for successful disease surveillance and outbreak response.

Moreover, the cross-border nature of the outbreak highlighted the necessity for regional collaboration and the sharing of critical health data among neighboring countries. However, the lack of harmonized data collection and analysis systems across Guinea, Liberia, and Sierra Leone significantly hampered collective surveillance efforts. The absence of a comprehensive regional strategy meant that the exchange of information regarding the disease's spread was often fragmented and insufficient, delaying timely responses.

Analyzing the responses to the outbreak, it becomes evident that reinforcing public health infrastructure is paramount. Lessons from the Ebola crisis underscore the importance of investing in robust health systems, including enhancing disease surveillance capabilities, training health workers, and establishing trust within communities. Strengthening these areas is vital for ensuring readiness against future public health emergencies.

In conclusion, the 2014-2016 Ebola outbreak in Guinea, Liberia, and Sierra Leone underscores the importance of establishing effective public health surveillance systems. The limitations of inadequate public health infrastructure, socio-political dynamics, and poor regional coordination must be comprehensively addressed. The insights gained from this case study provide an essential foundation for ongoing discussions about improving global health security and preparedness in the face of infectious disease threats. Thus, it is imperative that both national and international stakeholders collaborate on strategies that enhance health systems, foster community trust, and facilitate improved surveillance mechanisms to mitigate the impact of future health crises.

Strengths:

The case study of Guinea, Liberia, and Sierra Leone during the Ebola outbreak comprehensively illustrates the critical elements necessary for effective public health intervention. The collaboration among the Centers for Disease Control and Prevention (CDC), local ministries of health, and international partners stands as a cornerstone of this response, demonstrating the power of collaborative efforts in establishing functional Ebola surveillance systems. These systems were imperative in tracking the spread of the virus, allowing for timely identification and containment of potential outbreaks. The involvement of diverse stakeholders enhanced the technical capabilities and promoted a unified approach to tackling a common public health crisis.

Capacity building emerged as another vital component of this intervention. Through systematic efforts to strengthen epidemiological and data management capacities, the health infrastructures of these countries witnessed significant improvement. Enhanced routine surveillance systems provided the framework to monitor health trends and respond effectively to existing challenges. This proactive approach mitigated the immediate impacts of the Ebola outbreak and laid a robust foundation for addressing future public health emergencies. These nations developed a more resilient public health system by investing in local talent and resources to withstand future threats better.

Moreover, community engagement played a pivotal role in the overall success of the intervention. Implementing active surveillance and targeted health education initiatives empowered communities to participate in identifying suspected Ebola cases. This grassroots involvement proved instrumental in interrupting further transmission of the virus. Rapid identification of potential cases became feasible by fostering trust and encouraging open communication between health authorities and local populations (Stehling-Ariza et al., 2016). Such engagement heightened awareness around Ebola and cultivated a culture of vigilance that is essential for managing public health crises.

The concerted efforts by the CDC, local health authorities, and international partners in Guinea, Liberia, and Sierra Leone were foundational in effectively addressing the Ebola outbreak. Integrating collaboration, capacity building, and community engagement facilitated immediate response efforts and enhanced the long-term resilience of public health systems in these countries. The lessons learned from this case study underscore the importance of a multi-faceted approach in managing public health crises and provide a blueprint for future interventions.

Weaknesses:

The case studies of Guinea, Liberia, and Sierra Leone provide critical insights into the infrastructural challenges and community dynamics that significantly hindered effective surveillance during infectious disease outbreaks, particularly during the Ebola epidemic.

Infrastructure Limitations: A predominant issue highlighted in these case studies is insufficiently trained personnel, severely restricting public health response effectiveness. The lack of adequately trained staff meant that even when cases were identified, there were often not enough qualified individuals available to perform timely and thorough investigations. Moreover, limited information technology resources exacerbated this problem. The absence of robust data management systems hindered the ability to collect, analyze, and disseminate crucial health information. As a result, timely decision-making was compromised, further prolonging the public health crisis. Also, poor telephone and Internet services impeded communication among healthcare professionals and between these professionals and the communities they served. Without reliable communication channels, the dissemination of vital health information was delayed, leading to gaps in awareness about the disease and effective preventive measures.

Community Reticence: Another significant barrier to effective outbreak management was the reluctance of community members to report cases and contacts. This reticence stemmed from distrust of the healthcare system and fear of stigmatization. Consequently, delayed reporting hindered the immediate investigation and tracing of cases, allowing the virus to spread more rapidly within communities. McNamara et al. (2016) elucidate that this hesitation calls for a deeper understanding of community perceptions and the establishment of trust between health authorities and the population. Engaging communities through education and awareness campaigns is essential to encourage timely reporting and foster cooperation in outbreak response efforts.

The case studies of Guinea, Liberia, and Sierra Leone unequivocally underscore the critical importance of establishing robust surveillance systems and enhancing public health infrastructure. These findings reveal a compelling need for continuous improvement in training programs for healthcare professionals, developing information technology resources, and establishing reliable communication networks. Furthermore, engaging communities as active participants in public health initiatives is vital to break down barriers of mistrust and improve response times in future outbreaks. Addressing these multi-faceted challenges is imperative for strengthening public health systems globally and ensuring preparedness for emerging infectious diseases.

Conclusion

This statement encapsulates the critical interrelationship between healthcare financing and disease surveillance within the context of health systems in sub-Saharan Africa. These components are not merely parallel systems; they are deeply interconnected, influencing one another in ways that can significantly impact health outcomes.

Firstly, healthcare financing refers to the methods and systems through which funds are mobilized, allocated, and utilized to sustain health services. This encompasses a range of sources, such as government funding, private insurance, and out-of-pocket payments by individuals. Effective healthcare financing ensures that adequate resources are available to support health initiatives, improve service delivery, and foster equitable access to care.

On the other hand, disease surveillance involves systematically collecting, analyzing, and interpreting health data to monitor and respond to disease outbreaks and health trends. Strong surveillance systems provide critical insights that inform public health decisions, guide resource allocation, and shape healthcare policies. In sub-Saharan Africa, where infectious diseases remain prevalent, and health systems often struggle with limited resources, the ability to efficiently track and respond to health threats is paramount.

Despite notable advancements in healthcare financing and

disease surveillance in the region, significant challenges persist. For instance, many countries struggle with insufficient funds for health expenditure, hindering their ability to improve health services and implement robust surveillance systems. Additionally, existing surveillance mechanisms may be outdated or poorly integrated with healthcare financing systems, resulting in inefficiencies that undermine overall health system performance.

To effectively address these challenges, a multi-faceted approach is necessary. This includes the development of innovative financing mechanisms that can enhance resource mobilization, such as public-private partnerships, targeted grants, or the implementation of health financing reforms. Concurrently, there must be a commitment to improving disease surveillance systems by adopting advanced technologies, real-time data analytics, and training personnel in data collection and interpretation. Furthermore, enhancing integration between healthcare financing and disease surveillance is essential. A synergistic relationship can enable better resource allocation based on surveillance data, leading to more responsive and effective health interventions. For example, sustained investments in surveillance can yield timely information about disease outbreaks, guiding financial resources to areas of greatest need.

Finally, future research is crucial in identifying best practices and strategic approaches to overcoming barriers in healthcare financing and disease surveillance. By systematically examining successful models from various contexts and assessing the unique challenges faced within sub-Saharan Africa, researchers can significantly contribute to developing effective policies and practices.

In conclusion, healthcare financing and disease surveillance interdependence is fundamental to building resilient health systems in sub-Saharan Africa. By acknowledging their interconnected nature and addressing existing challenges through innovative solutions and research, we can pave the way for improved health outcomes and enhanced resilience against emerging health threats in the region.

Bibliography

Achieng, M.S. & Ogundaini, O.O., (2024). 'Big Data Analytics for Integrated Infectious Disease Surveillance in sub-Saharan Africa,' South African Journal of Information Management 26(1), a1668. https://doi.org/10.4102/sajim.v26i1.1668

Bennett, S., McPake, B., & Mills, A. (2018). The role of community-based health insurance in the health financing landscape of sub-Saharan Africa. Health Policy and Planning, 33(2), 234–241.

Beran, D., & Yudkin, J. (2006). Diabetes care in SSA. [The Lancet](https://www.thelancet.com/journals/lancet/article/PIIS0140-6736(06)69704-3/fulltext)

Biesma, C., Brugha, R., Harmer, A., Walsh, A., & Spicer, N. (2009). Donor funding for health system strengthening: A systematic review of the literature. Health Policy and Planning, 24(6), 417–428.

Brinkel, J., et al. (2014). Mobile health for surveillance in SSA. [MDPI](https://www.mdpi.com/1660-4601/11/11/11559)

Dieleman, J. L., et al. (2019). Global health financing: Transitioning from donor reliance. Health Policy and Planning.

Duran, A. C., Tavares, M. M., & de Souza, J. R. (2017). Financing health surveillance systems in Brazil: Challenges and perspectives. Cadernos de Saúde Pública, 33(8), e00108216.

Fasina, F.O., et al. (2021). One Health in SSA. [Elsevier](https://www.sciencedirect.com/science/article/pii/S2352771421001154)

Fawole, O.I., Bello, S., Adebowale, A.S. et al. (2023). COVID-19 surveillance in Democratic Republic of Congo, Nigeria, Senegal and Uganda: strengths, weaknesses and key Lessons. BMC Public Health 23, 835. https://doi.org/10.1186/s12889-023-15708-6

Fitzgerald, J. R., Kearney, M. H., & McCarthy, M. (2017). Digital health technologies for disease surveillance: A systematic review. Journal of Medical Internet Research, 19(1), e9.

Ifeagwu, S.C., Yang, J.C., Parkes-Ratanshi, R. et al. (2021). Health financing for universal health coverage in Sub-Saharan Africa: a systematic review. Glob Health Res policy 6, 8. https://doi.org/10.1186/s41256-021-00190-7

Kaburi, B.B., et al. (2024). Digitalization of disease surveillance in Africa. [Springer](https://link.springer.com/article/10.1186/s12889-024-19205-2)

Kariuki, S., et al. (2022). AMR surveillance in SSA. [Taylor & Francis] (https://www.tandfonline.com/doi/abs/10.2147/IDR.S342753)

Kumar, S., Bhatia, R., & Bhatnagar, T. (2016). Disease surveillance in India: Challenges and opportunities. Indian Journal of Public Health, 60(3), 197-202.

Kutzin, J. (2013). Health financing for universal coverage and health system performance: A global perspective. Health Systems & Reform, 1(1), 31–41.

Lu, C., et al. (2018). Achieving Universal Health Coverage in Rwanda: A success story. The Lancet Global Health.

Marmot, M., Friel, S., Bell, R., Houweling, T. A., & Taylor, S. (2008). Closing the gap in a generation: Health equity through action on the social determinants of health. The Lancet, 372(9650), 1661-1669.

McIntyre, D., et al. (2018). Challenges in financing universal health coverage in sub-Saharan Africa. [Oxford University Press](https://oxfordre.com/economics/display/10.1093/acrefore/9780190625979.001.0001/acrefore-9780190625979-e-28)

McNamara LA, Schafer IJ, Nolen LD, et al. Ebola Surveillance — Guinea, Liberia, and Sierra Leone. MMWR Suppl 2016;65(Suppl-3):35–43. DOI: http://dx.doi.org/10.15585/mmwr.su6503a6

Mills, A., et al. (2020). Financing equitable healthcare in sub-Saharan Africa. BMC Public Health.

Mremi, I.R., George, J., Rumisha, S.F. et al. Twenty years of integrated disease surveillance and response in Sub-Saharan Africa: challenges and opportunities for effective management of infectious disease epidemics. One Health Outlook 3, 22 (2021). https://doi.org/10.1186/s42522-021-00052-9

Mtei, G., Sanga, E., & Kiwara, A. (2014). Public financing for health in Tanzania: A systematic review. Health Policy and Planning, 29(4), 445-457.

Nkengasong, J. N., et al. (2021). COVID-19: Implications for Africa's health systems. Nature Medicine.

Novignon, J., & Nonvignon, J. (2012). Public and private health care expenditure in SSA. [Springer](https://link.springer.com/article/10.1186/2191-1991-2-22)

Nsubuga, P., et al. (2016). Integrated Disease Surveillance and Response in Africa. Emerging Infectious Diseases.

Nyaaba, G.N., et al. (2020). Integrating NCDs into routine surveillance. [Elsevier](https://www.sciencedirect.com/science/article/pii/S25

90229620300071)

O'Donnell, O., van Doorslaer, E., Wagstaff, A., & Lindelow, M. (2008). Analyzing health equity using household survey data: A guide to techniques and their implementation. World Bank Publications.

Oleribe, O. O., Momoh, J., Uzochukwu. B. S., Mbofana, F., Adebiyi, A., Barbera, T., Williams, R., & Taylor-Robinson, S. D. (2019). Identifying Key Challenges Facing Healthcare Systems In Africa And Potential Solutions. *International Journal of General Medicine*, 395–403. doi:https://doi.org/10.2147/IJGM.S223882

Otu, A. E., Ebenso, B. E., & Okwor, T. S. (2020). The state of disease surveillance in Nigeria: A systematic review. BMC Public Health, 20(1), 1–12.

Peters, D. H., Garg, A., Bloom, G., Walker, D. G., & Brieger, W. R. (2016). Poverty and access to health care in developing countries. Annals of the New York Academy of Sciences, 1136(1), 161-180.

Reid, S.E., et al. (2012). TB and HIV in SSA prisons. [OUP](https://academic.oup.com/jid/article-abstract/205/suppl_2/S265/804473)

Stehling-Ariza, T., Rosewell, A., Moiba, S.A., et al. (2016). The impact of active surveillance and health education on an Ebola virus disease cluster — Kono District, Sierra Leone, 2014–2015. BMC Infect Dis 16, 611. https://doi.org/10.1186/s12879-016-1941-0

Sullivan, R., Kearney, M. H., & McCarthy, M. (2017). Community-based surveillance of infectious diseases: A systematic review. BMC Public Health, 17(1), 1–10.

WHO. (2010). The World Health Report 2010: Health systems financing: The path to universal coverage. World Health Organization.

WHO. (2017). Surveillance and monitoring of infectious diseases: A global perspective. World Health Organization.

Witter, S., Fretheim, A., & Lindahl, A. K. (2017). Results-based financing for health: A systematic review. Health Policy and Planning, 32(1), 1-14.

Woldemariam, A., Woldemichael, K., & Wondimeneh, K. (2017). Out-of-pocket health expenditures in Ethiopia: Evidence from the Ethiopian household income, consumption, and expenditure survey. Health Policy and Planning, 32(6), 789–797.

Chapter 10: Healthcare Financing and Preventative Dental Care in sub-Saharan Africa

By Adebowale Awosika-Olumo MD., MS., MPH., PhD., FACE

Vignette: Bridging Gaps in Healthcare and Dental Care

The local market was bustling in a vibrant sub-Saharan African town. Stalls overflowed with colorful fruits, vegetables, and other local goods. Amidst the lively atmosphere, a small area was set aside for an important demonstration. A dental hygienist, dressed in a crisp uniform, stood before a group of curious onlookers, both adults and children.

The hygienist demonstrated proper toothbrushing techniques using a large model of a mouth and toothbrush. Educational posters around the area highlighted the importance of oral hygiene, preventative dental care, and the link between diet and dental health. The community members watched intently, some practicing the techniques, while others asked questions and shared their experiences.

In the background, market vendors and shoppers continued their daily routines, but many paused to listen and learn. The interaction between the health worker and the community underscored the significance of community-based programs in promoting health and well-being.

As the session concluded, the dental hygienist emphasized the importance of regular dental check-ups and maintaining a healthy diet. The community members left with new knowledge and a sense of empowerment, ready to take proactive steps toward better health.

Questions for Discussion:

1. What are the main barriers to accessing preventative dental care in sub-Saharan Africa, and how can they be addressed?
2. How does healthcare financing impact the availability and quality of dental care services in rural and urban areas?
3. How can community-based health insurance schemes be adapted to cover preventative dental care, and what must be done to ensure their sustainability?
4. How can preventative dental care be integrated into existing healthcare systems, especially in rural areas with limited resources?
5. What role can international NGOs and development organizations play in improving access to dental care, mainly through financing and resource allocation?

6. What role can community health workers play in improving oral hygiene and preventative care in their communities?
7. How can educational programs about oral health be effectively integrated into existing healthcare initiatives?
8. What are the potential benefits of using mobile clinics and telehealth services to provide dental care in remote areas?

Introduction

Healthcare financing and preventative dental care are critical components of health systems, particularly in sub-Saharan Africa, where oral health remains a significant public health challenge. Despite advancements in medical technology and increased awareness of the importance of oral health, many individuals in this region continue to face barriers to accessing preventative dental care. This chapter review explores the existing body of research on healthcare financing and preventative dental care in sub-Saharan Africa, highlighting key themes, challenges, and potential solutions.

In sub-Saharan Africa, healthcare financing is characterized by a mix of public, private, and out-of-pocket expenditures. Many countries in the region rely heavily on external funding and donor assistance, creating inconsistencies and vulnerabilities in the healthcare system. According to the World Health Organization (WHO), many sub-Saharan African nations allocate a disproportionately low percentage of their Gross Domestic Product (GDP) to healthcare, often falling short of the recommended 15% target set by the Abuja Declaration. This underfunding translates into insufficient resources for essential health services, including dental care. Consequently, oral health services are often relegated to the periphery of national health priorities, leading to a lack of trained professionals, inadequate facilities, and limited access to preventive care.

Preventative dental care is crucial for reducing the prevalence of oral diseases, such as dental caries, periodontal disease, and oral cancers. These conditions have direct health implications and significantly impact individuals' quality of life, productivity, and economic stability. In sub-Saharan Africa, the burden of oral diseases is exacerbated by factors such as poor dietary habits, lack of fluoride in drinking water, and limited access to dental services. Furthermore, cultural beliefs and stigma surrounding dental treatment often deter individuals from seeking timely care, leading to a cycle of neglect that worsens oral health issues across communities.

Integrating preventative dental care into primary healthcare systems is essential for addressing these challenges. Preventative measures, such as community education on oral hygiene, routine screenings, and fluoride treatments, can significantly reduce the incidence of oral diseases. However, the success of these initiatives is contingent on adequate healthcare financing. Countries that prioritize preventive care investment often experience improved health outcomes, reduced long-term healthcare costs, and enhanced overall productivity. In contrast, the lack of financial resources dedicated to oral health perpetuates a cycle of disease and poverty, particularly among marginalized populations.

The Importance of Preventative Dental Care

Preventative dental care encompasses a range of practices to prevent oral diseases, including regular dental check-ups, cleanings, fluoride treatments, and patient education on oral hygiene. The World Health Organization (WHO) emphasizes that preventative dental care is essential for reducing the burden of dental diseases, which can lead to pain, infection, and systemic health issues (WHO, 2020). In sub-Saharan Africa, dental caries, periodontal disease, and other oral health issues are comparatively high (Teshome et al., 2021). The oral health crisis in numerous African countries is a pressing issue that stems from its persistent marginalization within public health policies. This systemic neglect is starkly demonstrated by the inadequate financial and technical investments allocated to preventive and therapeutic dental services (WHO Africa, 2023). Such resource deficiencies foster a detrimental cycle, obstructing the effective development and implementation of essential oral health promotion strategies.

A significant indicator of this crisis is revealed in the WHO African region statistics of 2019, which states that approximately 70% of sub-Saharan African nations invested less than US$1 per person per year on oral healthcare treatment (WHO Africa, 2023). This figure not only underscores the severe limitations in financial commitment but also illustrates a substantial oversight regarding the importance of oral health in the broader healthcare spectrum. The ramifications of this minimal investment are profound, contributing to escalating rates of oral diseases, reduced quality of life for affected individuals, and rising healthcare costs as untreated oral health issues become more severe (WHO Africa, 2023).

The priorities—or lack thereof—in oral health are evident through several critical factors. Firstly, a significant shortage of trained healthcare professionals specializing in oral health severely hampers access to care. Secondly, insufficient funding directly obstructs the development of necessary infrastructure for oral health services, particularly in rural and underserved communities (WHO Africa, 2023). Additionally, the absence of comprehensive oral health policies and educational campaigns leaves vast segments of the population unaware of the importance of proper oral hygiene and the potential risks of neglecting oral health.

Governments and health organizations must implement a paradigm shift in their approach to oral health. Recognizing oral health as an integral component of overall health and well-being is vital. By elevating oral health within health policies and committing adequate resources to training, infrastructure, and public education, nations can cultivate a more equitable healthcare system. Such a shift would not only improve oral health outcomes but also enhance the overall health of the population. The importance of preventative dental care is underscored by its potential to improve overall health outcomes. These findings emphasize the need for an integrated healthcare approach that considers the impact of oral health on systemic conditions (Merza et al., 2024). Merza et al. (2024) concluded that incorporating dental screenings and preventive care as part of routine medical evaluations could allow healthcare providers to address potential systemic health risks comprehensively. Dental professionals, particularly periodontists, should be encouraged to collaborate with primary care and other medical specialists to manage systemic health conditions, especially in patients with known risk factors, such as diabetes or cardiovascular disease, which have been linked to various systemic conditions (Mills et al., 2023; Merza et al., 2024). Therefore, investing in preventative dental care can lead to significant long-term health benefits, reduced healthcare costs, and improved quality of life for individuals in sub-Saharan Africa.

Challenges in Accessing Preventative Dental Care

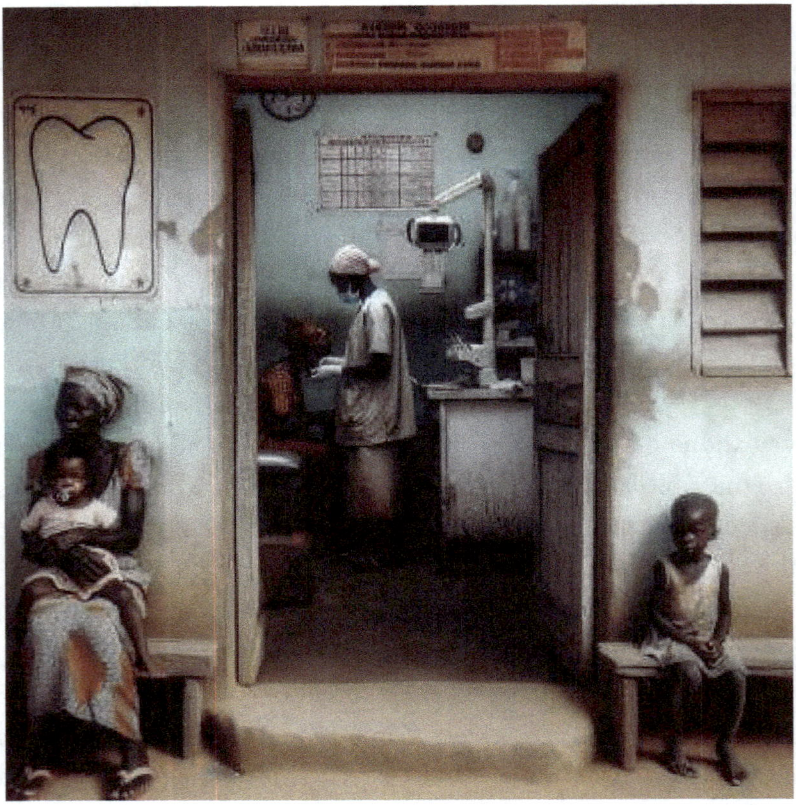

Economic Barriers

Economic barriers represent a formidable challenge to the accessibility of preventative dental care in sub-Saharan Africa. Many people, particularly in low-income communities, lack the financial means to procure necessary dental services.

According to the World Health Organization (WHO, 2020), the burden of out-of-pocket expenses associated with dental care is a formidable deterrent, dissuading individuals from seeking timely treatment. This economic strain often results in a tragic reliance on emergency care rather than a proactive approach emphasizing preventative measures. The widespread poverty in the region exacerbates this issue, with approximately 40% of individuals living on less than $1.90 per day, as reported by the World Bank (2021). Such financial constraints significantly limit the capacity of individuals and families to invest in their oral health, thereby perpetuating a cycle of neglect and crisis-oriented care.

Moreover, existing research elucidates that healthcare financing models in sub-Saharan Africa systematically prioritize curative services over preventative care. This predilection compounds the challenges faced by individuals seeking preventative dental care and reflects a misalignment of healthcare investment strategies.

Chough et al. (2020) articulate that regional health systems allocate limited resources to oral health initiatives, resulting in inadequate access to preventative services. This systemic neglect of preventative dental care intensifies disparities in oral health outcomes and imposes a greater long-term financial burden on healthcare systems.

In summary, the confluence of economic barriers, high poverty rates, and a healthcare financing model that favors curative care creates a multi-faceted challenge in providing adequate preventative dental services in sub-Saharan Africa. Addressing these issues is crucial to reducing oral health disparities and promoting a more sustainable healthcare model that values preventative care as an essential component of overall health and well-being.

Cultural and Educational Barriers

Cultural perceptions significantly influence the utilization of preventative dental care in sub-Saharan Africa, shaping individual and community behaviors regarding oral health. Traditional beliefs may contradict established modern dental practices in many of these communities. For instance, a study conducted by Lawal et al. (2015) highlights a prevalent belief among some individuals in Nigeria that dental problems are attributed to supernatural forces rather than being understood as preventable health conditions.

This perspective not only shapes personal attitudes toward dental health but also engenders a hesitance in seeking professional dental care, ultimately leading to untreated oral diseases. Moreover, the systemic issue of limited education and awareness about the importance of oral health further exacerbates the situation.

Research by Kassebaum et al. (2017) underscores that many sub-Saharan African countries suffer from a lack of educational resources and health literacy. This inadequacy significantly hinders individuals' comprehension of essential oral health practices and prevention strategies. The resulting knowledge gap directly influences individual behaviors, reinforcing cycles of poor oral health within these communities.

In summary, cultural beliefs and insufficient educational outreach create formidable barriers to effectively utilizing preventative dental care in sub-Saharan Africa. Addressing these challenges requires a multi-faceted approach that promotes modern dental practices while respecting and considering traditional beliefs. Enhancing health education and literacy will be crucial in bridging these gaps, ultimately fostering improved oral health outcomes across the region.

Infrastructure and Workforce Challenges

The healthcare infrastructure in sub-Saharan Africa is fraught with challenges that significantly hinder the provision of effective preventative dental care. A pervasive shortage of dental professionals is evident across many countries in the region, creating a pronounced disparity in access to care between urban and rural populations. For instance, research by Nair et al. (2020) highlights a concerning situation in rural Malawi, where entire communities lack access to trained dental personnel. This glaring insufficiency forces residents to undertake long and often burdensome journeys to obtain essential dental services, which can undermine their motivation to pursue preventative care altogether.

The inadequacies of the existing healthcare infrastructure further exacerbate these challenges. Many healthcare facilities in sub-Saharan Africa are equipped neither with the essential tools nor the necessary supplies to deliver comprehensive oral health services. As noted by the World Health Organization (WHO Africa, 2023), these deficiencies severely limit the capabilities of these facilities to implement adequate preventative dental care protocols. Moreover, the WHO (2020) has strongly advocated for strengthening regional healthcare systems. This recommendation emphasizes ensuring that preventative dental care is accessible to all populations.

Addressing systemic deficiencies—such as the scarcity of trained professionals, inadequate infrastructure, and lack of essential resources—will be crucial for advancing oral health in sub-Saharan Africa. Therefore, it is not merely advisable but essential for stakeholders at all levels to take decisive action to enhance dental care delivery and foster a more robust preventative care framework in the region.

Healthcare Financing Models

Healthcare financing in sub-Saharan Africa (SSA) presents unique challenges and opportunities, particularly in oral health. The current financing landscape is marked by a dual system of public and private funding, where government budgets aim to provide essential healthcare services but often fall short of meeting the comprehensive needs of the population. This shortfall is especially notable in oral healthcare, where public financing is frequently minimal, leading many individuals to rely heavily on private funding, including out-of-pocket payments. This reliance on private financing exacerbates existing inequities in access to preventive dental care, particularly for low-income individuals who may be unable to afford necessary treatments.

As highlighted by the World Health Organization (WHO Africa, 2023), these inequities are intensified by the varying levels of resources, equipment, and infrastructure across different regions, which can hinder effective service delivery. SSA's oral healthcare challenges differ significantly from those in developed countries, necessitating tailored solutions that address local contexts and needs. England et al. (2021) noted that volunteer organizations working in this space often face obstacles due to resource limitations, making it challenging to implement effective programs.

Innovative financing strategies are essential to bridge the gap in oral health services. The research by Ifeagwu et al. (2023) underscores the necessity for creative health financing mechanisms that can enhance financial risk protection and support sustainable health services. Strategies that integrate various funding sources—such as microfinance combined with health education—have shown promise in improving health outcomes, as evidenced by Lorenzetti et al. (2017). However, the authors emphasize the need for prolonged intervention periods to adequately assess impacts on health status and access to care.

Overall, for sub-Saharan Africa to advance toward universal health coverage, particularly in oral healthcare, it is critical to develop and implement appropriate health financing strategies that improve access, equity, and sustainability of health services in the long term.

Innovative Financing Solutions

Innovative financing solutions have emerged as crucial strategies for enhancing access to preventative dental care in sub-Saharan Africa. Among these solutions, Community-Based Health Insurance (CBHI) stands out as a contextually appropriate risk-pooling mechanism designed to offer financial protection to populations lacking access to formal health insurance (Artignan & Bellanger, 2021). This model seeks to address the unique health financing challenges faced by communities in this region, paving the way for improved health outcomes.

A systematic review of the barriers to CBHI uptake highlights several significant challenges that hinder enrollment and membership renewal in sub-Saharan African countries. These findings are pivotal, providing policymakers with evidence-based insights critical for informed decision-making (Shewamene et al., 2021). The identified barriers include a lack of awareness regarding the importance of health insurance, various socio-economic factors, deeply rooted health beliefs, and a notable lack of trust in the management of these schemes. Additionally, the quality of available health services and the perceived health status of individuals further complicate the uptake of CBHI. Limited entitlements to health benefits also pose significant obstacles, ultimately impeding access to essential services (Shewamene et al., 2021).

Alongside CBHI, microfinance initiatives have garnered attention as a promising approach to expanding access to healthcare services, including dental care. By providing small loans to individuals and communities, these programs have the potential to empower individuals to invest in their oral health proactively and seek preventative care. Integrating microfinance mechanisms into healthcare financing represents a significant shift in addressing the economic barriers faced by many individuals in sub-Saharan Africa.

Together, these innovative financing solutions underscore the urgent need to tackle economic obstacles that hinder access to preventative dental care in sub-Saharan Africa. By leveraging the strengths of CBHI and microfinance initiatives, stakeholders can create a more inclusive health system that supports better health outcomes for vulnerable populations. Addressing these barriers is not merely a financial challenge; it is a critical step toward advancing public health and ensuring that all individuals **can** achieve optimal oral health. Therefore, continued investment in and exploration of these financing solutions will be essential for fostering sustainable improvements in dental care access across the region.

Policy Implications and Recommendations

Strengthening healthcare systems in sub-Saharan Africa is imperative for enhancing access to preventative dental care. This approach necessitates a multi-faceted strategy, including increased public financing for oral health services and integrating preventative care within primary healthcare programs. The World Health Organization (2020) underscores the importance of prioritizing oral health as a vital component of comprehensive health systems. This prioritization calls for substantial investments in dental services and the ongoing training of the workforce to better equip health professionals in addressing oral health needs.

In this context, community engagement and education are pivotal in fostering a culture of preventative dental care. Effective public health campaigns that promote awareness about oral hygiene and the significance of regular dental check-ups are essential. These initiatives can effectively shift cultural perceptions regarding oral health, encouraging individuals to seek necessary care. By educating communities, we empower them with the knowledge needed to make informed decisions about their health, leading to a decrease in dental diseases and, consequently, a healthier population.

Moreover, intertwining oral health education with community practices cultivates a proactive approach to health rather than a reactive one. Engaging community leaders and employing culturally sensitive methods in educational campaigns can enhance participation and the overall effectiveness of these initiatives.

Ultimately, a strengthened healthcare system, supported by community engagement and education, is crucial for advancing preventative dental care in sub-Saharan Africa and achieving sustainable health outcomes.

Expanding Access to Dental Workforce

Addressing the critical shortage of dental professionals in sub-Saharan Africa is essential for enhancing the region's access to preventative dental care. The lack of dental practitioners significantly hampers many communities' ability to receive adequate dental services, which can lead to preventable dental diseases and poor overall health outcomes.

Therefore, targeted training programs must be developed specifically for dental professionals, focusing on underserved rural areas. These programs should aim to increase the number of qualified dental professionals and ensure they are well equipped to address the unique challenges of these communities. This includes understanding local health issues, cultural sensitivities, and the importance of preventative care. By equipping dental professionals with the necessary skills and knowledge, these programs will empower them to provide adequate and relevant services to populations that traditionally lack access to dental care.

In addition to training, implementing initiatives that incentivize dental professionals to work in underserved rural communities is a crucial strategy for bridging the gap in access to care. Financial incentives such as student loan forgiveness, competitive salaries, and housing support can motivate dental graduates to consider careers in areas that are often neglected due to economic or lifestyle factors. Furthermore, creating a supportive work environment that fosters professional growth and community involvement can enhance job satisfaction and retention among dental professionals.

Collectively, these strategies represent a proactive approach to rectifying disparities in dental care access in sub-Saharan Africa. By addressing both the training and retention of dental professionals, the availability of preventative dental care can be significantly improved, positively impacting the health outcomes of historically underserved populations.

Evidence suggests that with a concerted effort, it is possible to create a sustainable dental workforce that meets the needs of these communities (Nair et al., 2020). Consequently, policymakers, educational institutions, and healthcare organizations must collaborate and invest in these initiatives to yield long-term improvements in dental health across the region.

Conclusion

In sub-Saharan Africa, the landscape of healthcare financing and preventive dental care is fraught with uncertainties and challenges that necessitate immediate and robust intervention. Economic barriers, cultural perceptions, and infrastructural deficiencies significantly hamper access to essential dental services.

These factors not only restrict the availability of dental care but also perpetuate cycles of poor oral health, which can have far-reaching implications for overall health and well-being in the population.

Economic barriers fundamentally limit access to dental care in this region. Many individuals and families face significant financial obstacles that prevent them from seeking necessary treatment. The out-of-pocket expenses associated with dental care often exceed the financial capabilities of low-income households, leading to delays in seeking treatment and, ultimately, exacerbating dental health issues. Additionally, the scarcity of insurance coverage for dental services further compounds these challenges. As a result, the lack of financial resources effectively precludes a large segment of the population from receiving essential preventive dental care.

Cultural perceptions also influence how citizens in sub-Saharan Africa approach oral health. A significant lack of awareness exists regarding the importance of oral hygiene, preventive dental practices, and the implications of poor oral health. In many communities, dental issues are often viewed as minor inconveniences rather than serious health concerns that warrant professional intervention. These perceptions can hinder individuals from utilizing available services, further entrenching a cycle of neglect and inadequate oral health.

Infrastructure limitations are another critical factor that hinders access to preventive dental care. Many areas in sub-Saharan Africa lack the necessary healthcare facilities, skilled dental professionals, and basic dental supplies. Rural regions, in particular, may be underserved, prompting individuals to travel long distances to access dental care. This geographical disparity in dental service availability leads to significant inequities in health outcomes across different populations within the region.

Despite these challenges, promising pathways to improve access to preventive dental care are emerging. Innovative financing solutions, such as community-based insurance schemes and public-private partnerships, can potentially alleviate some of the current financial barriers. By pooling resources at the community level, these initiatives can reduce individual costs and enhance the affordability of dental services.

Moreover, engaging communities in health education and awareness campaigns can shift cultural perceptions, underscore the importance of preventive care, and promote proactive dental health practices. Strengthening healthcare systems is also paramount. This can be achieved through enhanced training programs for dental professionals, improved infrastructure, and the establishment of more accessible dental facilities. By prioritizing oral health within the broader healthcare agenda, policymakers can address immediate access issues and ensure that oral health is integrated into comprehensive health strategies.

This multi-faceted approach is essential for improving health outcomes, as the link between oral health and overall health has been well-documented. Addressing the challenges of healthcare financing and preventive dental care in sub-Saharan Africa is both a moral imperative and a critical strategic goal for enhancing public health. By implementing innovative financing solutions, fostering community engagement, and reinforcing healthcare systems, policymakers can significantly improve access to essential dental services. Ultimately, a concerted effort to prioritize oral health within the broader healthcare agenda will yield substantial benefits, enhancing the quality of life and health outcomes for individuals across sub-Saharan Africa.

Bibliography

Artignan, J., Bellanger, M (2021) Does community-based health insurance improve access to care in sub-Saharan Africa? A rapid review, Health Policy and Planning, Volume 36, Issue 4, Pages 572–584, https://doi.org/10.1093/heapol/czaa174

Chough SH (2020) A study on the status of dental and oral health in Malawi and its implication in achieving global health goals. Journal of Dental Research and Practice. doi: 10.15761/JDRP.1000127

Chou, R., Pappas, M., Dana, T., Selph, S., Hart, E., Fu, R. F., & Schwarz, E. (2021). Screening and Interventions to Prevent Dental Caries in Children Younger Than 5 Years: Updated Evidence Report and Systematic Review for the US Preventive Services Task Force. JAMA, 326(21), 2179–2192. https://doi.org/10.1001/jama.2021.15658

England, R., Paterson, A., & Jones, A. (2021). Delivering urgent oral healthcare in Sub-Saharan Africa: supporting sustainable local development. Primary Dental Journal, 10(3), 69–74. https://doi.org/10.1177/20501684211029420

Ifeagwu, S. C., Yang, J. C., Parkes-Ratanshi, R., & Brayne, C. (2021). Health financing for universal health coverage in Sub-Saharan Africa: a systematic review. Global health research and policy, 6(1), 8. https://doi.org/10.1186/s41256-021-00190-7

Kassebaum, N. J., Smith, A. G. C., Bernabé, E., Fleming, T. D., Reynolds, A. E., Vos, T., Murray, C. J. L., Marcenes, W., & GBD 2015 Oral Health Collaborators (2017). Global, Regional, and National Prevalence, Incidence, and Disability-Adjusted Life Years for Oral Conditions for 195 Countries, 1990-2015: A Systematic Analysis for the Global Burden of Diseases, Injuries, and Risk Factors. Journal of dental research, 96(4), 380–387.

https://doi.org/10.1177/0022034517693566.

Kumar, S., et al. (2018). Oral health and systemic diseases: A review of the literature. The Journal of Clinical Dentistry, 29(1), 1-8.

Lawal, F. B., Taiwo, J. O., & Oke, G. A. (2015). Factors influencing awareness and attendance of traditional oral health care practices by residents of a peri-urban community in Ibadan, Nigeria. African health sciences, 15(1), 233–239. https://doi.org/10.4314/ahs.v15i1.30

Lorenzetti, L. M. J., Leatherman, S., & Flax, V. L. (2017). Evaluating the effect of integrated microfinance and health interventions: an updated review of the evidence. Health policy and planning, 32(5), 732–756. https://doi.org/10.1093/heapol/czw170

Mills, A., Berlin-Broner, Y., & Levin, L. (2023). Improving Patient Well-Being as a Broader Perspective in Dentistry. International dental journal, 73(6), 785–792. https://doi.org/10.1016/j.identj.2023.05.005

Merza, R. fouad ., Alqahtani, N. S. ., Al-sulami, S. B. B. ., sindi, J. abid ., kabli, R. sadiq yousif ., alluqmani , S. hamoud ., Aljohani, R. B. ., Saleh, M. A. ., Hawsawi, S. M. A. ., Aljahdali , B. A. S. ., & Alata, A. J. A. . (2024). Oral Health and Systemic Disease: A Systematic Review of the Impact of Dental Care on Overall Health. Journal of Ecohumanism, 3(7), 2843–2852. https://doi.org/10.62754/joe.v3i7.4679

Nair, S. A., et al. (2020). Dental workforce in sub-Saharan Africa: A review of the literature. International Dental Journal, 70(2), 113-120.

Peres, M. A., Macpherson, L. M. D., Weyant, R. J., Daly, B.,

Venturelli, R., Mathur, M. R., Listl, S., Celeste, R. K., Guarnizo-Herreño, C. C., Kearns, C., Benzian, H., Allison, P., & Watt, R. G. (2019). Oral diseases: a global public health challenge. Lancet (London, England), 394(10194), 249–260. https://doi.org/10.1016/S0140-6736(19)31146-8

Shewamene, Z., Tiruneh, G., Abraha, A., Reshad, A., Terefe, M. M., Shimels, T., Lemlemu, E., Tilahun, D., Wondimtekahu, A., Argaw, M., Anno, A., Abebe, F., & Kiros, M. (2021). Barriers to uptake of community-based health insurance in sub-Saharan Africa: a systematic review. Health policy and planning, 36(10), 1705–1714. https://doi.org/10.1093/heapol/czab080

Teshome, A., Muche, A., & Girma, B. (2021). Prevalence of Dental Caries and Associated Factors in East Africa, 2000–2020: Systematic Review and Meta-Analysis. Frontiers in Public Health, 9, 645091. https://doi.org/10.3389/fpubh.2021.645091

World Bank. (2021). Poverty and equity data. Retrieved from https://www.worldbank.org/en/topic/poverty/overview

World Health Organization. (2020). Oral health. Retrieved from https://www.who.int/health-topics/oral-health

World Health Organization African Region (2023). Africa burdened with largest global increase of oral diseases. Retrieved from https://www.afro.who.int/news/africa-burdened-largest-global-increase-oral-diseases

Chapter 11: Healthcare financing and participation in clinical trials in Sub-Saharan Africa (SSA) Sayo Awosika-Olumo MD., MPH., PhD and Debo Awosika-Olumo MD., MS., MPH, PhD., FACE

Amara, a 34-year-old teacher in a rural community in sub-Saharan Africa, is diagnosed with an aggressive form of breast cancer. Her doctor informs her about a clinical trial in a nearby city, offering cutting-edge treatment that could save her life. The trial is funded by an international pharmaceutical company and facilitated by a local research institution. Participation in the trial would grant Amara free access to medication and regular medical check-ups, but she would need to cover her transportation and accommodation costs.

High healthcare expenses already burden Amara and her family due to her initial diagnosis. Despite her willingness to participate in the trial, she struggles to afford the logistical costs. Furthermore, she is uncertain about the ethical safeguards in place, given past concerns about exploitation in clinical trials across sub-Saharan Africa. Local community leaders encourage participation, seeing the trial as an opportunity to improve healthcare in the region, but many residents share Amara's apprehensions regarding the fairness of the financial arrangements.

This situation highlights the dual challenges of healthcare financing and equitable participation in clinical trials in sub-Saharan Africa. While clinical trials offer a vital avenue for accessing advanced treatments and improving regional healthcare infrastructure, financial barriers and mistrust often hinder participation. Addressing these issues requires innovative strategies that balance ethical research practices, community involvement, and sustainable financing models.

Questions

1. What strategies can be implemented to reduce financial barriers, such as transportation and accommodation costs, for participants in clinical trials in SSA?
2. How can research institutions and funding organizations ensure ethical practices in clinical trials, particularly in communities with a history of mistrust toward foreign-funded research?
3. What role can governments, private sectors, and international donors play in creating sustainable healthcare financing systems to support individuals like Amara?
4. How can researchers effectively engage and educate local communities about the benefits and risks of clinical trial participation to foster trust and informed decision-making?
5. What policies can be established to ensure that clinical trials in SSA contribute to long-term healthcare improvements for the region beyond the immediate benefits for participants?

Introduction

Sub-Saharan Africa (SSA) presents a complex landscape for healthcare financing and participation in clinical trials, influenced by myriad factors exacerbating health disparities. Healthcare financing and participation in clinical trials are critical components of the health systems in sub-Saharan Africa (Karamagi et al., 2023). However, the region faces unique challenges, including limited financial resources, inadequate infrastructure, and socio-economic disparities that significantly impact health outcomes and research participation.

This chapter aims to synthesize existing research on healthcare financing mechanisms and their influence on participation in clinical trials in SSA, highlighting gaps in the literature and suggesting areas for future research. Healthcare financing in SSA is characterized by a blend of public, private, and donor funding mechanisms. However, the reliance on out-of-pocket expenses remains alarmingly high, often leaving the most vulnerable populations without adequate healthcare services. Many SSA countries operate under constrained health budgets due to limited national revenues, forcing governments to prioritize spending in an environment where infectious diseases, maternal and child health, and rising non-communicable diseases need urgent attention (Knittel et al., 2023).

Initiating and implementing human experimental trials in SSA can be challenging. However, solutions exist, and successful execution requires careful planning, ongoing evaluation, responsiveness to new developments, and strict oversight of trial operations (Toto et al., 2020).

Despite financial challenges, several innovative financing mechanisms have emerged, including community-based health insurance schemes and public-private partnerships aimed at improving healthcare delivery. However, research indicates that these mechanisms often struggle with sustainability and scalability. Many low-income populations remain excluded from these initiatives, raising concerns about equity in access and the overall effectiveness of these financing strategies.

Healthcare Financing in Sub-Saharan Africa

Overview of Healthcare Financing Mechanisms

Healthcare financing in Sub-Saharan Africa (SSA) is a multi-faceted issue that involves various mechanisms. These mechanisms include government funding, out-of-pocket payments, private insurance, and donor funding. Each financing source plays a crucial role in shaping the accessibility and quality of healthcare services within the region. However, the overarching challenge remains: the high reliance on out-of-pocket payments, which has become the predominant model in many SSA nations.

As the World Health Organization (WHO, 2010) highlighted, this heavy dependence on out-of-pocket expenditures can lead to severe financial hardship for individuals and families. When healthcare costs are primarily borne by patients at the point of service, it creates a substantial barrier to accessing necessary medical care. The consequences of such a financing model are particularly severe for vulnerable populations, including low-income individuals, the elderly, and those with chronic health conditions. These groups often find themselves in a precarious situation, where the inability to afford healthcare can lead to deferred treatments, worsening health conditions, or even catastrophic health expenditures that plunge them into poverty.

Moreover, reliance on out-of-pocket payments exacerbates existing health inequities in SSA. Wagstaff (2002) and WHO (2024) noted that these inequities are starkly pronounced, disproportionately affecting marginalized communities that already face restrictions due to socio-economic, geographic, or cultural barriers. For instance, rural populations often need to travel long distances to access healthcare facilities. If significant fees are involved, they are more likely to forgo care, worsening health disparities between wealthier urban populations and poorer rural communities. This dynamic perpetuates a vicious cycle of inequality.

Private insurance offers some potential for alleviating these issues, but its penetration in SSA remains limited. This is often due to low income levels, a lack of public awareness about insurance options, and insufficient regulatory frameworks to facilitate the growth of a robust private insurance industry (WHO, 2024). Additionally, while donor funding provides much-needed resources, it is often tied to specific programs or initiatives, creating a fragmented healthcare financing landscape that fails to address systemic deficiencies.

In summary, the healthcare financing structure in sub-Saharan Africa is complex and presents significant challenges that must be addressed to improve health outcomes. Reliance on out-of-pocket payments imposes financial burdens and perpetuates health inequities. To create a more equitable and accessible healthcare system, policymakers must explore integrated financing strategies that balance government funding, private insurance, and sustainable donor contributions while ensuring that vulnerable populations can access healthcare without experiencing financial hardship.

Government Funding and Health Systems

Government funding is pivotal in financing healthcare systems across Sub-Saharan Africa (SSA). Despite its significance, many national governments in the region allocate a disproportionately small percentage of their Gross Domestic Product (GDP) to healthcare. This underinvestment often falls far short of the Abuja Declaration target of 15%, which was established to ensure that African nations prioritize healthcare funding as a critical component of national development (Azevedo, 2017).

The implications of such underfunding are manifold and profound, particularly regarding the availability and quality of healthcare services delivered to the population. The consequences of inadequate government funding manifest directly in various facets of the healthcare system. A notable study by Knittel et al. (2023) illuminates the correlation between insufficient funding and poor health outcomes among populations in SSA. Specifically, the findings indicate that under-resourced healthcare systems struggle to provide essential services, leading to increased morbidity and mortality rates.

Moreover, inadequate funding compromises the quality of healthcare delivery and limits opportunities for innovation within the sector. The study emphasizes the lack of participation in health-related research, including clinical trials, as a significant concern. Without substantial investment in health research, the potential for advancing medical science and improving public health outcomes is severely curtailed.

The underfunding of healthcare systems in SSA is not merely an administrative oversight; it represents a profound systemic issue affecting millions of individuals and communities. The failure to meet the Abuja Declaration target for health funding underscores a broader pattern of neglect regarding public health priorities in the region. Addressing this issue requires a concerted effort from both national governments and international partners to reassess budgetary allocations and recognize that healthcare investment is not merely an expenditure but a fundamental commitment to national well-being and future prosperity.

In conclusion, the evidence is clear: the extent of government funding dedicated to healthcare in SSA is critically inadequate, with alarming consequences for health outcomes and research advancement. There is an urgent need for increased financial commitment to health systems, which would not only improve accessibility and quality of care but also foster an environment conducive to research and innovation. The path forward demands bold policy decisions and a prioritization of healthcare funding to meet the pressing needs of the population effectively.

Donor Funding and Its Impact

The role of donor funding in healthcare financing within Sub-Saharan Africa (SSA) is a pivotal element that warrants thorough examination. As highlighted by Buse and Waxman (2001), such funding is particularly critical for specific disease programs, including HIV/AIDS, tuberculosis, and malaria. These targeted financial contributions have undeniably led to marked improvements in health outcomes, enabling countries to tackle these devastating diseases more effectively. However, critically assessing the broader implications of this funding model is essential.

One significant concern is that reliance on donor funding can cultivate dependency, ultimately undermining the sustainability of local health systems. Knittel et al. (2023) noted that this dependency can stifle the development of self-sustaining healthcare infrastructures. When health systems become overly reliant on external funding sources, they may lack the necessary resources and incentives to develop their own capacities and resilience. This dynamic can hinder long-term investments in local health initiatives, which are crucial for ensuring comprehensive care and responsiveness to evolving health challenges.

Moreover, focusing on specific disease programs may inadvertently divert attention and resources away from strengthening the broader health system, which is essential for fostering an environment conducive to clinical research and overall health improvement (Edem et al., 2021). Prioritizing certain diseases over others can lead to an imbalanced allocation of resources, resulting in a neglect of comprehensive healthcare challenges that extend beyond isolated programs. A holistic approach that integrates various health concerns is imperative for health systems to thrive and adapt to the multi-faceted nature of public health issues.

In summary, while donor funding has played a crucial role in addressing critical disease burdens in SSA, it is essential to recognize and address the dependency it may create and the potential implications for local health system sustainability. A balanced approach—targeting specific diseases while simultaneously strengthening the broader health infrastructure—will be necessary to ensure long-term health improvements and readiness for future challenges.

Private Health Insurance

The role of private health insurance in Sub-Saharan Africa (SSA) is notably limited, leading to significant coverage gaps for most of the population (Barasa et al., 2021). According to Mills (2014), a substantial portion of this region remains uninsured, which has profound implications for healthcare accessibility and equity. While private health insurance possesses the potential to inject additional resources into healthcare financing, its benefits are predominantly realized by urban populations and higher-income individuals. This dynamic perpetuates a cycle of inequity, as those who are uninsured or underinsured—often residing in rural areas or belonging to lower socio-economic strata—are systematically marginalized from essential health services.

One critical area affected by this inequitable landscape is access to clinical trials. Schmidt et al. (2016) argue that individuals without insurance may face significant financial barriers that discourage their participation in such studies. This limits their access to potentially beneficial treatments and narrows the diversity of trial participants, ultimately hindering the generalizability and applicability of research findings.

In their review of universal health insurance, Ly et al. (2022) concluded that public health insurance is more effective in contributing to universal health coverage (UHC) goals than community-based health insurance (CBHI), as it ensures better management and promotes the pooling of resources on a larger scale. The exclusion of uninsured populations from clinical research further exacerbates health disparities, as it stifles advancements in medical knowledge that could benefit a broader spectrum of society.

In summary, the limited reach of private health insurance in SSA creates pronounced inequities in healthcare access, particularly affecting participation in clinical trials. Addressing these disparities is crucial for fostering an inclusive health system that ensures equitable access to healthcare resources for all individuals, regardless of socio-economic status. Policymakers and stakeholders must prioritize initiatives to expand insurance coverage and facilitate broader participation in health research to mitigate these inequities and advance health outcomes across the region.

Participation in Clinical Trials in Sub-Saharan Africa

Importance of Clinical Trials

Clinical trials are fundamental to the progress of medical science and the enhancement of health outcomes. They serve as a crucial mechanism for gathering data regarding the efficacy and safety of new medical interventions, which is especially important in regions characterized by diverse populations and distinct disease burdens, as Nyirenda et al. (2021) highlighted. These trials contribute to our understanding of treatment efficacy and play a pivotal role in identifying potential adverse effects that can vary significantly across demographic groups.

Despite the critical importance of clinical trials, participation rates in Sub-Saharan Africa (SSA) remain disappointingly low (Dietrich et al., 2023). This limitation raises significant concerns regarding the generalizability of research findings to broader populations, particularly in a region home to many ethnicities and epidemiological profiles (Dietrich et al., 2023). The underrepresentation of SSA populations in clinical trials can result in a lack of applicable data for these communities, potentially leading to less effective and even harmful medical interventions that do not adequately account for regional health trends or genetic variances (Toto et al., 2020).

The ethical implications of such underrepresentation cannot be overstated. It poses a morally and scientifically untenable situation where the health interests of diverse populations are overlooked and jeopardized. Furthermore, underrepresenting SSA populations in clinical research contributes to a cycle of health inequity. When clinical trials do not include a representative population sample, the resulting data may inadvertently affirm biases in existing medical treatments and guidelines, further marginalizing already vulnerable communities.

Researchers and healthcare practitioners must prioritize equitable access to clinical trials while ensuring that the design and implementation of these studies are sensitive to the cultural and contextual realities of the populations being studied. While clinical trials are an indispensable element of advancing medical knowledge, the current limitations in participation from SSA populations present a significant barrier to achieving comprehensive and inclusive medical research (Toto et al., 2020). Addressing this gap is not only ethically imperative but is essential for generating valid data that can improve health outcomes for all populations, particularly those historically marginalized within the global health landscape. As such, stakeholders in the medical and research fields must actively work to mitigate these barriers and enhance participation in clinical trials across diverse communities.

Barriers to Participation

Several persistent barriers critically hinder clinical trial participation in Sub-Saharan Africa (SSA). Financial constraints represent a primary obstacle for many potential participants, as the costs associated with transportation, lost wages, and other related expenses can be prohibitive (Edem et al., 2021). Additionally, socio-cultural factors play a significant role, particularly the widespread mistrust of healthcare systems and a general lack of awareness regarding the nature and benefits of clinical trials (Dietrich et al., 2023; Diallo et al., 2021).

A study by Dietrich et al. (2023) underscores the importance of community engagement and education in overcoming these challenges and fostering higher participation rates. This evidence emphasizes that actively involving communities and providing educational initiatives are essential strategies for dismantling the barriers that deter individuals from participating in clinical research.

Clinical trials are essential for advancing medical science and improving health outcomes. They are vital for collecting data on the efficacy and safety of new medical interventions, which is especially crucial in regions marked by diverse populations and distinct disease burdens, as Nyirenda et al. (2021) observed. These trials enhance our understanding of treatment effectiveness and are key to pinpointing potential adverse effects that may vary significantly across different demographic groups. Despite their importance, participation rates in SSA remain unacceptably low (Dietrich et al., 2023). This trend raises significant concerns about the generalizability of research findings to broader populations.

The underrepresentation of SSA populations in clinical trials translates into a critical gap in applicable data for these communities. Consequently, interventions may be less effective or even harmful, failing to account for regional health trends and genetic variances. The ethical implications of this underrepresentation are profound. It creates a morally and scientifically indefensible situation where the health interests of diverse populations are marginalized and jeopardized.

More importantly, this underrepresentation perpetuates a cycle of health inequity. When clinical trials exclude representative populations, the resulting data may inadvertently reinforce biases in medical treatments and guidelines, further isolating vulnerable communities. To address these pressing concerns, researchers and healthcare practitioners must prioritize equitable access to clinical trials and ensure that the design and implementation of these studies are attuned to the cultural and contextual realities of the populations involved.

While clinical trials are indispensable for advancing medical knowledge, the existing limitations in participation from SSA populations represent a significant barrier to achieving comprehensive and inclusive medical research. Addressing this gap is not merely an ethical obligation; it is essential for generating valid data that can enhance health outcomes for all populations, particularly those historically marginalized within the global health landscape. Therefore, stakeholders in the medical and research fields must actively pursue strategies to mitigate these barriers and promote increased participation in clinical trials across diverse communities.

Ethical Considerations

The ethical considerations associated with clinical trials are paramount, particularly in low-resource settings such as Sub-Saharan Africa (SSA). The inherent vulnerabilities of specific populations in these regions necessitate rigorous ethical scrutiny to mitigate the potential exploitation of participants. Concerns surrounding informed consent and the equitable distribution of benefits from these trials are significant. The literature indicates that researchers often operate within complex ethical frameworks that demand a deep understanding of local contexts to ensure that participation is voluntary and informed (Joag et al., 2019; Garner et al., 2014).

The barriers to clinical trial participation in SSA are substantial and multi-faceted. Financial constraints emerge as a primary obstacle, with potential participants frequently unable to absorb the costs associated with transportation, lost wages, and other participation-related expenses (Edem et al., 2021). Furthermore, socio-cultural factors significantly complicate recruitment efforts. Mistrust of healthcare systems and a lack of awareness regarding the nature and potential benefits of clinical trials are pervasive issues that researchers must contend with (Dietrich et al., 2023; Diallo et al., 2021).

Recent investigations underscore the importance of community engagement and educational initiatives as effective strategies for overcoming these barriers and facilitating higher participation rates in clinical trials (Dietrich et al., 2023). Actively involving communities and elucidating the trials' processes and advantages are essential for dismantling the obstacles that deter individuals from engaging in clinical research.

Clinical trials are indispensable in advancing medical science and enhancing health outcomes, particularly in regions with diverse populations and unique disease burdens. Such research is critical for collecting vital data on the efficacy and safety of new medical interventions. This is especially important in SSA, where demographic diversity and distinct health challenges necessitate tailored solutions (Nyirenda et al., 2021).

Despite clinical trials' crucial role, participation rates among these populations remain alarmingly low, raising significant concerns about the generalizability of research findings and the applicability of interventions. The underrepresentation of SSA populations in clinical trials results in a troubling gap in relevant data, creating a morally and scientifically indefensible scenario. It marginalizes the health interests of these communities and perpetuates a cycle of health inequity.

The absence of representative populations in clinical trials undermines the validity of research outcomes and inadvertently reinforces biases in medical treatments and guidelines, further isolating vulnerable communities. To rectify this pressing issue, stakeholders within the medical and research fields must prioritize equitable access to clinical trials. The design and implementation of these studies must be attuned to the cultural and contextual realities of the populations involved.

Addressing these gaps is not merely an ethical imperative; it is essential for generating robust data that can substantially enhance health outcomes for all, particularly those historically marginalized in the global health landscape. In conclusion, it is essential that researchers and healthcare practitioners actively pursue and implement strategies to mitigate barriers to participation in clinical trials across diverse communities. Ensuring that inclusive and representative clinical research can foster a more equitable health environment that benefits all populations. This approach is not only vital for ethical research practices but is also crucial for the advancement of medical knowledge and the effective treatment of diverse health issues.

The Interplay Between Healthcare Financing and Clinical Trial Participation

Financial Incentives and Participation

The discussion surrounding financial incentives in clinical trial participation warrants thorough examination, as research has consistently shown that such incentives can significantly affect recruitment, particularly within economically disadvantaged populations. Compensation for participant time and travel expenses has been identified as a crucial strategy that may enhance recruitment efforts, especially among low-income groups (Schmidt et al., 2016). However, the ethical ramifications of introducing these incentives must be meticulously evaluated to prevent coercion and ensure voluntary participation (Joag et al., 2019). The ethical landscape concerning clinical trials is particularly complex in low-resource settings, such as Sub-Saharan Africa (SSA). Populations in these regions often exhibit inherent vulnerabilities, necessitating elevated ethical scrutiny to alleviate the potential exploitation of participants. Informed consent, a cornerstone of ethical research, must be safeguarded to ensure participants fully understand the implications of their involvement. Additionally, the equitable distribution of benefits resulting from these trials is a pressing concern that requires attention (Joag et al., 2019; Garner et al., 2014).

Several barriers hinder participation in clinical trials within SSA, with financial constraints emerging as a predominant obstacle. Prospective participants frequently encounter challenges in covering transportation costs, lost wages, and other expenses linked to trial involvement (Edem et al., 2021). Furthermore, socio-cultural factors complicate recruitment efforts. Widespread mistrust of healthcare systems and a lack of awareness regarding the nature and potential benefits of clinical trials pose significant challenges that researchers must overcome (Dietrich et al., 2023; Diallo et al., 2021). Recent studies underscore the critical role of community engagement and educational initiatives in mitigating these barriers and facilitating increased participation rates in clinical trials (Dietrich et al., 2023). Researchers can dismantle the obstacles that deter individuals from participating in medical research by actively involving communities and clarifying the processes and advantages associated with clinical trials.

The importance of clinical trials in advancing medical science and improving health outcomes, particularly in regions burdened with diverse populations and unique health challenges, cannot be overstated. Such research is vital for generating data on the efficacy and safety of new medical interventions, particularly in SSA, where demographic diversity and specific health issues require tailored solutions (Nyirenda et al., 2021). Despite the pivotal role of clinical trials, participation rates among SSA populations remain alarmingly low. This trend raises concerns about the generalizability of research findings and the relevance of interventions developed from these studies. The underrepresentation of SSA populations in clinical trials generates a troubling deficit in pertinent data, creating a scenario that is both morally and scientifically indefensible. This marginalization of health interests within these communities perpetuates a cycle of health inequity, compromising the validity of research outcomes and reinforcing biases in medical treatments and guidelines.

To address this pressing issue, stakeholders in the medical and research fields must prioritize equitable access to clinical trials. The design and implementation of these studies must be sensitively attuned to the cultural and contextual realities of the populations involved. Rectifying these disparities is not only an ethical obligation but also essential for generating robust data that can significantly improve health outcomes for all, particularly those historically marginalized in the global health landscape.

In conclusion, researchers and healthcare practitioners must actively pursue and implement strategies to mitigate barriers to participation in clinical trials across diverse communities. Ensuring that clinical research is inclusive and representative fosters a more equitable health environment and enhances the advancement of medical knowledge and the effective treatment of diverse health issues. Pursuing inclusive clinical research is not just a moral imperative but critical for developing sound and applicable medical interventions that benefit all populations.

Policy Implications

The text highlights a critical relationship between healthcare financing and clinical trial participation, particularly in Sub-Saharan Africa (SSA). It posits that effective policy-making must recognize this interconnectedness to address the region's significant health disparities.

To begin, it is essential to understand that healthcare financing plays a pivotal role in determining the accessibility and quality of healthcare services. In SSA, where health systems often face chronic underfunding, the lack of financial resources directly impacts the ability of healthcare facilities to provide quality care. This, in turn, affects the willingness and ability of individuals to participate in clinical trials. Policies that increase government funding for health systems are, therefore, vital. Increased funding can enhance infrastructure, improve service delivery, and foster a healthcare environment where clinical trials can be conducted safely and effectively.

Moreover, promoting community engagement in research is fundamental to creating equitable access. Engaging local communities in clinical research helps build trust and improve understanding of the importance and benefits of participating in clinical trials. This approach not only enhances recruitment but also ensures that the research is culturally relevant and addresses the specific health needs of the population. Policymakers must prioritize strategies that facilitate community involvement, ensuring that studies are designed with input from those they aim to benefit.

Furthermore, upholding ethical standards in clinical trials is non-negotiable (Dietrich et al., 2023; Kwizera et al., 2020). Ethical integrity ensures that participants are treated respectfully and their rights and welfare are safeguarded. Policies should explicitly outline the ethical guidelines that govern clinical trials while emphasizing responsible conduct among researchers. This commitment to ethics will engender community trust, increasing trial participation rates.

In summary, addressing health disparities in sub-Saharan Africa through healthcare financing and clinical trial participation necessitates comprehensive policy interventions. By increasing government funding, fostering community engagement in research, and ensuring rigorous ethical compliance, policymakers can create an environment conducive to equitable healthcare access and robust participation in clinical trials. This multi-faceted approach is essential for advancing regional health equity and improving overall health outcomes.

Gaps in the Literature

The interplay between healthcare financing mechanisms and clinical trial participation in Sub-Saharan Africa (SSA) represents a critical yet underexplored area of research that warrants further investigation. Recognizing various underlying issues, a notable scarcity of comprehensive studies that meticulously analyze the relationship between these two variables remains. Specifically, the lack of quantitative analyses correlating healthcare financing structures with clinical trial participation outcomes is a significant gap that needs addressing. Robust empirical data in this domain could elucidate causal relationships, subsequently informing targeted strategies to bolster participation rates.

Moreover, current research often fails to adequately examine how healthcare financing influences trial participation despite the dynamic nature of healthcare policies and funding. Understanding how shifts in these areas impact research engagement is essential for developing relevant and effective interventions. Furthermore, socio-cultural factors play an instrumental role in shaping patient decision-making regarding trial participation, yet many studies overlook these influences. A nuanced approach incorporating both qualitative and quantitative assessments could significantly enhance our understanding of these complex interactions.

Engaging in comparative studies across different nations or regions within SSA will provide valuable insights into optimal healthcare financing and clinical trial participation practices. The research landscape on this subject is evolving, yet critical gaps persist. Therefore, there is an urgent need for empirical studies that explore the intricate connections between healthcare financing mechanisms and clinical trial participation rates.

Moreover, it is vital to prioritize the perspectives of diverse populations regarding clinical trials. Investigating the specific factors that influence individuals' participation decisions will enrich our understanding of the barriers and facilitators present within various communities. As identified in the work of Edem et al. (2021), such an emphasis on diverse perspectives can lead to more effective recruitment strategies and improved participant retention. Addressing the complex relationship between healthcare financing and clinical trial participation in SSA demands comprehensive, multidisciplinary policy interventions. Policymakers must undertake the imperative steps of increasing governmental funding, fostering community engagement in research design, and ensuring adherence to ethical guidelines. By enacting these strategies, a conducive environment can be cultivated that enhances equitable access to healthcare and stimulates robust participation in clinical trials.

This multi-faceted approach is essential for advancing health equity and improving overall health outcomes in the region. With concerted efforts and a commitment to addressing these gaps, it is possible to transform the clinical research landscape in sub-Saharan Africa into one that is inclusive, effective, and ethically sound.

Conclusion

Healthcare financing mechanisms in sub-Saharan Africa play a pivotal role in shaping participation in clinical trials. While progress has been made, significant challenges that necessitate focused research remain. By bridging the existing gaps in the literature and exploring innovative or effective solutions, stakeholders can enhance both health outcomes and the landscape of clinical research in the region. As SSA grapples with health disparities, a strategic approach to integrating healthcare financing with clinical research initiatives will be critical in driving meaningful change.

Bibliography

Agula, C., Bawah, A. A., Asuming, P. O., Kyei, P., & Biney, A. (2024). Impact of health system strengthening interventions on child survival in sub-Saharan Africa: a systematic review protocol. Systematic reviews, 13(1), 15. https://doi.org/10.1186/s13643-023-02397-w

Azevedo M. J. (2017). The State of Health System(s) in Africa: Challenges and Opportunities. Historical Perspectives on the State of Health and Health Systems in Africa, Volume II: The Modern Era, 1–73. https://doi.org/10.1007/978-3-319-32564-4_1

Barasa, E., Kazungu, J., Nguhiu, P., & Ravishankar, N. (2021). Examining the level and inequality in health insurance coverage in 36 sub-Saharan African countries. BMJ global health, 6(4), e004712. https://doi.org/10.1136/bmjgh-2020-004712

Belay, S., Giday, M., & Manyazewal, T. (2021). Harnessing Clinical Trial Capacity to Mitigate Zoonotic Diseases: The Role of Expert Scientists in Ethiopia. Frontiers in public health, 9, 621433. https://doi.org/10.3389/fpubh.2021.621433

Buse, K., & Waxman, A. (2001). Global public-private partnerships: A strategy for WHO. *Bulletin of the World Health Organization, 2001, 79: 748–754.*

Diallo, B. A., Usuf, E., Ceesay, O., D'Alessandro, U., Roca, A., & Martinez-Alvarez, M. (2022). Clinical research on COVID-19: perceptions and barriers to participation in The Gambia. BMJ Global Health, 7(2), e007533. https://doi.org/10.1136/bmjgh-2021-007533

Dietrich, J. J., Munoz, J., Tshabalala, G., Makhale, L. M., Hornschuh, S., Rentas, F., Mulaudzi, M., Laher, F., & Andrasik,

M. P. (2023). A qualitative study of stakeholder and researcher perspectives of community engagement practices for HIV vaccine clinical trials in South Africa. Journal of Community Psychology, 51(3), 998–1015. https://doi.org/10.1002/jcop.22951

Edem, B., Onwuchekwa, C., Wariri, O., Nkereuwem, E., Nkereuwem, O. O., & Williams, V. (2021). Trends in clinical trial registration in sub-Saharan Africa between 2010 and 2020: a cross-sectional review of three clinical trial registries. Trials, 22(1), 472. https://doi.org/10.1186/s13063-021-05423-1

Garner, S. A., Anude, C. J., Adams, E., & Dawson, L. (2014). Ethical considerations in HIV prevention and vaccine research in resource-limited settings. Journal of acquired immune deficiency syndromes (1999), 67(1), 77–83. https://doi.org/10.1097/QAI.0000000000000248

Guidance for best practices for clinical trials. Geneva: World Health Organization; 2024. Licence: CC BY-NC-SA 3.0 IGO. https://iris.who.int/bitstream/handle/10665/378782/9789240097711-eng.pdf?sequence=1

Joag, K., Ambrosio, G., Kestler, E., Weijer, C., Hemming, K., & Van der Graaf, R. (2019). Ethical issues in the design and conduct of stepped-wedge cluster randomized trials in low-resource settings. Trials, 20(Suppl 2), 703. https://doi.org/10.1186/s13063-019-3842-1

Karamagi, H. C., Njuguna, D., Kidane, S. N., Djossou, H., Kipruto, H. K., Seydi, A. B., Nabyonga-Orem, J., Muhongerwa, D. K., Frimpong, K. A., & Nganda, B. M. (2023). Financing health system elements in Africa: A scoping review. PloS one, 18(9), e0291371. https://doi.org/10.1371/journal.pone.0291371

Knittel, B., Coile, A., Zou, A., Saxena, S., Brenzel, L., Orobaton, N., Bartel, D., Williams, C. A., Kambarami, R., Tiwari, D. P.,

Husain, I., Sikipa, G., Achan, J., Ajiwohwodoma, J. O., Banerjee, B., & Kasungami, D. (2023). Critical barriers to sustainable capacity strengthening in global health: a systems perspective on development assistance. Gates open research, 6, 116. https://doi.org/10.12688/gatesopenres.13632.2

Knottnerus J. A. (2021). New placebo-controlled Covid-19 vaccine trials are ethically questionable; it's now about comparative effectiveness and availability of registered vaccines. Journal of clinical epidemiology, 133, 175–176. https://doi.org/10.1016/j.jclinepi.2021.03.006

Kwizera, R., Sadiq, A., Ndyetukira, J. F., Nalintya, E., Williams, D., Rhein, J., Boulware, D. R., Meya, D. B., & COAT and ASTRO trial teams (2020). Impact of community engagement and social support on the outcomes of HIV-related meningitis clinical trials in a resource-limited setting. Research involvement and engagement, 6, 49. https://doi.org/10.1186/s40900-020-00228-z

Ly, M. S., Bassoum, O., & Faye, A. (2022). Universal health insurance in Africa: a narrative review of the literature on institutional models. BMJ global health, 7(4), e008219. https://doi.org/10.1136/bmjgh-2021-008219

Mills, A. (2014). Health Care Systems in Low- and Middle-Income Countries. N Engl J Med; 370:552-557. DOI: 10.1056/NEJMra1110897

Moffatt, S., White, M., Mackintosh, J., & Howel, D. (2006). Using quantitative and qualitative data in health services research - what happens when mixed method findings conflict? [ISRCTN61522618]. BMC health services research, 6, 28. https://doi.org/10.1186/1472-6963-6-28

National Institute of Health (2016). Guiding Principles for Ethical

Research

Pursuing: Potential Research Participants Protections. Retrieved from https://www.nih.gov/health-information/nih-clinical-research-trials-you/guiding-principles-ethical-research

Nyirenda, T., Bockarie, M., Machingaidze, S., Nderu, M., Singh, M., Fakier, N., Habarugira, J. M., Beattie, P., Pandya, L., Jajkowicz, D., Yazdanpanah, Y., Hankins, C., & Makanga, M. (2021). Strengthening capacity for clinical research in sub-Saharan Africa: partnerships and networks. International journal of infectious diseases: IJID: official publication of the International Society for Infectious Diseases, 110, 54–61. https://doi.org/10.1016/j.ijid.2021.06.061

Schmidt, H., & Hohmann, J. (2016). Financial incentives and participation in clinical trials: A systematic review. *Trials*, 17(1), 1-12. https://doi.org/10.1186/s13063-016-1467-0

Seward, N., Hanlon, C., Abdella, A., Abrahams, Z., Alem, A., Araya, R., Bachmann, M., Bekele, A., Bogale, B., Brima, N., Chibanda, D., Curran, R., Davies, J., Beyene, A., Fairall, L., Farrant, L., Frissa, S., Gallagher, J., Gao, W., Gwyther, L., … Prince, M. (2022). Health System Strengthening in four sub-Saharan African countries (ASSET) to achieve high-quality, evidence-informed surgical, maternal and newborn, and primary care: protocol for pre-implementation phase studies. Global health action, 15(1), 1987044. https://doi.org/10.1080/16549716.2021.1987044

Späth C, Schmidt B-M (2024) An unclosed loop: Perspectives of community engagement in infectious disease clinical trials in sub-Saharan Africa. PLoS ONE 19(8): e0308128. https://doi.org/10.1371/journal.pone.0308128

Toto, N., Douglas, E., Gmeiner, M., Barrett, L. K., Lindblad, R., Makhaza, L., Nedi, W., Phulusa, J., Quinnan, G. V., Sawyer, L. A., Thole, H., Van Voorhis, W. C., & Iroh Tam, P. Y. (2020). Conducting clinical trials in sub-Saharan Africa: challenges and lessons learned from the Malawi Cryptosporidium study. Trials, 21(1), 680. https://doi.org/10.1186/s13063-020-04620-8.

Wagstaff, A. (2002). Poverty and health sector inequalities. *Bulletin of the World Health Organization*, 80(2), 97-105. https://doi.org/10.1590/S0042-96862002000200003

World Health Organization. (2010). The World Health Report 2010: Health systems financing: The path to universal coverage. Geneva: World Health Organization. Retrieved from https://www.who.int/whr/2010/en/

World Health Organization (2024). Addressing health inequities among people living in rural and remote areas. Retrieved from https://www.who.int/activities/addressing-health-inequities-among-people-living-in-rural-and-remote-areas

Chapter 12: Healthcare Financing and Educational and Agricultural Policies Interconnections in Sub-Saharan Africa

Vignette: Interconnected Policies for Sustainable Development

In a rural community in sub-Saharan Africa, the local government is developing a comprehensive development plan that integrates healthcare financing, educational policies, and agricultural policies. By simultaneously addressing these critical areas, the goal is to improve the population's overall well-being.

Healthcare Financing: The government has introduced a national health insurance scheme to reduce out-of-pocket expenses and ensure access to essential health services. This scheme is funded through government spending, private contributions, and international aid.

Educational Policies: The government has implemented policies to improve educational outcomes and increase access to quality education. These include building new schools, training teachers, and providing scholarships for students from low-income families.

Agricultural Policies: Recognizing the importance of agriculture for food security and economic growth, the government has launched initiatives to support smallholder farmers. These initiatives include providing access to modern farming techniques, improving market access, and offering financial support for sustainable agricultural practices.

Questions

1. How does the national health insurance scheme impact children's educational attainment in the community?
2. Consider the effects of improved health on school attendance and academic performance.
3. In what ways can educational policies contribute to the success of agricultural initiatives in the region?
4. Think about how education can empower farmers with knowledge and skills for better agricultural practices.
5. How might improving agricultural productivity influence healthcare financing in the community?

6. Reflect on the potential economic benefits and how they could be reinvested in healthcare services.
7. What are the potential challenges in coordinating healthcare, education, and agricultural policies?
8. Identify possible obstacles and suggest strategies to overcome them.
9. How can community involvement enhance the effectiveness of these interconnected policies?

o Discuss the role of community participation in ensuring the success of integrated development plans.

Introduction

Healthcare financing in sub-Saharan Africa has become a crucial research focus due to the region's distinct socio-economic challenges and the interconnected nature of healthcare, education, and agricultural policies. This chapter highlights the complex interaction between these areas, showing that improved healthcare financing can enhance educational outcomes and agricultural productivity, fostering economic growth (World Health Organization [WHO], 2019).

The intricate relationship between healthcare financing, education, and agriculture in sub-Saharan Africa is crucial for addressing the region's socio-economic challenges. Adequate healthcare financing can lead to better health outcomes, which can bolster educational attainment. Healthier children are more likely to attend school regularly and perform better academically, suggesting a direct correlation between health and education (United Nations Educational, Scientific and Cultural Organization [UNESCO], 2020).

Moreover, agricultural productivity is likely to increase as the workforce becomes healthier and better educated. Improved health enables farmers to work more effectively and contribute to food security, directly impacting economic stability and growth (Food and Agriculture Organization [FAO], 2021). This interdependence underscores the necessity for integrated policy approaches, considering healthcare, education, and agriculture as intertwined sectors rather than isolated entities.

Sustainable development in sub-Saharan Africa depends on collaborative strategies that prioritize improvements in healthcare financing. Enhanced investments in health systems can reduce the disease burden, enabling individuals to engage more fully in education and economic activities. Consequently, the ripple effects of such improvements can manifest in heightened productivity, improved living standards, and robust economic growth.

In conclusion, a holistic approach to healthcare financing that recognizes its links to education and agriculture is vital for sustainable development in sub-Saharan Africa. Policymakers and stakeholders must work together to create synergies among these sectors, ultimately paving the way for a healthier, more educated, and economically prosperous population (World Bank, 2022). By systematically addressing the interconnections between these critical areas, the region can forge a path toward resilience and growth despite persistent challenges.

Healthcare Financing in Sub-Saharan Africa

Healthcare financing in sub-Saharan Africa is characterized by significant variability across countries, influenced by political conditions, economic progress, and historical frameworks. According to the World Health Organization (WHO, 2019), healthcare financing models are primarily categorized into out-of-pocket payments, social health insurance, and general taxation.

A predominant model in many sub-Saharan countries is out-of-pocket payment, where individuals pay for healthcare services at the time of use. This model frequently leads to disparities in healthcare access, as it disproportionately affects low-income populations who may be unable to afford necessary medical care (Kutzin, 2013). Consequently, out-of-pocket financing perpetuates inequities in health outcomes and reinforces existing socio-economic disparities.

Conversely, social health insurance schemes present a potentially equitable alternative, aiming to provide broader coverage and reduce financial barriers to care. However, these schemes encounter challenges related to coverage adequacy and long-term sustainability (Hofmarcher & Rack, 2019). Issues such as inadequate funding, administrative inefficiencies, and regulatory obstacles hinder the effective implementation of social health insurance in the region.

In summary, while sub-Saharan Africa's healthcare financing landscape is marked by reliance on out-of-pocket payments, the potential of social health insurance schemes remains constrained by significant systemic challenges. Addressing these challenges is critical to achieving equitable healthcare access across the region.

Challenges of Healthcare Financing

The ongoing challenges in healthcare financing in sub-Saharan Africa highlight the urgent need for practical solutions. The region faces issues such as inadequate infrastructure, limited human resources, and a heavy reliance on external funding, primarily international aid, which raises sustainability concerns (Morris et al., 2018; Ravishankar et al., 2009). This dependency undermines the autonomy of healthcare systems and can lead to fragmented service delivery, worsening existing healthcare disparities (Mills et al., 2017).

In response to these challenges, recent studies have explored various innovative financing mechanisms to improve healthcare access and quality. One notable approach is performance-based financing (PBF), which incentivizes healthcare providers to deliver quality services. This model is designed to create accountability and enhance health outcomes by linking financial rewards directly to performance metrics (Jacobs et al., 2020).

Furthermore, integrating digital technologies, particularly mobile payment systems, has emerged as a promising solution to improve financial access and operational efficiency in healthcare financing (Nanyonjo et al., 2019; Early et al., 2019). Greuel et al. (2023) state that smart mobile devices may augment community health workers' (CHWs') field performance and enhance face-to-face client interactions. However, these technologies also generate new challenges.

These innovations indicate a shift towards more adaptable and responsive healthcare financing models, potentially better suited to the unique challenges faced by sub-Saharan African countries. By fostering an environment that promotes accountability and utilizes technology, these models have the potential to transform healthcare delivery and ultimately improve health outcomes in the region.

Interconnections with Education Policies

The connection between healthcare and education is increasingly recognized as a critical factor in fostering development, especially in vulnerable populations. The literature articulates a strong link between quality healthcare and educational success. It is well established that poor health adversely affects cognitive development and school attendance, which are essential components of effective learning (Zimmerman et al., 2014; Basch, 2011).

In regions like sub-Saharan Africa, where children and adolescents face high rates of endemic diseases such as malaria and HIV/AIDS (WHO, 2022), the implications of health on educational achievement are profoundly significant (Gakidou et al., 2010). Moreover, investments in healthcare yield demonstrable improvements in educational outcomes. For instance, Filmer (2007) presents compelling evidence that better child health correlates with increased school enrollment and completion rates, highlighting the importance of reducing mortality and morbidity among this demographic.

The World Health Organization (WHO, 2019) further emphasizes this connection, asserting that healthy children are better equipped to perform academically, thereby establishing a positive feedback loop between health and educational success. Moving beyond individual health and education policies, integrating these two sectors is emerging as a key strategy for improving overall outcomes.

The Global Strategy for Women's, Children's, and Adolescents' Health (2016-2030) advocates for a multi-sectoral approach that explicitly recognizes the interdependencies between health and education (WHO, 2016). Successful implementations of policy integration are evident in countries such as Rwanda, where health initiatives—exemplified by school health programs—have demonstrably improved educational performance (Jean de Dieu et al., 2023; Wang et al., 2020).

The evidence strongly supports that bolstering health systems can significantly enhance educational outcomes. Therefore, policymakers must adopt a comprehensive approach that prioritizes both health and education separately while also recognizing their intrinsic link in driving sustainable development.

Interconnections with Agricultural Policies

Agriculture plays a fundamental role in the health and nutrition of populations in sub-Saharan Africa. The literature unequivocally emphasizes that food security is a cornerstone for promoting public health, as malnutrition is a significant factor contributing to morbidity and mortality rates, particularly among vulnerable populations, such as children (FAO, 2020). Given this context, agricultural policies must prioritize both food production and access. Such policies enhance food security and translate into considerable public health benefits, establishing agriculture as a critical sector for improving population health outcomes.

Research consistently demonstrates a reciprocal relationship between health investments and agricultural productivity (Zegeye et al., 2022). Zegeye et al. (2022) assert that developing the agricultural sector is critical for reducing poverty in poor countries (Habtewold, 2021). Studies show that agricultural technology can improve household welfare, especially for smallholder farmers (Habtewold, 2021). This finding is corroborated by the World Bank (2018), which highlights that effective health interventions—including vaccination programs and maternal health services—significantly reduce the disease burden. By alleviating health-related impediments, these interventions enable individuals to allocate more time and resources toward agricultural endeavors, effectively driving productivity within the sector.

Thus, integrating health initiatives into agricultural policy frameworks is beneficial and essential for optimizing agricultural output. For sustainable development to be realized in sub-Saharan Africa, the integration of health and agricultural policies is paramount. The "One Health" concept, which acknowledges the intricate interconnections between human, animal, and environmental health, has garnered considerable attention in policy dialogues (de Macedo Couto et al., 2020).

Countries such as Ethiopia exemplify the successful implementation of integrated policies that have yielded substantial improvements in both health and agricultural outcomes (Bach et al., 2020). This approach underscores the necessity of coordinated efforts across sectors, as synergies between health and agriculture enhance food security and foster a healthier society capable of driving economic growth. The imperative is clear: Strengthening agricultural policies that prioritize health and nutrition, combined with robust investment in health services, will indubitably enhance productivity and ensure that populations in sub-Saharan Africa thrive.

The path forward lies in recognizing and harnessing these synergies, fostering a holistic approach to sustainable development that benefits health and agriculture.

Conclusion

The intricate relationships between healthcare, education, and agriculture in sub-Saharan Africa underscore the need for a holistic perspective in addressing healthcare financing challenges. These sectors are not isolated; improvements in healthcare can lead to better educational outcomes, and vice versa, while a robust agricultural sector can enhance food security and economic stability, thereby influencing health and education systems.

To tackle healthcare financing issues effectively, policymakers must consider the socio-economic context governing these sectors. For instance, investing in education can empower communities to access health services better and understand health-related information, leading to improved health outcomes. Similarly, robust agricultural policies can enhance nutrition and food security, which are vital for overall health, particularly for vulnerable populations such as children and pregnant women.

Future research should prioritize investigating integrated policy frameworks that address healthcare financing and consider the synergies between health, education, and agricultural policies. Research can identify sustainable solutions that leverage resources across sectors by exploring innovative financing mechanisms—including public-private partnerships, community financing models, and international aid strategies.

Moreover, collaboration among stakeholders, including government entities, non-governmental organizations, and local communities, is essential to ensure policies are contextually appropriate and effectively implemented. Such a comprehensive approach will promote sustainable development and enhance population well-being, paving the way for resilient and thriving communities across sub-Saharan Africa.

In summary, tackling the interconnected challenges of healthcare financing, education, and agriculture requires a multi-faceted, collaborative framework that prioritizes integrated policies. Continued exploration of this synergy will be crucial for the region's long-term health and economic stability.

Bibliography

Bach, A., Gregor, E., Sridhar, S., Fekadu, H., & Fawzi, W. (2020). Multisectoral Integration of Nutrition, Health, and Agriculture: Implementation Lessons from Ethiopia. Food and Nutrition Bulletin. https://doi.org/10.1177/0379572119895097

Basch, C. E. (2011). Healthier Students Are Better Learners: High-Quality, Strategically Planned, and Effectively Coordinated School Health Programs Must Be a Fundamental Mission of Schools to Help Close the Achievement Gap. Journal of School Health, 81(10), 650–662. https://doi.org/10.1111/j.1746-1561.2011.00640.x

Berhe, H., et al. (2019). Integrated health and agricultural interventions in Ethiopia: A systematic review. BMC Public Health, 19(1), 1-15.

de Macedo Couto R, Brandespim DF (2020). A review of the One Health concept and its application as a tool for policymakers, Int. J. One Health, 6(1): 83-89. doi: www.doi.org/10.14202/IJOH.2020.83-89

Early, J., Gonzalez, C., Gordon-Dseagu, V., & Robles-Calderon, L. (2019). Use of Mobile Health (mHealth) Technologies and Interventions Among Community Health Workers Globally: A Scoping Review. Health promotion practice, 20(6), 805–817. https://doi.org/10.1177/1524839919855391

FAO (2021). The State of Food and Agriculture 2021. Making agrifood systems more resilient to shocks and stresses. Rome, FAO. https://doi.org/10.4060/cb4476en.

Filmer, D. (2007). If you build it, will they come? School availability and school enrollment in 21 poor countries. Journal of Development Studies, 43(5), 901–928.

Gakidou, E., et al. (2010). Increased educational attainment and its effect on child mortality in 175 countries between 1970 and 2009: a systematic analysis. The Lancet, 376 (9745), 959 – 974

Greuel, M., Sy, F., Bärnighausen, T., Adam, M., Vandormael, A., Gates, J., & Harling, G. (2023). Community Health Worker Use of Smart Devices for Health Promotion: Scoping Review. JMIR mHealth and uHealth, 11, e42023. https://doi.org/10.2196/42023

Habtewold T.M. (2021). Impact of climate-smart agricultural technology on multidimensional poverty in rural Ethiopia. J. Integr. Agric. 20(4):1021–1041. [Google Scholar]

Hofmarcher, M. M., & Rack, H. (2019). Health financing in sub-Saharan Africa: Challenges and opportunities. Health Policy and Planning, 34(7), 495-503.

Jacobs, E., Bertone, M. P., Toonen, J., Akwataghibe, N., & Witter, S. (2020). Performance-Based Financing, Basic Packages of Health Services and User-Fee Exemption Mechanisms: An Analysis of Health-Financing Policy Integration in Three Fragile and Conflict-Affected Settings. Applied health economics and health policy, 18(6), 801–810. https://doi.org/10.1007/s40258-020-00567-8

Jean de Dieu, H., Theogene, H., Emmanuel, N., Faustin, M., Abdou, M., Emmanuel, N., and Ke, Z. (2023). School feeding program implementation and its challenges in basic education schools in Rwanda. African Educational Research Journal, 11(3): 338-350.

Kutzin, J. (2013). Health financing for universal health coverage. World Health Organization.

Mills, A., et al. (2017). The challenges of health financing in sub-Saharan Africa. The Lancet Global Health, 5(5), e505-e506.

Morris, S. S., et al. (2018). The impact of health interventions on education outcomes in developing countries: A systematic review. Health Economics, 27(3), e1-e12.

Nanyonjo, A., Counihan, H., Siduda, S. G., Belay, K., Sebikaari, G., & Tibenderana, J. (2019). Institutionalization of integrated community case management into national health systems in low- and middle-income countries: a scoping review of the literature. Global health action, 12(1), 1678283. https://doi.org/10.1080/16549716.2019.1678283Ravishankar, N., et al. (2009). Financing of global health: Tracking development assistance for health from 1990 to 2007. The Lancet, 373(9681), 2113-2124.

United Nations Educational, Scientific and Cultural Organization [UNESCO] (2020). Global Education Monitoring Report: Inclusion and Education: All means All. Retrieved from https://www.unesco.at/en/education/education-2030/global-education-monitoring-gem-report/gem20.

Wang, D., & Fawzi, W. W. (2020). Impacts of school feeding on educational and health outcomes of school-age children and adolescents in low- and middle-income countries: protocol for a systematic review and meta-analysis. Systematic reviews, 9(1), 55. https://doi.org/10.1186/s13643-020-01317-6

World Bank. (2018). World Development Report 2018: Learning to realize education's promise.

World Bank Publications. WHO. (2016). Global strategy for women's, children's and adolescents' health (2016-2030).

World Bank (2022). The World Bank Annual Report (2022). Helping Countries Adapt to a Changing World (English). Washington, D.C. : World Bank Group. http://documents.worldbank.org/curated/en/099030009272214630/BOSIB0db37c9aa05a0961a08a83a0ea76ea

World Health Organization. WHO. (2019). World Health Statistics 2019: Monitoring health for the SDGs. World Health Organization.

World Health Organization. WHO. (2022). Child mortality (under 5 years). Retrieved from https://www.who.int/news-room/fact-sheets/detail/levels-and-trends-in-child-under-5-mortality-in-2020

Zegeye, M. B., Meshesha, G. B., & Shah, M. I. (2022). Measuring the poverty reduction effects of adopting agricultural technologies in rural Ethiopia: findings from an endogenous switching regression approach. Heliyon, 8(5), e09495. https://doi.org/10.1016/j.heliyon.2022.e09495

Zimmerman, E. and S. H. Woolf. 2014. Understanding the Relationship Between Education and Health. NAM Perspectives. Discussion Paper, National Academy of Medicine,

Washington, DC. https://doi.org/10.31478/201406a

Chapter 13: Healthcare Financing and Health Management Organization in sub-Saharan Africa

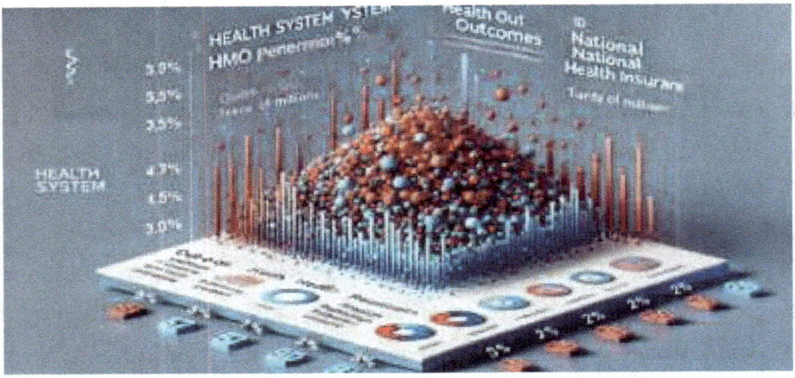

Vignette: The Weight of Choice

Aisha, a young mother in rural Malawi, cradles her feverish infant, David. The nearest health center is a two-hour walk away, and even then, it often lacks essential medicines. Aisha heard about a new Health Maintenance Organization (HMO) in a neighboring district. It promises comprehensive care for a fixed monthly fee, representing a significant portion of her family's meager income. David's condition worsens, and Aisha faces a heart-wrenching dilemma: risk depleting their savings on potentially inadequate treatment at the local clinic or gamble on the promises of a distant HMO. Her choice highlights the complex healthcare financing landscape in sub-Saharan Africa, where limited resources, underdeveloped infrastructure, and the allure of innovative financing models intersect, leaving vulnerable populations grappling with difficult decisions.

Questions:

1. Considering their limited financial resources and geographical constraints, how can HMO models be adapted to serve the rural poor in sub-Saharan Africa effectively? For example, could community-based micro-insurance schemes or mobile health technologies help bridge the affordability and accessibility gaps?
2. Given the projected decline in development assistance for health, what innovative financing mechanisms can sub-Saharan African countries explore to ensure sustainable healthcare funding? Could public-private partnerships, sin taxes, or diaspora bonds contribute meaningfully to domestic resource mobilization?
3. What regulatory frameworks are necessary to ensure the quality of care and financial stability of HMOs operating in sub-Saharan Africa, protecting vulnerable populations from potential exploitation or inadequate services?
4. How can health workforce shortages be addressed to support the expansion of HMOs and other healthcare delivery models across sub-Saharan Africa? Could task-shifting to community health workers or investing in training and retention programs alleviate the strain on limited human resources?
5. Beyond HMOs, what other health financing and service delivery innovations hold promise for achieving universal health coverage in sub-Saharan Africa, acknowledging the region's diverse contexts and challenges? For example, how can telemedicine, performance-based financing, and community-based health insurance contribute to the broader health system?

Introduction

In sub-Saharan Africa, healthcare financing and health management face multi-faceted challenges and opportunities as the region responds to shifting demographics, evolving disease burdens, and varying economic conditions (Wamai et al., 2022). Despite notable improvements in life expectancy, the region continues to lag behind other areas in critical health outcomes (Wamai et al., 2022). This gap is influenced by several interconnected factors, including pervasive poverty, underdeveloped health systems, persistent governance challenges, and a heavy reliance on external funding (Wamai et al., 2022).

One of the primary challenges is healthcare financing, where many countries allocate less than 5% of their gross domestic product (GDP) to health, leading to an overwhelming reliance on out-of-pocket payments by individuals. This financial model often results in significant economic strain for households (Apeagyei et al., 2024; Ifeagwu et al., 2021). Additionally, while external donor funding is crucial to healthcare financing, projections indicate that this aid may stagnate or decline (Krugman, 2024). Although GDP growth is anticipated, the share allocated to healthcare might diminish in several subregions, raising alarms about the long-term sustainability of healthcare funding (Apeagyei et al., 2024). Consequently, there is an urgent need for innovative and diversified financing mechanisms, such as enhancing national health insurance programs and exploring alternative strategies for mobilizing resources.

Moreover, effective health management is essential for optimizing limited resources. Inefficient organizational structures, weak leadership, and corruption obstruct equitable healthcare delivery. Strengthening primary healthcare systems is critical for addressing the dual burden of infectious diseases and ensuring comprehensive care. This goal necessitates investments in infrastructure, workforce development, and community health workers, which are pivotal in extending healthcare access to underserved populations.

Building leadership and management capacities within the health sector is equally vital for enhancing service delivery, fostering accountability, and advancing progress toward universal health coverage. Furthermore, robust research initiatives and systematic data collection are crucial for informed decision-making and monitoring advancements toward health-related Sustainable Development Goals. Collaborative partnerships involving governments, non-governmental organizations (NGOs), and international entities are essential for supporting health system-strengthening efforts and creating resilient healthcare systems that respond to the region's evolving health needs.

Overview of Healthcare Financing Models

Healthcare financing in sub-Saharan Africa is a complex landscape characterized by various funding sources with varying effectiveness (Ayadi et al., 2020; Karamagi et al., 2023). A significant portion, about 60%, comes from private spending, often in the form of out-of-pocket payments by individuals seeking care. This reliance on direct payments can substantially burden households, especially the poor. While public funding and health insurance play roles, they are often insufficient to meet the substantial health needs of the region. External donor funding supplements these sources but can be unpredictable and may not always align with local priorities.

Breakdown of the key financing models:

- **Out-of-Pocket Payments (OOP):** This is the most common form of healthcare financing in sub-Saharan Africa but can create financial hardship, especially for impoverished households. Studies indicate that OOP spending does not correlate with improved health outcomes.

- **Government Funding:** Public expenditure on healthcare varies significantly across countries in the region. While representing a crucial funding source, it often falls short of what is needed to provide comprehensive services. Strengthening institutions and improving efficiency in public healthcare systems are crucial for maximizing the impact of government spending.
- **Health Insurance:** Expanding health insurance coverage is a key strategy for improving financial protection and access to care. Studies suggest that increased health insurance funding correlates positively with improved health outcomes, such as increased life expectancy and reduced child mortality.
- **External Funding (Donor Aid):** Donor support plays a significant role in financing health initiatives in sub-Saharan Africa. This funding is often directed towards specific programs, such as disease control or infrastructure development. While valuable, its sustainability and alignment with local needs can be concerns.
- **Innovative Financing Mechanisms:** Exploring innovative approaches like health impact bonds is gaining traction. These bonds involve private investment in health programs, with government reimbursement tied to achieving pre-defined health outcomes (Donfouet et al., 2023). This model incentivizes efficiency and attracts private-sector resources (Donfouet et al., 2023).

Challenges and Opportunities:

Sub-Saharan Africa faces significant healthcare challenges, including a high disease burden, limited resources, and weak health systems. While private sector involvement is significant, particularly in service delivery, effective regulation and management are crucial.

Improving governance, strengthening institutions, and increasing public investment in healthcare are essential for achieving universal health coverage and better health outcomes. Innovative financing models and strategic partnerships between the public and private sectors can also play a vital role in addressing the healthcare financing gap and improving access to quality care.

Public financing, primarily through government budgets, is limited due to competing resource demands, leading to underfunded health systems (Apeagyei et al., 2024). In contrast, private financing has been growing, yet it often lacks regulation, resulting in disparities in access and quality of care (Kutzin, 2013; Kaiser et al., 2023).

Despite the potential benefits of health insurance, several challenges persist in healthcare financing in SSA. In SSA, quality of governance is associated with weak health systems, inadequate infrastructure, and a lack of trained personnel, which hinders effective implementation (Olafsdottir et al., 2011; African Development Bank Group, 2022; Agyei et al., 2024). Additionally, the informal nature of many employment sectors in SSA complicates the establishment of comprehensive health insurance schemes (Agyei et al., 2024).

Moreover, the reliance on external funding sources, such as international donors and non-governmental organizations (NGOs), can create dependency and undermine local ownership of health financing initiatives (World Health Organization, 2017; Gautier et al., 2017). This reliance raises questions about the sustainability of health financing in the region.

The Role of Health Insurance

Health insurance in sub-Saharan Africa is increasingly viewed as a crucial mechanism for achieving Universal Health Coverage (UHC) (Cashin et al., 2021). Many countries in the region are implementing or planning national health insurance (NHI) programs to address the financial barriers to healthcare access (Cashin et al., 2021; Apeagyei et al., 2024). The goal is to protect against financial risk, reduce catastrophic health expenditures, and expand access to treatment and preventative services (Apeagyei et al., 2024).

However, these programs face several challenges in terms of implementation and effectiveness (Olugbenga, 2017). While countries like Gabon, Ghana, and Rwanda have achieved significant population coverage with NHI, others struggle with low enrollment and financial sustainability (Olugbenga, 2017). One key issue is the underutilization of available claims data, which could offer valuable insights for program improvement (Apeagyei et al., 2024). Barriers to data analysis include inadequate technology, privacy concerns, and data quality issues (Apeagyei et al., 2024). Additionally, program administrators may not fully recognize the potential of this data.

Other challenges include the need for more financial resources for the health sector, the limited social financing compared to individual out-of-pocket payments, and the difficulties that direct payment systems create for access and affordability (Akokuwebe et al., 2022). Existing health systems also lack essential resources, such as drugs and adequately compensated professionals, making it difficult to provide necessary services (Akokuwebe et al., 2022). Moreover, the implementation of health insurance faces broader challenges related to socio-cultural, economic, and political contexts (Olugbenga, 2017).

Therefore, it is argued that simply adopting Western health insurance models may not be effective; countries need to develop strategies tailored to their specific circumstances. These strategies should be pragmatic, socially acceptable, and economically sustainable (Olugbenga, 2017). Key elements for success include transparent resource governance, strong accountability mechanisms, and the political will to drive these complex changes (Olugbenga, 2017).

Beyond national-level initiatives, other forms of health insurance, such as community-based and private insurance schemes, are emerging and expanding in the region (Carapinha et al., 2010). These play a role in expanding coverage and reducing out-of-pocket expenses, although their impact and integration within broader health systems require further examination.

The discussion around health insurance in sub-Saharan Africa is constantly evolving. New financing, management, and governance approaches are being explored, particularly in the informal sector (Akokuwebe et al., 2022; Zegeye et al., 2023; Bayked et al., 2024). The debate encompasses the adequacy of health insurance as a primary tool for UHC, the role of mutual health organizations, and the potential shift away from micro-insurance models (Al-Hanawi et al., 2021; Greer et al., 2015).

Health insurance schemes have been proposed to improve access to healthcare and reduce household financial burdens. In SSA, various models of health insurance exist, including community-based health insurance (CBHI) and social health insurance (SHI) (World Health Organization, 2020; Health Policy Project, 2015; 3ie, 2018; Jamal et al., 2020). CBHI has shown promise in increasing access to care, particularly in rural areas, but often struggles with sustainability and scalability (World Health Organization, 2020; Health Policy Project, 2015; 3ie, 2018; Agyei et al., 2024).

On the other hand, SHI has been implemented in several countries, such as Ghana and Rwanda, with varying degrees of success. While SHI can pool risks and improve financial protection, it requires strong governance and regulatory frameworks to ensure equitable access (World Health Organization, 2010; Agyei et al., 2024).

1.3 Challenges in Healthcare Financing

Healthcare financing in Sub-Saharan Africa (SSA) presents significant challenges, underlining the complexity of implementing effective health insurance systems in regions beset by systemic weaknesses. To begin with, Witter et al.'s (2016) argument supports the assertion that weak health systems serve as a barrier to health financing. In many SSA countries, health systems often suffer from insufficient infrastructure, which includes a lack of medical facilities, inadequate supply chains, and deficient healthcare technology. These limitations directly affect accessibility and the quality of care, thus undermining the effectiveness of health insurance schemes dependent on a robust healthcare delivery system.

Furthermore, the lack of trained healthcare personnel exacerbates these challenges. Many SSA nations grapple with a shortage of skilled workers, including doctors, nurses, and other healthcare professionals. This shortage impedes the delivery of insurance-covered care and impairs overall health system performance. Consequently, even when health insurance schemes are established, their effectiveness is severely compromised by the inability to provide adequate services to beneficiaries.

Another critical obstacle is the informal nature of employment in SSA (Agyei et al., 2024). A significant portion of the workforce is employed in informal sectors that are not typically covered by formal health insurance schemes (Agyei et al.,

2024). This informal employment complicates the establishment of comprehensive health insurance programs, as these workers may not contribute to or benefit from conventional insurance models. As a result, a large part of the population remains unprotected, exacerbating health disparities and undermining the effectiveness of health financing initiatives (Agyei et al., 2024).

The reliance on external funding sources, such as international donors and non-governmental organizations (NGOs), introduces additional complications, as highlighted by Mills et al. (2016). While these external sources provide crucial financial support, such dependence can erode local ownership of health financing initiatives. Local governments and communities may become less invested in developing sustainable health financing solutions, leading to a lack of accountability and responsiveness to local health needs. This dynamic raises significant concerns regarding the long-term sustainability of health financing in the region, as continued reliance on external funding may not be viable.

In conclusion, the challenges of implementing adequate healthcare financing in SSA are multi-faceted and deeply intertwined with systemic issues such as weak health systems, the informal nature of employment, and reliance on external funding. Addressing these challenges requires a comprehensive approach that enhances infrastructure, invests in human resources, and fosters local ownership of health financing initiatives. Without such measures, the potential benefits of health insurance remain unattainable for a large portion of the population, leaving significant gaps in healthcare access and equity.

Health Maintenance Organizations (HMOs) in Sub-Saharan Africa

Health Maintenance Organizations (HMOs) are a key component of managed care systems, offering health insurance coverage through established provider networks. Members typically pay a fixed premium for access to a broad range of healthcare services, emphasizing preventive care and cost efficiency (George, S., 2021). The HMO model has been adapted in various ways across Sub-Saharan Africa (SSA), reflecting the region's diverse healthcare contexts.

In SSA, HMOs primarily focus on healthcare delivery. A notable example is Hygeia HMO in Nigeria, founded in 1984, which offers health coverage through a comprehensive network of clinics and hospitals (IFHA Fund, n.d.). Hygeia also operates Lagoon Hospitals, an accredited group recognized by the Joint Commission International (IFHA Fund, n.d.).

Though integrated HMO models that provide insurance alongside preferred providers are becoming more common throughout SSA, comprehensive data on their prevalence and impact remains scarce and often outdated. These HMOs utilize capitation models or in-house care strategies to manage costs and mitigate fraud effectively (International Finance Corporation, 2007). Additionally, community health insurance schemes are gaining momentum and may significantly enhance access to healthcare services across the region (Girard, 2012).

While the HMO landscape in SSA is evolving, ongoing research and updated data are crucial for understanding their full impact on healthcare access and delivery in the region.

2.2 Implementation of HMOs in SSA

The implementation of HMOs in SSA has yielded mixed results. In Nigeria, for example, the National Health Insurance Scheme (NHIS) was established in 2005 to promote the HMO model. However, it has faced significant challenges, including low enrollment rates and limited provider networks (Ogunbekun et al., 2017).

Similarly, in South Africa, the introduction of managed care organizations has led to criticisms regarding access and the quality of care, particularly for vulnerable populations (McIntyre et al., 2014).

Benefits of HMOs in sub-Saharan Africa

Despite the challenges, HMOs offer several potential benefits for healthcare financing in SSA. By promoting preventive care and managing chronic diseases, HMOs can reduce healthcare costs and improve health outcomes (George, S., 2021). Furthermore, the HMO model encourages the efficient use of resources, as providers are incentivized to focus on preventive care and early intervention (Baker et al., 2016).

Health Maintenance Organizations (HMOs) hold considerable promise for enhancing healthcare delivery in SSA. Their potential benefits, particularly in improving access and the quality of care, are crucial in a region facing numerous health challenges. Below is a more detailed exploration of the advantages and challenges associated with HMOs in this context.

Advantages of HMOs in Sub-Saharan Africa

1. Improved Access to Healthcare: HMOs can bridge gaps in healthcare access, especially for populations that have

historically faced financial and geographical barriers. By pooling resources and leveraging their size to negotiate better rates with providers, HMOs can offer more affordable healthcare options, making it easier for low-income individuals and those in remote areas to receive necessary medical services.

2. Focus on Preventative Care: A core principle of HMOs is a strong emphasis on preventative care, including vaccinations, health education, and early screenings. By prioritizing prevention, HMOs can help manage and reduce the incidence of diseases, especially infectious diseases, and ultimately lower healthcare costs associated with advanced treatments.
3. Standardized Quality of Care: HMOs can set consistent quality standards for healthcare services within their networks. Establishing accreditation processes ensures that healthcare providers meet specific criteria, enhancing the overall quality of care patients receive (Asres Ioab et al., 2021).
4. Cost Containment: HMOs can negotiate bulk purchasing rates and manage healthcare utilization effectively, reducing costs for consumers and employers. These cost-containment strategies help alleviate some of the financial burdens that healthcare expenditures place on individuals and families.
5. Enhanced Data Collection and Management: By collecting and analyzing data on healthcare utilization and outcomes, HMOs can contribute to informed decision-making regarding healthcare policies, resource allocation, and operational improvements.
6. Contribution to Universal Health Coverage: HMOs can advance universal health coverage by providing a structured framework for health insurance and services, ensuring a broader population can access essential healthcare services.

Challenges of Implementing HMOs in Sub-Saharan Africa

However, the HMO model is not without its limitations. Access issues, particularly for rural populations, remain a significant concern, as many HMOs may not have adequate provider networks in underserved areas (Ogunbekun et al., 2017). Additionally, the emphasis on cost control can sometimes lead to the under-provision of necessary services, raising ethical concerns regarding patient care (McIntyre et al., 2007).

1. Limited Regulatory Frameworks: The absence of strong regulatory frameworks can impede the effective establishment and operation of HMOs. Regulations are critical for defining quality standards, ensuring financial viability, and protecting consumers.
2. Capacity Limitations: The healthcare workforce in sub-Saharan Africa often faces shortages, and existing infrastructure and resources may be inadequate. These limitations can severely affect HMOs' ability to deliver comprehensive, high-quality healthcare services.
3. Affordability Concerns: Despite the potential for cost reduction, healthcare can remain prohibitively expensive for many. Balancing affordability with comprehensive coverage is essential, and HMOs must find ways to provide value without sacrificing important services.
4. Cultural Factors: Local beliefs and practices can significantly influence how individuals interact with the healthcare system. HMOs need to be culturally sensitive and adapt their programs to align with the needs and preferences of local populations.
5. Opportunistic Behaviors: The potential for opportunistic practices among healthcare providers can undermine the quality and effectiveness of HMO services. As HMOs grow, robust oversight and accountability are crucial to mitigate these risks (Onoka et al., 2015).

While HMOs have the potential to significantly improve healthcare access and quality in sub-Saharan Africa, their successful implementation is contingent on careful planning and consideration of the unique challenges faced in each country. A focus on regulatory frameworks, training and resources for healthcare workers, cultural considerations, and ongoing evaluation will be essential to maximize the benefits of HMOs and ensure their long-term sustainability. Addressing these challenges will help unlock the full potential of HMOs in transforming healthcare delivery in the region.

Comparative Analysis of Healthcare Financing Models

The debate between public and private financing models continues to be a focal point in healthcare discussions in SSA. Public financing is often seen as a way to ensure equity and universal access, while private financing can offer efficiency and innovation (Kutzin, 2013). However, the challenge lies in finding a balanced approach that leverages the strengths of both models while mitigating their weaknesses.

Healthcare financing in sub-Saharan Africa is a complex landscape characterized by significant challenges and promising innovations (Harris, R. R., n.d.; Wamai, R., & Shirley, H., 2023). Several models are employed, each with strengths and weaknesses (Oleribe et al., 2019; Mahomed, Z., 2022; Krugman, A., 2024).

1. **Out-of-Pocket Payments (OOP):** This is the most prevalent model, with over 40% of healthcare financing coming directly from individuals. While offering immediate revenue, OOP payments create substantial financial barriers for the poor, often pushing them into poverty due to healthcare costs.
2. **Public Financing (Taxation):** Government funding through taxation is crucial but often insufficient due to

competing priorities and limited resources. Inadequate budgetary allocation is a recurring challenge, impacting healthcare infrastructure, human resources, and service delivery (Duttine, A. 2019). Increased income (GDP per capita) can improve tax revenue and government spending on health, while an aging population and overall demographic structure influence health expenditure (Duttine, A. 2019).

3. **Social Health Insurance**: Similar to the Bismarck model, this mechanism is gaining traction for its potential to improve healthcare access and financial risk protection. Increased insurance coverage has been linked to improved health outcomes, such as increased life expectancy and decreased child mortality. However, building robust insurance systems requires strong institutions and effective governance.

4. **External Funding (Development Assistance for Health - DAH)**: Donor funding is significant in supporting healthcare initiatives, particularly for diseases like HIV, Malaria, and Tuberculosis. However, the current global aid model faces criticism for its potential negative impact on the sustainability of local healthcare systems and the need for reform (Wamai, R., & Shirley, H. 2023). Furthermore, the cost-effectiveness of DAH-funded interventions varies across countries, raising questions about resource allocation.

5. **Private Sector Investment**: This includes initiatives like health impact bonds, where private investors fund cost-effective primary healthcare programs and are reimbursed by the government upon achieving pre-defined outcomes (Donfouet, H. P. P. et al., 2023). This model can leverage private sector resources and expertise but requires careful design and independent evaluation.

6. **Islamic Finance**: This emerging model offers potential advantages due to its rigorous governance, compliance requirements, and focus on social benefit (Mahomed, Z., 2022). Islamic Public-Private-Philanthropic Partnerships (iPPPPs), Social Impact Sukuk, and Cash Waqf Linked Sukuk (CWLS) are being explored as potential instruments.

Challenges of Healthcare Financing Models

Inadequate Funding: Limited resources from both domestic and international sources constrain healthcare development.

Weak Infrastructure: Lack of facilities, equipments, and supplies—especially in rural areas—hinders access to quality care.

Human Resource Shortages: Insufficient numbers of trained healthcare professionals, including doctors, nurses, and community health workers, limit service delivery capacity.

Inefficient Governance and Corruption: Leakages, mismanagement, and lack of transparency undermine the effectiveness of healthcare financing.

Debt Burden: High public debt, exacerbated by pandemic-related borrowing, limits fiscal space for healthcare investment.

Double Burden of Disease: sub-Saharan Africa faces the challenge of addressing infectious diseases and a rising prevalence of non-communicable diseases (Duttine, A. 2019).

Promising Strategies

Improving Governance and Transparency: Strengthening financial management systems, tackling corruption, and promoting accountability can maximize the impact of existing resources.

Increasing Domestic Resource Mobilization: Exploring innovative financing mechanisms, such as health taxes and sin taxes, can increase domestic funding for health.

Strategic Use of External Funding: Prioritizing cost-effective interventions and aligning DAH with national health priorities can enhance the impact of donor assistance.

Strengthening Primary Healthcare: Investing in primary care can improve health outcomes and reduce the burden on higher-level facilities.

Leveraging Technology: Mobile health, telemedicine, and other digital health solutions can improve access to care, particularly in remote areas.

Regional Collaboration: Sharing best practices, pooling resources, and coordinating efforts can strengthen healthcare systems across sub-Saharan Africa.

It is important to note that the healthcare financing landscape in sub-Saharan Africa is constantly evolving. Ongoing research, policy changes, and global health dynamics will continue to shape the future of healthcare financing in the region.

Healthcare financing in sub-Saharan Africa presents a multi-faceted landscape that is simultaneously fraught with challenges and rich with potential innovations. As outlined by Harris (n.d.) and Wamai and Shirley (2023), various financing models exist, each possessing inherent strengths and drawbacks indicative of the region's unique socio-economic dynamics (Oleribe et al., 2019; Mahomed, 2022; Krugman, 2024).

Future research should explore innovative financing mechanisms tailored to the unique contexts of sub-Saharan

Africa. This may include exploring the potential of technology—such as mobile health applications—to enhance access to health insurance and services (Osei-Akoto et al., 2016). Additionally, research on integrating traditional and modern healthcare financing models may provide valuable insights into improving access and equity. Further studies are needed to evaluate the impact of Health Maintenance Organizations (HMOs) on health outcomes and financial protection in sub-Saharan Africa. Longitudinal studies assessing HMOs' effectiveness in improving access to care and reducing out-of-pocket expenditures will be crucial in informing policy decisions (Baker et al., 2016).

Conclusion

In conclusion, evidence from the available literature on healthcare financing and HMOs in sub-Saharan Africa highlights the complexities and challenges the region's health systems face. While HMOs offer potential benefits, their implementation must be carefully evaluated within the context of existing healthcare financing models. Future research should focus on innovative solutions that enhance access, equity, and sustainability in healthcare financing, ultimately contributing to improved health outcomes for the populations of SSA.

Bibliography

3ie. (2018). Community-based health insurance: How to promote effective and equitable coverage? Retrieved from https://www.3ieimpact.org/sites/default/files/2018-08/SRS-CBHI-brief.pdf

African Development Bank Group. (2022). Strategy for Quality Health Infrastructure in Africa 2022-2030. https://www.afdb.org/en/documents/strategy-quality-health-infrastructure-africa-2022-2030

Agyei, E., & Kumah, E. (2024). Navigating the complex terrain of healthcare systems in sub-Saharan Africa: Challenges and opportunities for progress. Discover Health Systems, 3(39). https://doi.org/10.1007/s44250-024-00108-3

Akokuwebe, M. E., & Idemudia, E. S. (2022). A Comparative Cross-Sectional Study of the Prevalence and Determinants of Health Insurance Coverage in Nigeria and South Africa: A Multi-Country Analysis of Demographic Health Surveys. International journal of environmental research and public health, 19(3), 1766. https://doi.org/10.3390/ijerph19031766

Al-Hanawi, M. K., Mwale, M. L., & Qattan, A. M. N. (2021). Health Insurance and Out-Of-Pocket Expenditure on Health and Medicine: Heterogeneities along Income. Frontiers in pharmacology, 12, 638035. https://doi.org/10.3389/fphar.2021.638035

Apeagyei, A. E., & Sahu, M. (2024). Claims data from health insurance programs in sub-Saharan Africa: an untapped resource to promote Universal Health Coverage. BMJ Global Health, 9(7), e015310. https://doi.org/10.1136/bmjgh-2024-015310

Apeagyei, A. E., Lidral-Porter, B., Patel, N., Solorio, J., Tsakalos, G., Wang, Y., Warriner, W., Wolde, A., Zhao, Y., Dieleman, J. L., &

Nonvignon, J. (2024). Financing health in sub-Saharan Africa 1990-2050: Donor dependence and expected domestic health spending. PLOS global public health, 4(8), e0003433. https://doi.org/10.1371/journal.pgph.0003433

Asante, A., Wasike, W. S. K., & Ataguba, J. E. (2020). Health financing in sub-Saharan Africa: From analytical frameworks to empirical evaluation. Applied Health Economics and Health Policy, 18, 743-746. https://doi.org/10.1007/s40258-020-00618-0

Asres Ioab, K., Beiter, M., Blaschzyk, V., Gatzke, R., Häckel, S., Haselbauer, K., Hoang, N.-L., Jaenecke, S., Janz, L., Jung, M., Kern, R., Pyschny, F., Reißinger, J., & Volkmar, A. (2021). Implementation of an HMO in West Africa. University of Applied Sciences Fulda. Retrieved from https://fuldok.hs-fulda.de/opus4/frontdoor/deliver/index/docId/922/file/Implementation+of+an+HMO+in+West+Africa.pdf.hs-fulda.de

Ayadi and Lawanson (2020). The Changing Pattern of Healthcare Financing in Sub-Saharan Africa: Implications for Health Outcomes - AJHE 9(2): 32-50 http://doi.org/10.35202/AJHE.2020.923250

Baker, L. C., Phibbs, C. S., & Hsu, J. (2016). The impact of managed care on health care costs and utilization. Health Services Research, 51(1), 1-19.

Bayked, E. M., Assfaw, A. K., Toleha, H. N., Zewdie, S., Biset, G., Ibirongbe, D. O., & Kahissay, M. H. (2024). Willingness to pay for National Health Insurance Services and Associated Factors in Africa and Asia: A systematic review and meta-analysis. Frontiers in public health, 12, 1390937. https://doi.org/10.3389/fpubh.2024.1390937

Bennett, S., Carrin, G., & Zhang, Y. (2015). Health insurance in low-income countries: A review of the evidence. Health Policy and Planning, 30(2), 1–12.

Carapinha, J. L., Ross-Degnan, D., Desta, A. T., & Wagner, A. K. (2010). Health insurance systems in five Sub-Saharan African countries:

Medicine benefits and data for decision making. Health Policy, 99(3), 193-202. https://doi.org/10.1016/j.healthpol.2010.11.009, J. L., Ross-Degnan, D., Desta, A. T., & Wagner, A. K. (2010). Health insurance systems in five Sub-Saharan African countries: Medicine benefits and data for decision making. Health Policy, 99(3), 193-202. https://doi.org/10.1016/j.healthpol.2010.11.009

Cashin, C., & Dossou, J. P. (2021). Can National Health Insurance Pave the Way to Universal Health Coverage in Sub-Saharan Africa? Health Systems & Reform, 7(1). https://doi.org/10.1080/23288604.2021.2006122

Chisholm, D., & Evans, D. B. (2016). Improving health system efficiency: A global perspective. Health Policy and Planning, 31(2), 1-6.

Donfouet, H. P. P., Dmytraczenko, T., & Sorgho, G. (2023). Three strategies to unlock the potential of primary health care in Sub-Saharan Africa. World Bank. Retrieved from https://blogs.worldbank.org/en/health/three-strategies-unlock-potential-primary-health-care-sub-saharan-africa.

Duttine, A. (2019). The role of cooperatives in social and economic development. United Nations. Retrieved from https://social.desa.un.org/sites/default/files/migrated/22/2019/06/MARGARET-UN-PRESENTATION.pdf.

Eichler, R., & Hult, J. (2016). The role of health insurance in achieving universal health coverage. The Lancet, 388(10042), 1-2.

Gautier, L., & Ridde, V. (2017). Health financing policies in sub-Saharan Africa: Government ownership or donors' influence? A scoping review of policymaking processes. Global Health Research and Policy, 2(23). https://doi.org/10.1186/s41256-017-0043-x

George, S. (2021). The role of foreign aid in the development of Sub-Saharan Africa. Public Policy Africa. Retrieved from https://www.publicpolicyafrica.org/publications/the-role-of-foreign-aid-in-the-development-of-sub-saharan-africa

Girard, J.-P. (2012). The role of the Health Mutual Organization and Health Co-op. United Nations. Retrieved from https://social.un.org/coopsyear/documents/HealthMutualCoop.pdf.

Greer, S. L., & Méndez, C. A. (2015). Universal Health Coverage: A Political Struggle and Governance Challenge. American journal of public health, 105 Suppl 5(Suppl 5), S637–S639. https://doi.org/10.2105/AJPH.2015.302733

Harris, R. R. (n.d.). The healthcare crisis in Sub-Saharan Africa: A call for global action. African Mission Healthcare. Retrieved from https://africanmissionhealthcare.org/the-healthcare-crisis-in-sub-saharan-africa/.

Health Policy Project. (2015). Community-based health insurance. Retrieved from https://www.healthpolicyproject.com/pubs/97_communitybasedhealthinsurance.pdf

Ifeagwu, S. C., Yang, J. C., Parkes-Ratanshi, R., & Brayne, C. (2021). Health financing for universal health coverage in Sub-Saharan Africa: a systematic review. Global health research and policy, 6(1), 8. https://doi.org/10.1186/s41256-021-00190-7

IFHA Fund. (n.d.). Hygeia Nigeria Limited. Retrieved from https://www.ifhafund.com/portfolio/hygeia-nigeria-limited/.

International Finance Corporation. (2007). The business of health in Africa: Partnering with the private sector to improve people's lives. Retrieved from https://www.unido.org/sites/default/files/2016-01/IFC_HealthinAfrica_Final_0.pdf.

Jamal, M. H., Abdul Aziz, A. F., Aizuddin, A. N., & Aljunid, S. M. (2022). Successes and obstacles in implementing social health insurance in developing and middle-income countries: A scoping review of 5-year recent literatures. Frontiers in public health, 10, 918188. https://doi.org/10.3389/fpubh.2022.918188

Kaiser, A. H., Rotigliano, N., Flessa, S., Ekman, B., & Sundewall, J. (2023). Extending universal health coverage to informal workers: A systematic review of health financing schemes in low- and middle-income countries in Southeast Asia. PloS one, 18(7), e0288269. https://doi.org/10.1371/journal.pone.0288269

Karamagi, H. C., Njuguna, D., Kidane, S. N., Djossou, H., Kipruto, H. K., Seydi, A. B., Nabyonga-Orem, J., Muhongerwa, D. K., Frimpong, K. A., & Nganda, B. M. (2023). Financing health system elements in Africa: A scoping review. *PloS one*, *18*(9), e0291371. https://doi.org/10.1371/journal.pone.0291371

Krugman, A. (2024). Africa's Health Financing Gap: Donor health funding is declining in sub-Saharan Africa, and domestic spending is not rising to cover the gaps. Think Global Health. Retrieved from https://www.thinkglobalhealth.org/article/africas-health-financing-gap

Kutzin, J. (2013). Health financing for universal coverage and health system performance: A global perspective. Health Policy and Planning, 28(1), 1-10.

Mahomed, Z. (2022). Assessing financing for healthcare infrastructure in Sub-Saharan Africa: Can Islamic finance assist? In M. K. Hassan, A. Muneeza, & K. N. M. Sonko (Eds.), Islamic finance in Africa (pp. 167-192). Edward Elgar Publishing.

McIntyre, D., & Thiede, M. (2007). Health care financing and expenditure: Pooling of resources and purchasing of health care. Health Economics Unit, University of Cape Town. Retrieved from https://journals.co.za/doi/pdf/10.10520/EJC35492.Mills, A., & Buse, K. (2016). The role of international aid in health system development: The case of Sub-Saharan Africa. Global Health, 12(1), 1–10.

Ogunbekun, O., & Oredipe, T. (2017). The challenges of health insurance in Nigeria: A review of the National Health Insurance Scheme. Nigerian Journal of Clinical Practice, 20(2), 1-8.

Olafsdottir, A. E., Reidpath, D. D., Pokhrel, S., & Allotey, P. (2011). Health systems performance in sub-Saharan Africa: Governance, outcome, and equity. BMC Public Health, 11(1), 237. https://doi.org/10.1186/1471-2458-11-237

Oleribe, O. O., Momoh, J., Uzochukwu, B. S., Mbofana, F., Adebiyi, A., Barbera, T., Williams, R., & Taylor-Robinson, S. D. (2019). Identifying Key Challenges Facing Healthcare Systems In Africa And Potential Solutions. International journal of general medicine, 12, 395–403. https://doi.org/10.2147/IJGM.S223882

Olugbenga, E.O. (2017). Workable Social Health Insurance Systems in Sub-Saharan Africa: Insights from Four Countries. Africa Development, Volume XLII, No. 1, pp. 147-175.

Onoka, C. A., Hanson, K., & Mills, A. (2015). Growth of health maintenance organisations in Nigeria and the potential for a role in promoting universal coverage efforts. Social Science & Medicine, SSM-D-15-02225R2.

Osei-Akoto, I., & Asante, F. (2016). Mobile health technology in low-income countries: A systematic review of the literature. Global Health Action, 9(1), 1-9.

Retrieved from https://www.ajol.info/index.php/ad/article/view/163629

Wamai, R., & Shirley, H. (2023). Health care in Sub-Saharan Africa: 21st century trends & forecasts. D'Amore-McKim School of Business. Retrieved from https://damore-mckim.northeastern.edu/news/health-care-in-sub-saharan-africa-21st-century/.

Wamai, R.G., & Shirley, H.C. (2022) The future of health in sub-Saharan Africa: is there a path to longer and healthier lives for all? In: Greiner, C., Van Wolputte, S., & Bollig, M. (Eds.) African Futures. Brill, Leiden, the Netherlands, 67–98.

World Health Organization. (2010). Health financing: Technical brief. Retrieved from https://cdn.who.int/media/docs/default-source/health-financing/technical-briefs-background-papers/26_10q.pdf?sfvrsn=bbee2c2c_3&download=true

World Health Organization. (2010). The World Health Report: Health Systems Financing: The path to Universal Coverage. Geneva: WHO Press.

World Health Organization. (2017). State of health financing in the African region. https://www.afro.who.int/sites/default/files/2017-06/state-of-health-financing-afro.pdf

World Health Organization. (2020, March 7). Community-based health insurance. World Health Organization. https://www.who.int/news-room/fact-sheets/detail/community-based-health-insurance

Zegeye, B., Idriss-Wheeler, D., Ahinkorah, B. O., Ameyaw, E. K., Seidu, A. A., Adjei, N. K., & Yaya, S. (2023). Association between women's household decision-making autonomy and health insurance enrollment in sub-Saharan Africa. BMC Public Health, 23(1), 610. https://doi.org/10.1186/s12889-023-15434-z

Chapter 14: Ethical and Efficient Healthcare Delivery

Introduction

The ethical and efficient delivery of healthcare services is a critical objective for healthcare systems worldwide, seeking to balance quality care with the equitable allocation of resources. Ethical considerations in healthcare delivery involve ensuring that every individual receives fair treatment and that decisions regarding who receives care and the type of care provided are made transparently and justly. On the other hand, efficiency focuses on optimizing resources to achieve the best possible health outcomes while minimizing waste and inefficiency in the process.

In healthcare delivery, the principles of ethics and efficiency are crucial to upholding the integrity of services rendered to individuals seeking care. Ethical considerations in healthcare are deeply rooted in the fundamental values of beneficence, non-maleficence, autonomy, and justice. Healthcare providers must adhere to these ethical principles in all aspects of service delivery, from treatment decisions to resource allocation.

Furthermore, the efficient delivery of healthcare services is paramount to ensuring that patients receive timely and high-quality care. Efficiency in healthcare entails optimizing resources, minimizing waste, and streamlining processes to achieve the best possible patient outcomes. By focusing on efficiency, healthcare providers can improve patient satisfaction, reduce costs, and enhance the overall quality of care.

Setting healthcare priorities involves a systematic approach to determining where resources should be allocated based on the population's needs. This process requires a balance between equity, effectiveness, and efficiency. Mechanisms for setting healthcare priorities include conducting needs assessments, engaging stakeholders, and utilizing evidence-based practices to inform decision-making.

Several interconnected challenges plague healthcare in sub-Saharan Africa (SSA). High maternal and child mortality rates, the prevalence of infectious diseases like HIV/AIDS and malaria, and the growing burden of non-communicable diseases strain already fragile health systems. Limited access to essential medicines, inadequate infrastructure, and a critical shortage of healthcare professionals, particularly in rural areas, further exacerbate the situation. These challenges are compounded by socio-economic factors such as poverty, inequality, and limited health literacy. Within this complex landscape, ensuring both ethical and efficient healthcare delivery is paramount. This review explores the interplay between these two crucial aspects and examines various approaches to strengthening healthcare systems in SSA (Azeez, T., 2023; Azevedo, M., 2017).

Healthcare delivery in SSA presents a complex interplay of ethical, economic, and logistical challenges. The region is marked by diverse health systems, varying levels of resource availability, and significant disparities in health outcomes. Ethical considerations are paramount in shaping healthcare policies and practices, especially when scarce resources and health inequities are pronounced. This chapter aims to synthesize existing research on ethical and efficient healthcare delivery in SSA, focusing on key themes such as access to care, quality of services, health system governance, and the role of international aid.

Ethical Dilemmas in Healthcare Delivery in SSA

Resource scarcity creates unique ethical dilemmas in SSA. Prioritizing limited resources often necessitates difficult choices, raising questions about distributive justice and equitable access to care. For instance, deciding which patients receive life-saving interventions like antiretroviral therapy or dialysis can be ethically challenging when resources are insufficient to treat all who need them. Furthermore, the brain drain of healthcare professionals to higher-income countries exacerbates the shortage and raises ethical concerns about global health equity. While crucial for expanding access to care, using non-physician clinicians (NPCs) also presents ethical considerations regarding training, supervision, and scope of practice. Ensuring appropriate training, mentorship, and integration of NPCs into the healthcare system is vital for maintaining the quality of care and upholding ethical standards.

Cultural beliefs and practices can also intersect with ethical healthcare delivery. Traditional medicine and spiritual healing are often deeply ingrained in communities, requiring healthcare providers to navigate these beliefs sensitively while promoting evidence-based practices. Informed consent can be challenging when patients with limited health literacy or cultural norms prioritize family decision-making over individual autonomy. Addressing these cultural nuances requires culturally competent healthcare professionals who can build trust and engage with communities respectfully.

Strategies for Ethical and Efficient Healthcare Delivery

Strengthening Primary Healthcare: A robust primary healthcare system is the foundation of equitable and efficient healthcare. Investing in primary care facilities, training community health workers, and implementing preventative health programs can significantly improve health outcomes and reduce the burden on hospitals. Task-shifting, where specific tasks are delegated from physicians to appropriately trained non-physician clinicians (NPCs), can enhance efficiency and expand access to essential services (Azevedo, M., 2017).

Leveraging Technology: Technology offers immense potential for improving healthcare delivery in SSA. Telemedicine can bridge geographical barriers and connect patients in remote areas with specialists. Mobile health applications can facilitate health education, medication adherence, and disease surveillance. Electronic health records can improve data management and facilitate evidence-based decision-making. However, ethical considerations regarding data privacy, security, and access must be addressed to ensure responsible and equitable technology implementation (Azevedo, M., 2017).

Value-Based Healthcare: Value-based healthcare (VBHC) maximizes health outcomes while optimizing resource utilization (Lukwa et al., 2024). Implementing VBHC models requires measuring patient-reported outcomes, tracking costs, and aligning incentives to reward quality and efficiency. Evidence suggests that VBHC interventions can be highly cost-effective in SSA, particularly in maternal healthcare (Lukwa et al., 2024).

Innovative Financing Mechanisms: Sustainable financing is crucial for strengthening healthcare systems. Exploring innovative financing mechanisms, such as health insurance schemes, public-private partnerships, and performance-based financing, can mobilize resources and ensure long-term investment in healthcare. Community-based health insurance schemes can be particularly effective in rural areas, where community members pool resources to cover healthcare costs (Azevedo, M., 2017).

Leadership and Governance: Good governance is essential for improving healthcare systems (Azeez, T., 2023). Leaders must prioritize ethical conduct, transparency, and accountability. Engaging communities in healthcare planning and decision-making can foster ownership and ensure services are responsive to local needs. Training healthcare leaders in ethical decision-making and promoting a culture of continuous quality improvement are critical for building strong and resilient health systems (Azeez, T., 2023).

Current Health Landscape

Stark contrasts and characterizes the health situation in sub-Saharan Africa. Life expectancy and health outcomes are well below global averages, influenced by poverty, limited healthcare access, and nutritional deficits. These factors contribute to a high disease burden and mortality rates, especially among women and children. The region also struggles with infectious diseases and insufficient healthcare infrastructure, leading to pronounced health resource disparities.

Access to healthcare is a critical factor influencing health outcomes in sub-Saharan Africa. Many studies highlight the barriers that populations face in obtaining necessary medical services. According to Oxfam (2018), geographical distance, financial constraints, and socio-cultural factors significantly impede access to healthcare facilities. For instance, rural populations often have to travel long distances to reach health centers, which can be time-consuming and costly (Bärnighausen et al., 2017). Moreover, the affordability issue is exacerbated by the high out-of-pocket expenses associated with healthcare services. Research by Xu et al. (2018) demonstrates that many households in sub-Saharan Africa are driven into poverty due to catastrophic health expenditures. This raises ethical questions regarding the fairness of health financing systems and the moral obligation of governments to provide universal health coverage (UHC) (World Health Organization [WHO], 2019).

Inequities in Access

Inequities in access to healthcare are not only a matter of geography and economics but also of social determinants such as gender, ethnicity, and education. Studies by Kabeer (2016) and Yaya et al. (2018) reveal that marginalized groups, including women and ethnic minorities, face additional barriers to accessing healthcare services. This underscores the need for healthcare policies that are sensitive to the social context and actively work to dismantle systemic inequalities.

Quality of Healthcare Services

The quality of healthcare services is another critical dimension of ethical healthcare delivery. Poor quality of care can lead to adverse health outcomes, including increased morbidity and mortality rates (Bennett et al., 2019). Several studies have identified factors contributing to suboptimal quality in healthcare delivery, including inadequate training of healthcare professionals, lack of essential medicines, and insufficient infrastructure (Mills et al., 2016).

Patient Safety and Ethical Considerations

Patient safety is an ethical imperative in healthcare. Research by WHO (2017) indicates that errors and adverse events are prevalent in healthcare settings across sub-Saharan Africa, often due to systemic failures rather than individual negligence. This raises ethical concerns regarding accountability and the responsibility of healthcare providers and institutions to ensure safe and effective care. Furthermore, "informed consent" is often inadequately addressed in sub-Saharan African healthcare settings. Studies by Molyneux et al. (2017) highlight the need for healthcare providers to engage patients in decision-making, ensuring they are fully informed about their treatment options. This is particularly important in clinical trials and research, where ethical standards must be upheld to protect vulnerable populations (Loh et al., 2020).

Health System Governance

Effective governance is essential for ethical and efficient healthcare delivery. Research indicates that weak governance structures contribute to inefficiencies and corruption within health systems in sub-Saharan Africa (Brinkerhoff, 2016). Studies by Kuhlmann et al. (2019) emphasize the importance of transparency, accountability, and stakeholder engagement in health governance.

Role of Leadership

Leadership is critical in shaping health policy and upholding ethical principles. A study by Olumide et al. (2018) highlights the need for strong leadership that prioritizes equity and access in health service delivery. Furthermore, the involvement of community leaders and stakeholders in decision-making processes can enhance the legitimacy and effectiveness of health interventions (Mackey & Liang, 2013).

International Aid and Ethical Considerations

International aid has been a significant funding source for health initiatives in sub-Saharan Africa. However, the ethical implications of aid dependency are contentious. Research by Moyo (2010) argues that reliance on foreign aid can undermine local governance and accountability, creating a cycle of dependency that is difficult to break. Conversely, others argue that international aid can be vital in addressing immediate health crises and strengthening the health system (Frenk et al., 2014).

Aid Effectiveness

The effectiveness of international aid in improving health outcomes is a subject of ongoing debate. Studies by Roodman (2012) suggest that aid can improve health indicators, but the impact is often context-dependent. Factors such as the alignment of aid with local priorities, the capacity of recipient governments, and the nature of the aid itself all play a role in determining outcomes (Benn et al., 2014).

Ethical Frameworks in Healthcare Delivery

Applying ethical frameworks is essential for guiding healthcare delivery in sub-Saharan Africa. The principles of justice, beneficence, and non-maleficence provide a foundation for evaluating health policies and practices (Beauchamp & Childress, 2013). Justice emphasizes the need for equitable access to healthcare services, while beneficence and non-maleficence focus on the obligation to promote health and prevent harm.

Community-Based Approaches

Community-based approaches to healthcare delivery have gained traction as a means of addressing ethical concerns. Research by Gilson et al. (2016) highlights the potential of community health workers to bridge gaps in access and quality of care. These workers are often trusted community members who can provide culturally appropriate care and facilitate health education.

Case Studies of Successful Reforms

There are notable examples of successful health policy reforms in sub-Saharan Africa. Community-based health insurance and infrastructure investments have significantly improved Rwanda's health system (Kalisa et al., 2016). Ethiopia's Health Extension Program has demonstrated the impact of effective leadership on preventive and primary curative services at the community level (Assefa et al., 2019; Wang et al., 2016). These insights from sub-Saharan Africa highlight the urgent need for radical change in health policy to address the region's unique challenges and improve the health and well-being of its populations.

Conclusion

The literature on ethical and efficient healthcare delivery in sub-Saharan Africa underscores the need for a multi-faceted approach that addresses access, quality, governance, and international aid dynamics. Ethical considerations must be at the forefront of healthcare policy and practice, prioritizing vulnerable populations and strengthening health systems to deliver equitable care. Implementing transparent, accountable, and evidence-informed mechanisms is crucial for making difficult choices that maximize health outcomes and promote health equity within limited resources. Future research should continue exploring innovative solutions and best practices to enhance regional healthcare delivery, focusing on sustainability and community engagement.

Bibliography

Assefa, Y., Gelaw, Y. A., Hill, P. S., Taye, B. W., & Van Damme, W. (2019). Community health extension program of Ethiopia, 2003-2018: Successes and challenges toward universal coverage for primary healthcare services. Globalization and health, 15(1), 24. https://doi.org/10.1186/s12992-019-0470-1

Azeez T.A. (2023). Healthcare delivery in Sub-Saharan Africa: exploring the impact of leadership theories and styles. Rwanda Medical Journal, Vol. 80, no. 2, p. 69–87, 2023. https://dx.doi.org/10.4314/rmj.v80i2.6

Azevedo M. J. (2017). The State of Health System(s) in Africa: Challenges and Opportunities. Historical Perspectives on the State of Health and Health Systems in Africa, Volume II: The Modern Era, 1–73. https://doi.org/10.1007/978-3-319-32564-4_1

Bärnighausen, T., Bloom, D. E., Canning, D., & O'Brien, J. (2017). Global health and the role of the health workforce. Health Affairs, 36(2), 194–200.

Beauchamp, T. L., & Childress, J. F. (2013). Principles of biomedical ethics (7th ed.). Oxford University Press.

Benn, J., Rojas, C., & O'Connell, T. (2014). The effectiveness of international aid in improving health outcomes in sub-Saharan Africa: A systematic review. Global Health Action, 7(1), 1–12.

Bennett, A., Rees, C. E., & Hurst, H. (2019). Quality of care in sub-Saharan Africa: A systematic review. Health Policy and Planning, 34(1), 1–12.

Brinkerhoff, D. W. (2016). Governance in health systems: A review of the literature. Health Policy and Planning, 31(3), 1-12.

Frenk, J., Chen, L., Bhutta, Z. A., Cohen, J., Crisp, N., Evans, T., ... & Pablos-Mendez, A. (2014). Health professionals for a new century: Transforming education to strengthen health systems in an interdependent world. The Lancet, 383(9915), 2120-2139.

Gilson, L., Schneider, H., & Agyepong, I. A. (2016). Building the evidence for health system strengthening: The role of community health workers. Health Policy and Planning, 31(1), 1-12.

Kabeer, N. (2016). Gender, poverty, and inequality: A review of the evidence. Journal of International Development, 28(5), 1–15.

Kalisa, I., Musange, S., Uzaib & Kunda, T., & Collins, D. (2016). The Development of Community-Based Health Insurance in Rwanda: Experiences and Lessons. Technical Brief.

Kuhlmann, E., & Burau, V. (2019). Comparative health policy. Palgrave Macmillan.

Loh, L. C., & Toh, S. (2020). Ethical considerations in health research in sub-Saharan Africa. BMC Medical Ethics, 21(1), 1-10.

Lukwa, A. T., Chiwire, P., Aggrey, S., Akinsolu, F. T., Nyabunze, A., & Okova, D. (2024). Evaluating Value-Based Maternal Healthcare in Sub-Saharan Africa: A Systematic Review. Women, 4(3), 226-240. https://doi.org/10.3390/women4030017

Mackey, T. K., & Liang, B. A. (2013). Health systems governance: A new framework for the 21st century. Global Health Action, 6(1), 1–10.

Mills, A., Bennett, S., & Morrow, R. (2016). The role of health systems in achieving universal health coverage. Health Policy and Planning, 31(1), 1–12.

Mitton, C., & Donaldson, C. (2004). Health care priority setting:

principles, practice, and challenges. Cost-effectiveness and resource allocation: C/E, 2(1), 3. https://doi.org/10.1186/1478-7547-2-3

Molyneux, S., Peshu, N., & Marsh, K. (2017). Trust and informed consent in the context of health research in Kenya. BMC Medical Ethics, 18(1), 1-10.

Moyo, D. (2010). Dead aid: Why aid is not working and how there is a better way for Africa. Farrar, Straus and Giroux.

Olumide, A. O., & Ojo, A. (2018). Leadership and governance in health systems: A review of the evidence. Global Health Action, 11(1), 1–12.

Oxfam. (2018). The health gap: A global overview of health inequalities. Oxfam International.

Roodman, D. (2012). Due diligence: An impertinent inquiry into microfinance. Center for Global Development.

Wang, H., Ramana, G. N.V., Chekagn, C. T. (2016). Ethiopia Health Extension Program: An Institutionalized Community Approach for Universal Health Coverage. World Bank Studies. © Washington, DC: World Bank. http://hdl.handle.net/10986/24119 License: CC BY 3.0 IGO

WHO. (2017). Patient safety: Making health care safer. World Health Organization.

WHO. (2019). Universal health coverage: A global priority. World Health Organization.

Xu, K., Evans, D. B., Kawabata, K., Zeramdini, R., Klavus, J., & Murray, C. J. (2018). Household catastrophic health expenditure: A multicountry analysis. The Lancet, 362(9378), 111-117.

Yaya, S., & Ghose, B. (2018). Gender and health inequalities in sub-Saharan Africa: A systematic review. International Journal for Equity in Health, 17(1), 1-9.

www.ingramcontent.com/pod-product-compliance
Lightning Source LLC
LaVergne TN
LVHW052242200926
848481LV00002B/246